EYEWITNESS HISTORY OF THE CIVIL WAR
War in the West

WAR IN THE WEST

Shiloh to Vicksburg, 1862-1863

edited by

John Cannan

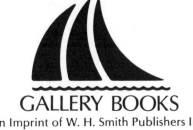

GALLERY BOOKS
An Imprint of W. H. Smith Publishers Inc.
112 Madison Avenue
New York City 10016

Prepared by Combined Books, Inc.
26 Summit Grove Avenue, Suite 207
Bryn Mawr, PA 19101

Produced by Wieser & Wieser, Inc.
118 East 25th Street
New York, NY 10010

Published by Gallery Books
A division of W. H. Smith Publishers, Inc.
112 Madison Avenue
New York, NY 10016

ISBN 0-8317-3084-6

CONTENTS

PREFACE TO THE SERIES

Well over a century after its conclusion, the Civil War still remains the gravest crisis in the history of the Republic since the attainment of independence. It was a vast complex struggle which touched the lives of far more Americans than any other war in which the nation has fought. A conflict of momentous import, it still retains an immediate and continuing impact on the life of the nation. The story of the Civil War has been told on numerous occasions and in numerous ways. The literature is enormous, ranging from erudite scholarly tomes to dry official reports, from informative popular histories to vicious partisan tracts. All these have their value. Yet none can ever be entirely satisfactory. After all these years there exists no better way of looking at the Civil War than to see it through the eyes of those who lived through it, the thousands upon thousands for whom the war was a daily reality.

The Civil War was probably the first war in history in which most of the troops could read and write. As a result, there exists an enormous number of firsthand accounts. The range of materials is equally large, from private letters to multi-volume memoirs. These cover everything from the minutia of daily* life to serious historical treatments, from amusing anecdotes to vituperative personal attacks. Nothing surpasses such original documents for developing an understanding of the events as they were perceived by the people who lived through them, for the flavor of the times, the emotions of the struggle, the force of the issues, the impact of the events. Such materials have been drawn upon several times already for the creation of a number of anthologies of firsthand accounts of the war, or of particular aspects of it. Yet the amount of material available is so vast, the stories to be told so numerous, that there still remains much material which has not received wide circulation. It was an awareness of this fact which led to the creation of the present series, *Eyewitness to the Civil War.*

In preparing *Eyewitness to the Civil War,* the editor has made no effort to attempt a "balanced" presentation. As a consequence, many events are treated from only a Northern point of view, while others have a Southern slant, and still others are seen from two or three different perspectives. The purpose of the work is neither to achieve historical accuracy nor political balance, but to see events as they were experienced and understood by some of the people who lived through them. There will thus be redundancies, contradictions, and errors, not to mention outright falsehoods.

All of the selections appear almost exactly as they did on their original publication, save for the occasional eliding of extraneous materials. Where necessary, the editor has created titles for selections which lacked such. For the most part, he has avoided the inclusion of explanatory notes, confining himself to the insertion of occasional comments in brackets. Where explanatory notes appear in the original, they have been included only when they seemed of particular importance. In addition, the editor has refrained from modernizing the many little differences in spelling, capitalization, grammar, usage and syntax, which have developed since the Civil War. Needless to say, there has been no attempt to impose a uniformity of style. Thus, in *Eyewitness to the Civil War* the participants speak for themselves in their own voices.

FORT HENRY AND FORT DONELSON

After the disaster at First Bull Run, the advocates of the Union were heartened over the first great victories of Federal armies in the West. There Ulysses S. Grant, in a campaign lasting from 2 to 16 February 1862, boldly captured a Confederate force of some 12,000 men at Forts Henry and Donelson guarding the Tennessee and Cumberland Rivers respectively. The victory effectively opened the waterways for a Federal invasion of the Volunteer State, pierced the Tennessee-Kentucky line and forced the Confederate forces under Albert Sidney Johnston to fall back from Kentucky and most of Tennessee.

★★★

HENRY WALKE

Gunboats on the Tennessee

In campaigning against Forts Henry and Donelson, Grant decided to employ a fleet of shallow-draft ironclad gunboats under the command of Flag Officer Andrew Foote. A bombardment from Foote's fleet, overpowering Federal numbers, and the weakness of the Confederate position at Fort Henry forced the garrison's com-mander Brigadier General Lloyd Til-ghman to surrender on 6 February, but not before he had sent most of his troops to reinforce Fort Donelson. The skipper of the Union gunboat Carondelet, Comman-der Henry Walke, described the naval action against Fort Henry in Battles and Leaders of the Civil War.

During the winter of 1861–62, an expedition was planned by Flag-Officer Foote and Generals Grant and McClernand against Fort Henry, situated on the east-ern bank of the Tennessee River, a short distance south of the line between Kentucky and Tennessee. In January the iron-clads were brought down to Cairo, and great efforts were made to prepare them for im-mediate service, but only four of the iron-clads could be made ready as soon as required.

On the morning of the 2d of February the flag-officer left Cairo with the four armored vessels above named, and the wooden gun-boats *Tyler, Lexington,* and *Conestoga,* and in the evening reached the Ten-nessee River. On the 4th the fleet anchored six miles below Fort Henry. The next day, while reconnoitering, the *Essex* received a shot which passed through the pantry and the officers' quarters, addressed them, and offered a prayer.

Heavy rains had been falling, and the river had risen rapidly to an unusual height; the swift current brought down an immense quantity of heavy drift-wood, lumber, fences, and large trees, and it required all the steam-power of the *Carondelet,* with both an-chors down, and the most strenuous exertions of the officers and crew, working day and night, to prevent the boat from being dragged downstream. This adver-sity appeared to dampen the ardor of our crew, but when the next morning they saw a large number of white objects, which through the fog looked like polar bears, coming down the stream, and ascertained that they were the enemy's torpedoes forced from their moorings by the powerful current, they took heart, regarding the freshet as providential and as a presage of victory. The overflowing river, which opposed our progress, swept away in broad daylight this hidden peril; for if the torpedoes had not been disturbed, or had broken loose at night while we were shoving the drift-wood from our bows, some of them would surely

*Commander Henry Walke, skipper of the **Carondelet** during the naval bombardments of both Fort Henry and Fort Donelson.*

have exploded near or under our vessels.

The 6th dawned mild and cheering, with a light breeze, sufficient to clear away the smoke. At 10:20 the flag-officer made the signal to prepare for battle, and at 10:50 came the order to get under way and steam up to Panther Island, about two miles below Fort Henry. At 11:35, having passed the foot of the island, we formed in line and approached the fort four abreast,—the *Essex* on the right, then the *Cincinnati, Carondelet,* and *St. Louis.* For want of room the last two were interlocked, and remained so during the fight.

As we slowly passed up this narrow stream, not a sound could be heard nor a moving object seen in the dense woods which overhung the dark and swollen river. The gun-crews of the *Carondelet* stood silent at their posts, impressed with the serious and important character of the service before them. About noon the fort and the Confederate flag came suddenly into view, the barracks, the new earth-works, and the great guns well manned. The captains of our guns were men-of-war's men, good shots, and had their men well drilled.

The flag-steamer, the *Cincinnati,* fired the first shot as the signal for the others to begin. At once the fort was ablaze with the flame of her eleven heavy guns. The wild whistle of their rifle-shells was heard on every side of us. On the *Carondelet* not a word was spoken more than at ordinary drill, except when Matthew Arthur, captain of the starboard bow-gun, asked

permission to fire at one or two of the enemy's retreating vessels, as he could not at that time bring his gun to bear on the fort. He fired one shot, which passed through the upper cabin of a hospital-boat, whose flag was not seen, but injured no one. The *Carondelet* was struck in about thirty places by the enemy's heavy shot and shell. Eight struck within two feet of the bow-ports, leading to the boilers, around which barricades had been built—a precaution which I always took before going into action, and which on several occasions prevented an explosion. The *Carondelet* fired 107 shell and solid shot; none of her officers or crew was killed or wounded.

The firing from the armored vessels was rapid and well sustained from the beginning of the attack, and seemingly accurate, as we could occasionally see the earth thrown in great heaps over the enemy's guns. Nor was the fire of the Confederates to be despised; their heavy shot broke and scattered our iron-plating as if it had been putty, and often passed completely through the casemates. But our old men-of-war's men, captains of the guns, proud to show their worth in battle, infused life and courage into their young comrades. When these experienced gunners saw a shot

The gunboat **Essex** *which, during the bombardment of Fort Henry, received a calamitous shot in its middle boiler that killed several on board and severely damaged the ship. All in all the crew of the vessel suffered 32 casualties during the battle.*

coming toward a port, they had the coolness and discretion to order their men to bow down, to save their heads.

After nearly an hour's hard fighting, the captain of the *Essex*, going below, and complimenting the First Division for their splendid execution, asked them if they did not want to rest and give three cheers, which were given with a will.

The *Essex* had fired seventy shots from her two 9-inch guns. A powder boy, Job Phillips, fourteen years of age, coolly marked down upon the casemate every shot his gun had fired, and his account was confirmed by the gunner in the magazine. Her loss in killed, wounded, and missing was thirty-two.

The *St. Louis* was struck seven times. She fired one hundred and seven shots during the action. No one on board the vessel was killed or wounded.

Flag-Officer Foote during the action was in the pilot-house of the *Cincinnati*, which received thirty-two shots. Her chimneys, after-cabin, and boats were completely riddled. Two of her guns were disabled. The only fatal shot she received passed through the larboard front, killing one man and wounding several others. I happened to be looking at the flag-steamer when one of the enemy's heavy shot struck her. It had the effect, apparently, of a thunder-bolt, ripping her side-timbers and scattering the splinters over the vessel. She did not slacken her speed, but moved on as though nothing unexpected had happened.

From the number of times the gun-boats were struck, it would appear that the Confederate artillery practice, at first, at least, was as good, if not better, than ours. This, however, was what might have been expected, as the Confederate gunners had the advantage of practicing on the ranges the gun-boats would probably occupy as they approached the fort. The officers of the gun-boats, on the contrary, with guns of different caliber and unknown range, and without practice, could not point their guns with as much accuracy. To counterbalance this advantage of the enemy, the gun-boats were much better protected by their casemates for distant firing than the fort by its fresh earthworks. The Confederate soldiers fought as valiantly and as skillfully as the Union sailors. Only after a most determined resistance, and after all his heavy guns had been silenced, did General Tilghman lower his flag. The Confederate loss, as reported, was 5 killed, 11 wounded, and 5 missing. The prisoners, including the general and his staff, numbered 78 in the fort and 16 in a hospital-boat; the remainder of the garrison, a little less than 2600, having escaped to Fort Donelson.

Our gun-boats continued to approach the fort until General Tilghman, with two or three of his staff, came off in a small boat to the *Cincinnati* and surrendered the fort to Flag-Officer Foote, who sent for me, introduced me to General Tilghman, and gave me orders to take command of the fort and hold it until the arrival of General Grant.

General Tilghman was a soldierly-looking man, a little above medium height, with piercing black eyes and a resolute, intelligent expression of countenance.

Brigadier General Lloyd Tilghman, chief of the ill-fated Fort Henry.

He was dignified and courteous, and won the respect and sympathy of all who became acquainted with him. In his official report of the battle he said that his officers and men fought with the gravest bravery until 1:50 P.M., when seven of his eleven guns were disabled; and, finding it impossible to defend the fort, and wishing to spare the lives of his gallant men, after consultation with his officers he surrendered the fort.

It was reported at the time that, in surrendering to Flag-Officer Foote, the Confederate general said, "I am

Union gunboats under the command of Flag-Officer Andrew Foote descend upon Fort Henry on 6 February 1862.

Below: *Rebels on the retreat from Fort Henry. General Tilghman realized his position there was untenable and therefore ordered an evacuation of the 2,500-man garrison leaving some 90 men behind to man the fort's guns.*

glad to surrender to so gallant an officer," and that Foote replied, "You do perfectly right, sir, in surrendering, but you should have blown my boat out of the water before I would have surrendered to you." I was with Foote soon after the surrender, and I cannot believe that such a reply was made by him. He was too much of a gentleman to say anything calculated to wound the feelings of an officer who had defended his post with signal courage and fidelity, and whose spirits were clouded by the adverse fortunes of war.

When I took possession of the fort the Confederate surgeon was laboring with his coat off to relieve and save the wounded; and although the officers and crews of the gun-boats gave three hearty cheers when the Confederate flag was hauled down, the first inside view of the fort sufficed to suppress every feeling of exultation and to excite our deepest pity. On every side the blood of the dead and wounded was intermingled with the earth and their implements of war. Their largest gun, a 128-pounder, was dismounted and

Foote's gunboats duel with Tilghman's batteries at close range. Confederate guns managed to damage the Federal fleet putting one ship out of action, but were forced to capitulate under the superior fire power of the attacking vessels.

A gruesome visage of the Federal bombardment of Fort Henry. In actuality, only five rebels were killed while 11 more were wounded.

Walke's vessel, the **Carondelet** *approaches its target of Fort Henry.*

filled with earth by the bursting of one of our shells near its muzzle; the carriage of another was broken to pieces, and two dead men lay near it, almost covered with heaps of earth; a rifled gun had burst, throwing its mangled gunners into the water. But few of the garrison escaped unhurt.

General Grant, with his staff, rode into the fort about 3 o'clock on the same day, and relieved me of the command. The general and staff then accompanied me on board the *Carondelet* (anchored near the fort), where he complimented the officers of the flotilla in the highest terms for the gallant manner in which they had captured Fort Henry. He had expected his troops to take part in a land attack, but the heavy rains had made the direct roads to the fort almost impassable.

The wooden gun-boats *Conestoga*, Commander S. L. Phelps, *Tyler*, Lieutenant-Commander William Gwin, and *Lexington*, Lieutenant J. W. Shirk, engaged the enemy at long range in the rear of the iron-clads. After the battle they pursued the enemy's transports up the river, and the *Conestoga* captured the steamer *Eastport*. The news of the capture of Fort Henry was received with great rejoicing all over the North.

The Stars and Stripes fly triumphantly over Fort Henry after Tilghman bowed to the inevitable and surrendered.

★★★

H. L. BEDFORD

The Defense of Fort Donelson

Following the swift capitulation of Fort Henry, Grant and Foote believed the use of gunboats against the fortifications at Fort Donelson might lead to the surrender of that position as well. As Grant's troops

began sealing off the garrison from escape by land, the naval war vessels attempted to bombard the fort's guns at close range on 14 February. The move met with disappointing failure as two ships were disabled and another heavily damaged. Foote was injured with a wound that would eventually kill him. An instructor of artillery at the fort, H.L. Bedford witnessed the repulse of the

Federal flotilla and recounted his experiences in an address which was originally published in the Southern Society Historical Papers.

The operations of the army at this place having proved disastrous to the Confederate cause, it has been condemned as a strategic point, and no one seems particularly anxious to acknowledge the responsibility of its selection. It was the general impression at the Fort that its location had been ordered by the Tennessee authorities as being the most eligible point on the Cumberland River, in close proximity to Fort Henry, on the Tennessee. The original intention evidently was the obstruction of the Cumberland. The engineer in charge, Lieutenant Dixon, while tracing the outlines of the earthworks, never dreamed that a persistent stand against an invading army would ever be attempted, and I feel warranted in suggesting that General A. S. Johnston regarded it simply as a protection to his rear.

When I received orders in October, 1861, to report there as Instructor of Artillery, Colonel E. W. Mun-

ford, aide to General Johnston, informed me that he was instructed by his chief to impress upon me that the Cumberland river cut his rear, and the occupation of Bowling Green was dependent upon the proper guarding of that stream. If, then, Fort Donelson was intended to prevent the passage of gunboats, its location was an admirable one; it accomplished its mission, and its founder need feel no hesitation in claiming its paternity. Nor does the final result of the operations of the land forces necessarily convict General Johnston of a mistake in the reinforcement of Donelson. At that time he was believed to possess the ability as a general which events soon verified, and his condemnation will have to rest on surer proofs than the charges of flippant writers. To the average mind the whole matter resolves itself into the simple question: Whether General Johnston sufficiently reinforced Fort Donelson to successfully resist the forces

Ulysses S. Grant. At the beginning of the war he held the rank of a mere colonel before being promoted to brigadier general. The capture of Fort Henry and Fort Donelson proved to be a great boon to the military career of this former store clerk.

The skipper of the Federal flotilla at both Fort Henry and Fort Donelson, Flag-Officer Andrew Foote.

that invaded the State of Tennessee under General Grant by way of Fort Henry; and, if so, is he fairly chargeable with the blunders of his generals, in allowing themselves to be cooped in temporary trenches until reinforcements to the enemy could come up the Cumberland? Any close student of the "Operations at Fort Donelson," embraced in series No. 1, Vol. 7, of the "Records of the Rebellion," will probably detect by whom the mistakes were made. It is doubtless there recorded when and where the opportunity of withdrawing the Confederate forces was disregarded; that General Johnston was unfortunate in the selection, or rather the grouping of his lieutenants, on this occasion, is beyond controversy. His army consisted of raw recruits; his generals were ready made for him; their commissions were presumptions of merit; there had been no opportunity for development, and he had no alternative but to accept the patents of ability issued to them by the War Department. The senior general arrived at the eleventh hour, and seems to have been lacking in disposition or in power to hold his second in due subjection. The latter had been on the ground for about a week; he was full of energy and physical activity, and possessed rare executive ability. He was restless under restraint, probably prone to insubordination, and it was almost impossible for him to yield his sceptre to a new comer. He gave orders affecting the whole army without any known rebuke or remonstrance from his chief. The performances of these two chieftains afford an apt illustration of a very homely old saying that will readily recur to most of you. This rule of duality of commanders, according to some of the official reports, seems to have obtained in the heavy batteries, but as it was not then known or recognized, it did not create any confusion. When I reported there for duty very little in the way of defence had been accomplished. Two 32-pounder carronades had been mounted on the river, and three 32-pounders were temporarily mounted on the crest of the bluff. The carronades were utterly useless, except against wooden boats at close quarters, while the three guns on the hill, on account of position, could not be made effectual against ironclads. The garrison, in command of Lieutenant-Colonel Randle McGavock, consisted of a part of Colonel Heiman's

Tenth Tennessee regiment, the nucleus of Colonel Sugg's Fiftieth Tennessee (then called Stacker's regiment), and Captain Frank Maney's light battery.

As there were no heavy artillerists, Captain Beaumont's company of Fiftieth Tennessee had been detailed for that duty. At the time of my arrival, there was considerable excitement at the Fort. Smoke was seen rising a few miles down the river, the long-roll was being beat, and there was hurrying to and fro; companies were getting under arms and into line with the rapidity of zealots, though wanting in the precision of veterans. The excitement subsided as the smoke disappeared. In a short while the companies were dismissed, and the men resumed their wonted avocations. The local engineer was also in charge of the works at Fort Henry, and was, necessarily, often absent. His duties were onerous and manifold; I, therefore, volunteered to remount the three 32-pounders and place them in the permanent battery; and as the completion of the defence was considered of more importance than the drilling of artillery, I was kept constantly on engineering duty until after the investment. General Tilghman arrived about the middle of December, and took command. He manifested a good deal of interest in forwarding the work. The Fiftieth Tennessee regiment (Colonel Suggs) was organized; the Thirtieth Tennessee (Colonel Head), and the Forty-ninth Tennessee (Colonel Bailey), reported, and these, with Maney's light battery, constituted the garrison, Lieutenant-Colonel McGavock having rejoined Colonel Hieman at Fort Henry.

The work for the completion of the defences and for the comfort of the soldiers, was pushed on as rapidly as the means at hand would permit. There was no lagging, nor lukewarmness, nor shirking of duty. As one of the many evidences of the zeal manifested by the garrison, I would state that whenever a detail for work of any magnitude was made from any of the regiments, a field officer usually accompanied it, in

The interior works of Fort Donelson. After the fall of Fort Henry, Fort Donelson was the next objective for Grant's army and Foote's gunboats.

order to secure promptness and concert of action. This, I believe, was the invariable rule with the Forty-ninth Tennessee. At the time of the arrival of reinforcements, the water batteries were not in that state of incompleteness and disorder which the report of a general officer charges, nor was there any gloom or despondency hanging over the garrison. It is true there was some delay in getting the 10-inch Columbiad in working condition, but no one connected with the Fort was responsible for it. The gun was mounted in ample time, but upon being tested it came very nearly being dismounted by the running back of the carriage against the hurters. It was necessary to increase the inclination of the chassis, which was accomplished by obtaining larger rear traverse wheels from the iron works just above Dover. It was still found, even with a reduced charge of powder, that the recoil of the carriage against the counter-hurters was of sufficient force to cut the ropes tied there as bumpers. There was no alternative but to dismount the piece and lower the front half of the traverse circle; by this means the inclination of the chassis was made so steep that the piece was in danger of getting away from the gunners when being run into battery, and of toppling off in front.

Any paper upon the subject of Fort Donelson would be incomplete without the mention of Lieutenant-Colonel Wilton A. Haynes, of the Tennessee artillery. He was, in the nomenclature of the volunteers, a "West Pointer," and was an accomplished artillerist. He came to Fort Donelson about the middle of January, and found the "Instructor of Artillery" engaged in engineering duty, and nothing being done in familiarizing the companies detailed for artillery service with their pieces. He organized an artillery battalion, and made a requisition on General Polk, at Columbus, for two drill officers, and whatever of proficiency these companies attained as artillerists is due to him. He was physically unable to participate in the engagements and this may account for the failure of recognition in the official reports.

The artillery battalion as organized by Colonel Haynes was fully competent to serve the guns with success, but General Pillow deemed otherwise and proceeded to the mistake of assigning Lieutenant Dixon to the command of the heavy batteries, instead of attaching him to his personal staff, and availing himself of that officer's familiarity as an engineer with the topography of the battleground and of the surrounding country. The assignment was particularly unfortunate, inasmuch as Dixon was killed before the main fight and the batteries were not only deprived of his services for that occasion, but the Confederate army lost an able engineer. It must be remembered, however, that the great fear was of the gunboats. It was apprehended that their recent achievements at Fort Henry would be repeated at Donelson, and it was natural that the commanding gen-

The inner workings of a Federal ironclad gunboat of the type commanded by Flag Officer Foote in his bombardment of Fort Donelson.

*Another member of Foote's powerful fleet of
ironclads, the* **Cincinnati.**

*Fort Donelson's powerful batteries guard the
approaches to the Cumberland River from the
incursions of Federal ships.*

eral should make every other interest subservient to the efficiency of the heavy batteries. The river defenses consisted of two batteries. The upper one was on the river bank immediately abreast of the earthworks; It was crescent shaped, and contained one 32-pound calibre rifle gun and two 32-pounder carronades. The other battery was some hundred and fifty yards lower down and consisted of eight 32-pounders and one 10-inch Columbiad. This lower battery, although essentially a straight line, ran *en echelon* to the left over the point of a hill that made down obliquely from the earthworks to the river, with the right piece resting on the brink of the river bank, and the Columbiad over in the valley of a stream, emptying into the river, some hundred and fifty yards lower down. The back water in this stream protected the batteries from a direct assault. About nine hundred yards below the lower battery, a floating abattis was placed in the river for the purpose of preventing the passage of boats. This was done by anchoring full length trees by the roots and allowing the tops to float. In ordinary stages of water this might have offered some impediment, but at the time of the attack the river was very high and the boats passed over without the least halt or break in their line of approach.

In all the accounts that I have seen from the Federal side, the armament of the water batteries is over-estimated. Flag-Officer Foot reports that there must have been about twenty heavy guns, and General Lew Wallace places it at seventeen. Admiral Walke, while correctly stating the number in the lower battery, is in error in claiming that the upper was about the same in strength.

On the morning of the 12th of February the finishing touches were put to the Columbiad, and the batteries were pronounced ready for gunboats, whereupon Lieutenant Dixon proceeded to the assignment of the guns. Captain R. R. Ross, of the Maury Company Light Artillery, whose company had been ordered to heavy batteries by General Pillow, was placed in command of the rifle gun and the two corronades. Captain Beaumont's company, A, Fiftieth Tennessee, and Captain Bidwell's company, Thirtieth Tennessee, worked the 32-pounders, and the Columbiad was turned over to my command, with a detachment of twenty men under Lieutenant Sparkman, from Captain Ross's company, to work it. I received private instructions to continue the firing with blank cartridges, in the event the gun should dismount itself in action. The drill officers, Lieutenants McDaniel and Martin, were assigned to the 32-pounders, while Captains Culbertson and Shaster had special assignments or instructions, the nature of which I never knew.

As the artillerists, who were to serve the rifle and Columbiad, had no experience with heavy guns, most of them probably never having seen a heavy battery until that morning, it was important that they should be instructed in the manual of their pieces. Drilling, therefore, began immediately, but had continued for a short time only when it was most effectually interrupted by the appearance of a gunboat down the river,

Confederate gunners prepare their artillery to fight off Foote's formidable naval attack. The batteries at Fort Donelson consisted of ten 32-pounders, one 32-pound rifled gun and one 10-inch Columbiad.

which subsequently was ascertained to be the Caron-delet. She fired about a dozen shots with remarkable precision, and retired without any response from the batteries.

On the morning of the 13th drilling was again interrupted by the firing of this boat, and the same thing happened in the afternoon. It really appeared as if the boat was diabolically inspired, and knew the most opportune times to annoy us. Sometime during the day, probably about noon, she delivered her fire with such accuracy that forbearance was no longer endurable, and Lieutenant Dixon ordered the Colum-biad and rifle to respond. The first shot from the Columbiad passed immediately over the boat, the sec-ond fell short, but the third was distinctly heard to strike. A cheer of course followed, and Lieutenant Dixon, in the enthusiasm of the moment, ordered the

Foote's flagship during the battle of Fort Donelson, the formidable **St. Louis.** *After suffering 59 hits from Rebel guns, the vessel was incapacitated and floated helplessly downstream.*

A veteran of the battle against Fort Donelson, the **Conestoga,** *an unarmored gunboat skippered by Lieutenant Commander S.L. Phelps.*

32-pounders to open fire, although the enemy was clearly beyond their range. The Carondelet, nothing daunted, continued the action, and soon one of her shells cut away the right cheek of one of Captain Bidwell's guns, and a flying nut passed through Lieutenant Dixon's head, killing him instantly. In this engagement the flange of one of the front traverse wheels of the Columbiad was crushed, and a segment of the front half of the traverse circle was cupped, both of which proved serious embarrassments in the action next day.

On the morning of the 14th, dense volumes of smoke were seen rising from down the river; it was evident that transports were landing troops. Captain Ross became impatient to annoy them, but having no fuse shells to his guns, he came over to the Columbiad and advised the throwing of shells down the river. The commander declined to do so without orders, whereupon Captain Culbertson, who had succeeded Lieutenant Dixon in the command of the batteries, was looked up, but he refused to give the order, upon the ground that it would accomplish no good, and that he did not believe in the useless shedding of blood. Captain Ross, not to be outdone, set himself to the task of procuring the necessary order and returned to the Columbiad about 3 o'clock P.M. with a verbal order form General Floyd to harass the transports. In obedience to this order, we prepared to shell the smoke. A shell was inserted, the gun was given the proper elevation, the lanyard was pulled, and the missile went hissing over the bend of the river, plunged into a bank of smoke, and was lost to view. This was called by an army correspondent, claiming to have been on one of the gunboats, "a shot of defiance." Before the piece could be reloaded, the prow of a gunboat made its appearance around the bend, quickly followed by three others, and arranging themselves in line of battle, steamed up to the attack. When they had arrived within a mile and a half of the batteries, a solid shot having been substituted for a shell, the Columbiad began the engagement with a ricochet shot, the rifle gun a ready second. The gunboats returned the fire, right centre boat opening, the others following in quick succession. After the third discharge the rifle remained silent on account of becoming accidentally spiked. This had a bad effect on the men at the Columbiad, causing them considerable uneasiness for their comrades at the upper battery. The Columbiad continued the action unsupported until the boats came within the range of the 32-pounders, when the engagement became general, with ten guns of the batteries opposed to the twelve bow guns of the ironclads, supplemented by those of the two wooden boats that remained in the rear throwing curvated shells. As the boats drew nearer, the firing on both sides became faster, until it appeared as if the battle had dwindled into a contest of speed in firing. When they arrived within three hundred yards of the lower battery they came to a stand, and then it was that the bombardment was truly terrific. The roar of cannons was continuous and deafening, and commands, if necessary, had to be given by

signs. Pandemonium itself would hardly have been more appalling, but neither chaos nor cowardice obtruded themselves, and I must insist that General Wallace and Admiral Walke are mistaken in their assertions that the gunners were seen running from their guns. It is true there was some passing from the batteries to the Fort, but not by the artillerists in action, and as the passage was over an exposed place, in fact across the field of fire of the gunboats, it is a fair presumption that the transit was made as swiftly as possible. Of one thing I am certain, there was no fleeing from the Columbiad, and although her discharges were necessarily very slow, I think every one in hearing that day will testify that her boom was almost as regular as the swinging of a pendulum. If these two Federal officers saw her condition when surrendered, they will admit that it was not likely that panic-stricken cannoniers could have carried her safely through such a furious bombardment, especially to have done the execution with which she is accredited. In his contribution to the *Century*, of December, 1884, doubtless by the cursory reading of Captain Bidwell's report, General Wallace is lead into the mistake of saying that each gunner selected his boat and stuck to her during the engagement. I am satisfied that the experienced officers who acted as gunners did not observe this rule. The Columbiad was rigidly impartial, and fired on the boats as chance or circumstances dictated, with the exception of the last few shots, which were directed at the Carondelet. This boat was hugging the eastern shore, and was a little in advance of the others. She offered her side to the Columbiad, which was on the left and the most advanced gun of the batteries. Several well-directed shots raked the side and tore away her armor, according to the report of Lieutenant Sparkman, who was on the lookout. Just as the other boats began to drift back, the Carondelet forged ahead for about a half length, as though she intended making the attempt to pass the battery, and it is presumable that she then received the combined fire of all the guns.

It is claimed that if Hannibal had marched on Rome immediately after the battle of Cannæ, he could have taken the city, and by the same retrospective reasoning, it is probable that if Admiral Foote had stood beyond the range of 32-pounders he could have concentrated his fire on two guns. If his boats had fired with the deliberation and accuracy of the Carondelet on the previous day, he could have dismounted those guns, demolished the 32-pounders at his leisure, and shelled the Fort to his heart's content. But flushed with his victory at Fort Henry, his success there paved the way for his defeat at Donelson, a defeat that might have proved more disastrous could the Columbiad have used a full charge of powder and the rifle gun participated in the fight. After the battle three of the gunboats were seen drifting helplessly down the stream, and a shout of exultation leaped from the lips of every soldier in the fort. It was taken up by the men in the trenches, and for awhile a shout of victory, the sweetest strain to the ears of those who win, reverberated over the hills and hollows around the little vil-

lage of Dover.

While the cannoniers were yet panting from their exertion, Lieutenant-Colonel Robb, of the Forty-ninth Tennessee, who fell mortally wounded the next day, ever mindful of the comfort of those around him, sent a grateful stimulant along the line of guns. Congratulations were the order of the hour. Generals Floyd and Pillow personally complimented the artillerists. They came to the Columbiad, called for the commander, and after congratulating him upon the performances of that day, promised that if the batteries would continue to keep back the gunboats, the infantry of their command would keep the land forces at a safe distance. That officer, who had been watching the smoke of the transports landing reinforcements, as he stood there before these generals, just thirty-six hours before surrender, receiving their assurances of protection, wondered if they were able to fulfill the promise, or if they were merely indulging an idle habit of braggadocio.

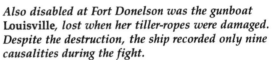

Walke's terrifying monster of a floating vessel, the **Carondelet.** *At Fort Donelson, her crew lost 33 men in killed and wounded.*

Sister ship to the **Conestoga,** *the* **Tyler.**

Also disabled at Fort Donelson was the gunboat **Louisville,** *lost when her tiller-ropes were damaged. Despite the destruction, the ship recorded only nine causalities during the fight.*

★★★

LEW WALLACE

Fort Donelson Surrenders

Though Grant commanded an army of 15,000 troops, he ably managed to besiege Fort Donelson, commanded by three generals: John B. Floyd, Gideon Pillow, and Simon Bolivar Buckner. Brigadier General Lew Wallace who commanded a division in Grant's army would be for-ever remembered not for his military prowess, but for his celebrated work, Ben Hur. Evidence of his romantic penmanship can be found in this article taken from Battles and Leaders of the Civil War that describes the Federal operations at Fort Donelson.

The village of Dover was—and for that matter yet is—what our English cousins would call the "shire-town" of the county of Stewart, Tennessee. In 1860 it was a village unknown to fame, meager in population, architecturally poor. There was a court-house in the place, and a tavern, remembered now as double-storied, unpainted, and with windows of eight-by-ten glass, which, if the panes may be likened to eyes, were both squint and cataractous. Looking through them gave the street outside the appearance of a sedgy slough of yellow backwater. The entertainment furnished man and beast was good of the kind; though at the time mentioned a sleepy traveler, especially if he were of the North, might have been somewhat vexed by the explosions which spiced the good things of a debating society that nightly took possession of the bar-room, to discuss the relative fighting qualities of the opposing sections.

If there was a little of the romantic in Dover itself, there was still less of poetic quality in the country round about it. The only beautiful feature was the Cumberland River, which, in placid current from the south, poured its waters, ordinarily white and pure as those of the springs that fed it, past the village on the east. Northward there was a hill, then a small stream, then a bolder hill round the foot of which the river swept to the west, as if courteously bent on helping Hickman's Creek out of its boggy bottom and cheerless ravine. North of the creek all was woods. Taking in the ravine of the creek, a system of hollows, almost wide and deep enough to be called valleys, inclosed the town and two hills, their bluffest ascents being on the townward side. Westward of the hollows there were woods apparently interminable. From Fort Henry, twelve miles north-west, a road entered the village, stopping first to unite itself with another wagon-way, now famous as the Wynn's Ferry road, coming more directly from the west. Still another road, leading off to Charlotte and Nashville, had been

The hapless commander of Fort Donelson, Brigadier General John B. Floyd. After botching the breakthrough attempt against Grant's besieging army, Floyd chose to surrender the reins of command to his subordinate Gideon Pillow, opting to flee the fort and leaving his men to face an ignominious fate.

cut across the low ground near the river on the south. These three highways were the chief reliances of the people of Dover for communication with the country, and as they were more than supplemented by the river and its boatage, the three were left the year round to the guardianship of the winds and rains.

However, when at length the Confederate authorities decided to erect a military post at Dover, the town entered but little into consideration. The real inducement was the second hill on the north—more properly a ridge. As it rose about a hundred feet above the level of the inlet, the reconnoitering engineer, seeking to control the navigation of the river by a fortification, adopted it at sight. And for that purpose the bold bluff was in fact a happy gift of nature, and we shall see presently how it was taken in hand and made terrible.

It is of little moment now who first enunciated the idea of attacking the rebellion by way of the Tennessee River; most likely the conception was simultaneous with many minds. The trend of the river; its navigability for large steamers; its offer of a highway to the rear of the Confederate hosts in Kentucky and the State of Tennessee; its silent suggestion of a secure passage into the heart of the belligerent land, from which the direction of movement could be changed toward the Mississippi, or, left, toward Richmond; its many advantages as a line of supply and of general communication, must have been discerned by every military student who, in the summer of 1861, gave himself to the most cursory examination of the map. It is thought better and more consistent with fact to conclude that its advantages as a strategic line, so actually obtrusive of themselves, were observed about the same time by thoughtful men on both sides of the contest. With every problem of attack there goes a counter problem of defense.

A peculiarity of the most democratic people in the world is their hunger for heroes. The void in that respect had never been so gaping as in 1861. General Scott was then old and passing away, and the North caught eagerly at the promise held out by George B. McClellan; while the South, with as much precipitation, pinned its faith and hopes on Albert Sidney Johnston. There is little doubt that up to the surrender of Fort Donelson the latter was considered the foremost soldier of all who chose rebellion for their part. When the shadow of that first great failure fell upon the veteran, President Davis made haste to reassure him of his sympathy and unbroken confidence. In the official correspondence which has survived the Confederacy there is nothing so pathetic, and at the same time so indicative of the manly greatness of Albert Sidney Johnston, as his letter in reply to that of his chief.

When General Johnston assumed command of the Western Department, the war had ceased to be a new idea. Battles had been fought. Preparations for battles to come were far advanced. Already it had been accepted that the North was to attack and the South to defend. The Mississippi River was a central object; if opened from Cairo to Fort Jackson (New Orleans), the

Second in command at Fort Donelson, the spineless Brigadier General Gideon Pillow. After receiving command of the fort from his superior John B. Floyd, Pillow opted to hand over his responsibilities to Simon Bolivar Buckner.

Brigadier General Simon Bolivar Buckner. With his superiors fleeing their command, Buckner agreed to stay with his men to surrender Fort Donelson to Grant. Subsequently, he was the first Confederate general to surrender during the war.

Confederacy would be broken into halves, and good strategy required it to be broken. The question was whether the effort would be made directly or by turning its defended positions. Of the national gun-boats afloat above Cairo, some were formidably iron-clad. Altogether the flotilla was strong enough to warrant the theory that a direct descent would be attempted; and to meet the movement the Confederates threw up powerful batteries, notably at Columbus, Island Number Ten, Memphis, and Vicksburg. So fully were they possessed of that theory that they measurably neglected the possibilities of invasion by way of the Cumberland and Tennessee rivers. Not until General Johnston established his headquarters at Nashville was serious attention given to the defense of those streams. A report to his chief of engineers of November 21st, 1861, establishes that at that date a second battery on the Cumberland at Dover had been completed; that a work on the ridge had been laid out, and two guns mounted; and that the encampment was then surrounded by an abatis of felled timber. Later, Brigadier-General Lloyd Tilghman was sent to Fort Donelson as commandant, and on January 25th he reports the batteries prepared, the entire field-works built with a trace of 2900 feet, and rifle-pits to guard the approaches were begun. The same officer speaks further of reënforcements housed in four hundred log-cabins, and adds that while this was being done at Fort Donelson, Forts Henry and Heiman, over on the Tennessee, were being thoroughly strengthened. January 30th, Fort Donelson was formally inspected by Lieutenant-Colonel Gilmer, chief engineer of the Western Department, and the final touches were ordered to be given it.

It is to be presumed that General Johnston was satisfied with the defenses thus provided for the Cumberland River. From observing General Buell at Louisville, and the stir and movement of multiplying columns under General U. S. Grant in the region of Cairo, he suddenly awoke determined to fight for Nashville at Donelson. To this conclusion he came as late as the beginning of February; and thereupon the brightest of the Southern leaders proceeded to make a capital mistake. The Confederate estimate of the Union force at that time in Kentucky alone was 119 regiments. The force at Cairo, St. Louis, and the towns near the mouth of the Cumberland River was judged to be about as great. It was also known that we had unlimited means of transportation for troops, making concentration a work of but few hours. Still General Johnston persisted in fighting for Nashville, and for that purpose divided his thirty thousand men. Fourteen thousand he kept in observation of Buell at Louisville. Sixteen thousand he gave to defend Fort Donelson. The latter detachment he himself called "the best part of his army." It is difficult to think of a great master of strategy making an error so perilous.

Henry Wager Halleck, commander of the Federal war effort in the West until he was appointed General in Chief of the entire Union War effort in July of 1862.

Having taken the resolution to defend Nashville at Donelson, he intrusted the operation to three chiefs of brigade—John B. Floyd, Gideon J. Pillow, and Simon B. Buckner. Of these, the first was ranking officer, and he was at the time under indictment by a grand jury at Washington for malversation as Secretary of War under President Buchanan, and for complicity in an embezzlement of public funds. As will be seen, there came a crisis when the recollection of the circumstance exerted an unhappy influence over his judgment. The second officer had a genuine military record; but it is said of him that he was of a jealous nature, insubordinate, and quarrelsome. His bold attempt to supersede General Scott in Mexico was green in the memories of living men. To give pertinency to the remark, there is reason to believe that a personal misunderstanding between him and General Buckner, older than the rebellion, was yet unsettled when the two met at Donelson. All in all, therefore, there is little doubt that the junior of the three commanders was the fittest for the enterprise intrusted to them. He was their equal in courage; while in devotion to the cause and to his profession of arms, in tactical knowledge, in military bearing, in the faculty of getting the most service out of his inferiors, and inspiring them with confidence in his ability,—as a soldier in all the higher meanings of the word,—he was greatly their superior.

The 6th of February, 1862, dawned darkly after a thunder-storm. Pacing the parapets of the work on the hill above the inlet formed by the junction of Hickman's Creek and the Cumberland River, a sentinel, in the serviceable butternut jeans uniform of the Confederate army of the West, might that day have surveyed Fort Donelson almost ready for battle. In fact, very little was afterward done to it. There were the two water-batteries sunk in the northern face of the bluff, about thirty feet above the river; in the lower battery 9 32-pounder guns and 1 10-inch Columbiad, and in the upper another Columbiad, bored and rifled as a 32-pounder, and 2 32-pounder carronades. These guns lay between the embrasures, in snug revetment of sand in coffee-sacks, flanked right and left with stout traverses. The satisfaction of the sentry could have been nowise diminished at seeing the backwater lying deep in the creek; a more perfect ditch against assault could not have been constructed. The fort itself was of good profile, and admirably adapted to the ridge it crowned. Around it, on the landward side, ran the rifle-pits, a continuous but irregular line of logs, covered with yellow clay. From Hickman's Creek they extended far around to the little run just outside the town on the south. If the sentry thought the pits looked shallow, he was solaced to see that the followed the coping of the ascents, seventy or eighty feet in height, up which a foe must charge, and that, where they were weakest, they were strengthened by trees felled outwardly in front of them, so that the interlacing limbs and branches seemed impassable by men under fire. At points inside the outworks, on the inner slopes of the hills, defended thus from view of an enemy as well as from

his shot, lay the huts and log-houses of the garrison. Here and there groups of later comers, shivering in their wet blankets, were visible in a bivouac so cheerless that not even morning fires could relieve it. A little music would have helped their sinking spirits, but there was none. Even the picturesque effect of gay uniforms was wanting. In fine, the Confederate sentinel on the ramparts that morning, taking in the whole scene, knew the jolly, rollicking picnic days of the war were over.

To make clearer why the 6th of February is selected to present the first view of the fort, about noon that day the whole garrison was drawn from their quarters by the sound of heavy guns, faintly heard from the direction of Fort Henry, a token by which every man of them knew that a battle was on. The occurrence was in fact expected, for two days before a horseman had ridden to General Tilghman with word that at 4:30 o'clock in the morning rocket signals had been exchanged with the picket at Bailey's Landing, announcing the approach of gun-boats. A second courier came, and then a third; the latter, in great haste, requesting the general's presence at Fort Henry. There was quick mounting at headquarters, and, before the

camp could be taken into confidence, the general and his guard were out of sight. Occasional guns were heard the day following. Donelson gave itself up to excitement and conjecture. At noon of the 6th, as stated, there was continuous and heavy cannonading at Fort Henry, and greater excitement at Fort Donelson. The polemicists in Dover became uneasy and prepared to get away. In the evening fugitives arrived in groups, and told how the gun-boats ran straight upon the fort and took it. The polemicists hastened their departure from town. At exactly midnight the gallant Colonel Heiman marched into Fort Donelson with two brigades of infantry rescued from the ruins of Forts Henry and Heiman. The officers and men by whom they were received then knew that their turn was at hand; and at daybreak, with one mind and firm of purpose, they set about the final preparation.

Brigadier-General Pillow reached Fort Donelson on the 9th; Brigadier-General Buckner came in the night of the 11th; and Brigadier-General Floyd on the 13th. The latter, by virtue of his rank, took command.

The morning of the 13th—calm, spring-like, the very opposite of that of the 6th—found in Fort Donelson a garrison of 28 regiments of infantry: 13 from

Camp Butler in Springfield, Illinois, where Grant drilled farmers, clerks and schoolboys in the arts of war. Dressed in the Federal uniform, these citizen soldiers fought the war in the West.

Tennessee, 2 from Kentucky, 6 from Mississippi, 1 from Texas, 2 from Alabama, 4 from Virginia. There were also present 2 independent battalions, 1 regiment of cavalry, and artillerymen for 6 light batteries, and 17 heavy guns, making a total of quite 18,000 effectives.

General Buckner's division—6 regiments and 2 batteries—constituted the right wing, and was posted to cover the land approaches to the water-batteries. A left wing was organized into six brigades, commanded respectively by Colonels Heiman, Davidson, Drake, Wharton, McCausland, and Baldwin, and posted from right to left in the order named. Four batteries were distributed amongst the left wing. General Bushrod R. Johnson, an able officer, served the general commanding as chief-of-staff. Dover was converted into a depot of supplies and ordnance stores. These dispositions made, Fort Donelson was ready for battle.

It may be doubted if General Grant called a council of war. The nearest approach to it was a convocation held on the *New Uncle Sam*, a steamboat that was afterward transformed into the gun-boat *Blackhawk*. The morning of the 11th of February, a staff-officer visited each commandant of division and brigade

with the simple verbal message: "General Grant sends his compliments, and requests to see you this afternoon on his boat." Minutes of the proceedings were not kept; there was no adjournment; each person retired when he got ready, knowing that the march would take place next day, probably in the forenoon.

There were in attendance on the occasion some officers of great subsequent notability. Of these Ulysses S. Grant was first. The world knows him now; then his fame was all before him. A singularity of the volunteer service in that day was that nobody took account of even a first-rate record of the Mexican War. The battle of Belmont, though indecisive, was a much better reference. A story was abroad that Grant had been the last man to take boat at the end of that affair, and the addendum that he had lingered in face of the enemy until he was hauled aboard with the last gangplank, did him great good. From the first his silence was remarkable. He knew how to keep his temper. In battle, as in camp, he went about quietly, speaking in a conversational tone; yet he appeared to see everything that went on, and was always intent on business. He had a faithful assistant adjutant-general, and appreciated him; he preferred, however, his own eyes, word, and hand. His aides were little more than messengers. In dress he was plain, even negligent; in partial amendment of that his horse was always a good one and well kept. At the council—calling it such by grace—he smoked, but never said a word. In all probability he was framing the orders of march which were issued that night.

Charles F. Smith, of the regular army, was also present. He was a person of superb physique, very tall, perfectly proportioned, straight, square-shouldered, ruddy-faced, with eyes of perfect blue, and long snow-white mustaches. He seemed to know the army regulations by heart, and caught a tactical mistake, whether of command or execution, by a kind of mental *coup d'œil*. He was naturally kind, genial, communicative, and never failed to answer when information was sought of him; at the same time he believed in "hours of service" regularly published by the adjutants as a rabbi believes in the Ten Tables, and to call a court-martial on a "bummer" was in his eyes a sinful waste of stationery. On the occasion of a review General Smith had the bearing of a marshal of France. He could ride along a line of volunteers in the regulation uniform of a brigadier-general, plume, chapeau, epaulets and all, without exciting laughter—something nobody else could do in the beginning of the war. He was at first accused of disloyalty, and when told of it, his eyes flashed wickedly; then he laughed, and said, "Oh, never mind! They'll take it back after our first battle." And they did. At the time of the meeting on the *New Uncle Sam* he was a brigadier-general, and commanded the division which in the land operations against Fort Henry had marched up the left bank of the river against Fort Heiman.

Another officer worthy of mention was John A. McClernand, also a brigadier. By profession a lawyer, he was in his first of military service. Brave, industrious, methodical, and of unquestioned cleverness, he was rapidly acquiring the art of war.

There was still another in attendance on the *New Uncle Sam* not to be passed—a young man who had followed General Grant from Illinois, and was seeing his first of military service. No soldier in the least

familiar with headquarters on the Tennessee can ever forget the slender figure, large black eyes, hectic cheeks, and sincere, earnest manner of John A. Rawlins, then assistant adjutant-general, afterward major-general and secretary of war. He had two special devotions—to the cause and to his chief. He lived to see the first triumphant and the latter first in peace as well as in war. Probably no officer of the Union was mourned by so many armies.

Fort Henry, it will be remembered, was taken by Flag-Officer Foote on the 6th of February. The time up to the 12th was given to reconnoitering the country in the direction of Fort Donelson. Two roads were discovered: one of twelve miles direct, the other almost parallel with the first, but, on account of a slight divergence, two miles longer.

By 8 o'clock in the morning, the First Division, General McClernand commanding, and the Second, under General Smith [see page 429], were in full march. The infantry of this command consisted of twenty-five regiments in all, or three less than those of the Confederates. Against their six field-batteries General Grant had seven. In cavalry alone he was materially stronger. The rule in attacking fortifications is five to one; to save the Union commander from a charge of rashness, however, he had also at control a fighting quality ordinarily at home on the sea rather than the land. After receiving the surrender of Fort Henry, Flag-Officer Foote had hastened to Cairo to make preparation for the reduction of Fort Donelson. With six of his boats, he passed into the Cumberland River; and on the 12th, while the two divisions of the army were marching across to Donelson, he was hurrying, as fast as steam could drive him and his following, to a second trial of iron batteries afloat against earth batteries ashore. The *Carondelet*, Commander Walke, having preceded him, had been in position below the fort since the 12th. By sundown of the 12th, McClernand and Smith reached the point designated for them in orders.

On the morning of the 13th of February General Grant, with about twenty thousand men, was before Fort Donelson. We have had a view of the army in the works ready for battle; a like view of that outside and about to go into position of attack and assault is not so easily to be given. At dawn the latter host rose up from the bare ground, and, snatching bread and coffee

Foote's gunboats unsuccessfully engage the batteries of Fort Donelson with little success. While unable to shut down the enemy guns, the Federal fleet took a severe pounding.

as best they could, fell into lines that stretched away over hills, down hollows, and through thickets, making it impossible for even colonels to see their regiments from flank to flank.

Pausing to give a thought to the situation, it is proper to remind the reader that he is about to witness an event of more than mere historical interest; he is about to see the men of the North and North-west and of the South and South-west enter for the first time into a strife of arms; on one side the best blood of Tennessee, Kentucky, Alabama, Mississippi, and Texas, aided materially by fighting representatives from Virginia; on the other, the best blood of Illinois, Ohio, Indiana, Iowa, Missouri, and Nebraska.

We have now before us a spectacle seldom witnessed in the annals of scientific war—an army behind field-works erected in a chosen position waiting quietly while another army very little superior in numbers proceeds at leisure to place it in a state of siege. Such was the operation General Grant had before him at daybreak of the 13th of February. Let us see how it was accomplished and how it was resisted.

In a clearing about two miles from Dover there was a log-house, at the time occupied by a Mrs. Crisp. As the road to Dover ran close by, it was made the head-quarters of the commanding general. All through the night of the 12th, the coming and going was incessant. Smith was ordered to find a position in front of the enemy's right wing, which would place him face to face with Buckner. McClernand's order was to establish himself on the enemy's left, where he would be opposed to Pillow.

A little before Birge's sharp-shooters were astir. Theirs was a peculiar service. Each was a preferred marksman, and carried a long-range Henry rifle, with sights delicately arranged as for target practice. In action each was perfectly independent. They never manœuvered as a corps. When the time came they were asked, "Canteens full?" "Biscuits for all day?" Then their only order, "All right; hunt your holes, boys." Thereupon they dispersed, and, like Indians, sought cover to please themselves behind rocks and stumps, or in hollows. Sometimes they dug holes; sometimes they climbed into trees. Once in a good location, they remained there the day. At night they would crawl out and report in camp. This morning, as I have said, the sharp-shooters dispersed early to find places within easy range of the breastworks.

The movement by Smith and McClernand was begun about the same time. A thick wood fairly screened the former. The latter had to cross an open valley under fire of two batteries, one on Buckner's left, the other on a high point jutting from the line of outworks held by Colonel Heiman of Pillow's command. Graves commanded the first, Maney the second; both were of Tennessee. As always in situations where the advancing party is ignorant of the ground and of the designs of the enemy, resort was had to skirmishers, who are to the main body what antennæ are to insects. Theirs it is to unmask the foe. Unlike sharp-shooters, they act in bodies. Behind the skirmishers, the batteries started out to find positions,

and through the brush and woods, down the hollows, up the hills the guns and caissons were hauled. Nowadays it must be a very steep bluff in face of which the good artillerist will stop or turn back. At Donelson, however, the proceeding was generally slow and toilsome. The officer had to find a vantage-ground first; then with axes a road to it was hewn out; after which, in many instances, the men, with the prolongs over their shoulders, helped the horses along. In the gray of the dawn the sharp-shooters were deep in their deadly game; as the sun came up, one battery after another opened fire, and was instantly and gallantly answered; and all the time behind the hidden sharp-shooters, and behind the skirmishers, who occasionally stopped to take a hand in the fray, the regiments marched, route-step, colors flying, after their colonels.

About 11 o'clock Commander Walke, of the *Carondelet*, engaged the water-batteries. The air was then full of the stunning music of battle, though as yet not a volley of musketry had been heard. Smith, nearest the enemy at starting, was first in place; and there, leaving the fight to his sharp-shooters and skirmishers and to his batteries, he reported to the chief in the log-house, and, like an old soldier, calmly waited orders. McClernand, following a good road, pushed on rapidly to the high grounds on the right. The appearance of his column in the valley covered by the two Confederate batteries provoked a furious shelling from them. On the double-quick his men passed through it; and when, in the wood beyond, they resumed the route-step and saw that nobody was hurt, they fell to laughing at themselves. The real baptism of fire was yet in store for them.

When McClernand arrived at his appointed place and extended his brigades, it was discovered that the Confederate outworks offered a front too great for him to envelop. To attempt to rest his right opposite their extreme left would necessitate a dangerous attenuation of his line and leave him without reserves. Over on their left, moreover, ran the road already mentioned as passing from Dover on the south to Charlotte and Nashville, which it was of the highest importance to close hermetically so that there would be no communication left General Floyd except by the river. If the road to Charlotte were left to the enemy, they might march out at their pleasure.

The insufficiency of his force was thus made apparent to General Grant, and whether a discovery of the moment or not, he set about its correction. He knew a reënforcement was coming up the river under convoy of Foote; besides which a brigade, composed of the 8th Missouri and the 11th Indiana infantry and Battery A, Illinois, had been left behind at Forts Henry and Heiman under myself. A courier was dispatched to me with an order to bring my command to Donelson. I ferried my troops across the Tennessee in the night, and reported with them at headquarters before noon the next day. The brigade was transferred to General Smith; at the same time an order was put into my hand assigning me to command the Third Division, which was conducted to a position between Smith and McClernand, enabling the latter to extend his line well to the left and cover the road to Charlotte.

Thus on the 14th of February the Confederates were completely invested, except that the river above Dover remained to them. The supineness of General Floyd all this while is to this day incomprehensible. A vigorous attack on the morning of the 13th might have thrown Grant back upon Fort Henry. Such an achievement would have more than offset Foote's conquest. The *morale* to be gained would have alone justified the attempt. But with McClernand's strong division on the right, my own in the center, and C. F. Smith's on the left, the opportunity was gone. On the side of General Grant, the possession of the river was all that was wanting; with that Grant could force the fighting, or wait the certain approach of the grimmest enemy of the besieged—starvation.

It is now—morning of the 14th—easy to see and understand with something more than approximate exactness the oppositions of the two forces. Smith is on the left of the Union army opposite Buckner. My division, in the center, confronts Colonels Heiman, Drake, and Davidson, each with a brigade. McClernand, now well over on the right, keeps the road to Charlotte and Nashville against the major part of Pillow's left wing. The infantry on both sides are in cover behind the crests of the hills or in thick woods, listening to the ragged fusillade which the sharpshooters and skirmishers maintain against each other almost without intermission. There is little pause in the exchange of shells and round shot. The careful chiefs have required their men to lie down. In brief, it looks as if each party were inviting the other to begin.

These circumstances, the sharp-shooting and cannonading, ugly as they may seem to one who thinks of them under comfortable surroundings, did in fact serve a good purpose the day in question in helping the men to forget their sufferings of the night before. It must be remembered that the weather had changed during the preceding afternoon: from suggestions of spring it turned to intensified winter. From lending a gentle hand in bringing Foote and his iron-clads up the river, the wind whisked suddenly around to the north and struck both armies with a storm of mixed rain, snow, and sleet. All night the tempest blew mercilessly upon the unsheltered, fireless soldier, making sleep impossible. Inside the works, nobody had overcoats; while thousands of those outside had marched from Fort Henry as to a summer fête, leaving coats, blankets, and knapsacks behind them in the camp. More than one stout fellow has since admitted, with a laugh, that nothing was so helpful to him that horrible night as the thought that the wind, which seemed about to turn his blood into icicles, was serving the enemy the same way; they, too, had to stand out and take the blast. Let us now go back to the preceding day, and bring up an incident of McClernand's swing into position.

About the center of the Confederate outworks there was a V-shaped hill, marked sharply by a ravine on its right and another on its left. This Colonel Heiman occupied with his brigade of five regiments— all of Tennessee but one. The front presented was about 2500 feet. In the angle of the V, on the summit of the hill, Captain Maney's battery, also of Tennessee, had been planted. Without protection of any kind, it nevertheless completely swept a large field to the left, across which an assaulting force would have to come in order to get at Heiman or at Drake, next on the south.

Maney, on the point of the hill, had been active throughout the preceding afternoon, and had succeeded in drawing the fire of some of McClernand's guns. The duel lasted until night. Next morning it was renewed with increased sharpness, Maney being assisted on his right by Graves's battery of Buckner's division, and by some pieces of Drake's on his left.

McClernand's advance was necessarily slow and trying. This was not merely a logical result of unacquaintance with the country and the dispositions of the enemy; he was also under an order from General Grant to avoid everything calculated to bring on a general engagement. In Maney's well-served guns he undoubtedly found serious annoyance, if not a positive obstruction. Concentrating guns of his own upon the industrious Confederate, he at length fancied him silenced and the enemy's infantry on the right thrown into confusion—circumstances from which he hastily deduced a favorable chance to deliver an assault. For that purpose he reënforced his Third Brigade, which was nearest the offending battery, and gave the necessary orders.

Up to this time, it will be observed, there had not been any fighting involving infantry in line. This was now to be changed. Old soldiers, rich with experience, would have regarded the work proposed with gravity; they would have shrewdly cast up an account of the chances of success, not to speak of the chances of coming out alive; they would have measured the distance to be passed, every foot of it, under the guns of three batteries, Maney's in the center, Graves's on their left and Drake's on their right—a direct line of fire doubly crossed. Nor would they have omitted the reception awaiting them from the rifle-pits. They were to descend a hill entangled for two hundred yards with underbrush, climb an opposite ascent partly shorn of timber; make way through an abatis of tree-tops; then, supposing all that successfully accomplished, they would be at last in face of an enemy whom it was possible to reënforce with all the reserves of the garrison—with the whole garrison, if need be. A veteran would have surveyed the three regiments selected for the honorable duty with many misgivings. Not so the men themselves. They were not old soldiers. Recruited but recently from farms and shops, they accepted the assignment heartily and with youthful confidence in their prowess. It may be doubted if a man in the ranks gave a thought to the questions, whether the attack was to be supported while making, or followed up if successful, or whether it was part of a general adavnce. Probably the most they knew was that the immediate objective before them was the capture of the battery on the hill.

The line when formed stood thus from the right: the 49th Illinois, then the 17th, and then the 48th,

Failing to invest the fort by water, Brigadier General Ulysses S. Grant attempted to take it by siege. While Federal troops surrounded Donelson, Union batteries pounded the Confederates in their earthworks.

Confederate entrenchments come under a heavy assault from Colonel Jacob Lauman's brigade of Brigadier General Charles F. Smith's division. Several unfortunate soldiers fell wounded only to freeze to death on the field or be consumed in flames of burning thickets set afire by bursting shells and musketry.

Colonel Haynie. At the last moment, a question of seniority arose between Colonels Morrison and Haynie. The latter was of opinion that he was the ranking officer. Morrison replied that he would conduct the brigade to the point from which the attack was to be made, after which Haynie might take the command, if he so desired.

Down the hill the three regiments went, crashing and tearing through the undergrowth. Heiman, on the lookout, saw them advancing. Before they cleared the woods, Maney opened with shells. At the foot of the descent, in the valley, Graves joined his fire to Maney's. There Morrison reported to Haynie, who neither accepted nor refused the command. Pointing to the hill, he merely said, "Let us take it together." Morrison turned away, and rejoined his own regiment. Here was confusion in the beginning, or worse, an assault begun without a head. Nevertheless, the whole line went forward. On a part of the hillside the trees were yet standing. The open space fell to Morrison and his 49th, and paying the penalty of the exposure, he outstripped his associates. The men fell rapidly; yet the living rushed on and up, firing as they went. The battery was the common target. Maney's gunners, in relief against the sky, were shot down in quick succession. His first lieutenant (Burns) was one of the first to suffer. His second lieutenant (Massie) was mortally wounded. Maney himself was hit; still he staid, and his guns continued their punishment; and still the farmer lads and shop boys of Illinois clung to their purpose. With marvelous audacity they pushed through the abatis and reached a point within forty yards of the rifle-pits. It actually looked as if the prize were theirs. The yell of victory was rising in their throats. Suddenly the long line of yellow breastworks before them, covering Heiman's five regiments, crackled and turned into flame. The forlorn-hope stopped—staggered—braced up again—shot blindly through the smoke at the smoke of the new enemy, secure in his shelter. Thus for fifteen minutes the Illinoisans stood fighting. The time is given on the testimony of the opposing leader himself. Morrison was knocked out of his saddle by a musket-ball, and disabled; then the men went down the hill. At its foot they rallied around their flags and renewed the assault. Pushed down again, again they rallied, and a third time climbed to the enemy. This time the battery set fire to the dry leaves on the ground, and the heat and smoke became stifling. It was not possible for grave men to endure more. Slowly, sullenly, frequently pausing to return a shot, they went back for the last time; and in going their ears and souls were riven with the shrieks of their wounded comrades, whom the flames crept down upon and smothered and charred where they lay.

Considered as a mere exhibition of courage, this assault, long maintained against odds,—twice repulsed, twice renewed,—has been seldom excelled. One hundred and forty-nine men of the 17th and 49th were killed and wounded. Haynie reported 1 killed and 8 wounded.

There are few things connected with the operations against Fort Donelson so relieved of uncertainty as this: that when General Grant at Fort Henry became fixed in the resolution to undertake the movement, his primary object was the capture of the force to which the post was intrusted. To effect their complete environment, he relied upon Flag-Officer Foote and his gun-boats, whose astonishing success at Fort Henry justified the extreme of confidence.

Foote arrived on the 14th, and made haste to enter upon his work. The *Carondelet* (Commander Walke) had been in position since the 12th. Behind a low output of the shore, for two days, she maintained a fire from her rifled guns, happily of greater range than the best of those of the enemy.

Troops of the 2nd Iowa Regiment attempt to storm the Confederate entrenchments with bayonets fixed in a failed assault of 15 February 1862.

At 9 o'clock on the 14th, Captain Culbertson, looking from the parapet of the upper battery, beheld the river below the first bend full of transports landing troops under cover of a fresh arrival of gun-boats. The disembarkation concluded, Foote was free. He waited until noon. The captains in the batteries mistook his deliberation for timidity. The impinging of their shot on his iron armor was heard distinctly in the fort a mile and a half away. The captains began to doubt if he would come at all. But at 3 o'clock the boats took position under fire: the *Louisville* on the right, the *St. Louis* next, then the *Pittsburgh*, then the *Carondelet*, all iron-clad.

Five hundred yards from the batteries, and yet Foote was not content! In the Crimean war the allied French and English fleets, of much mightier ships, undertook to engage the Russian short batteries, but little stronger than those at Donelson. The French on that occasion stood off 1800 yards. Lord Lyons fought his *Agamennon* at a distance of 800 yards. Foote forged ahead within 400 yards of his enemy, and was still going on. His boat had been hit between wind and water; so with the *Pittsburgh* and *Carondelet*. About

the guns the floors were slippery with blood, and both surgeons and carpenters were never so busy. Still the four boats kept on, and there was great cheering; for not only did the fire from the shore slacken; the lookouts reported the enemy running. It seemed that fortune would smile once more upon the fleet, and cover the honors of Fort Henry afresh at Fort Donelson. Unhappily, when about 350 yards off the hill a solid shot plunged through the pilot-house of the flag-ship, and carried away the wheel. Near the same time the tiller-ropes of the *Louisville* were disabled. Both vessels became unmanageable and began floating down the current. The eddies turned them round like logs. The *Pittsburgh* and *Carondelet* closed in and covered them with their hulls.

Seeing this turn in the fight, the captains of the batteries rallied their men, who cheered in their turn, and renewed the contest with increased will and energy. A ball got lodged in their best rifle. A corporal and some of his men took a log fitting the bore, leaped out on the parapet, and rammed the missile home. "Now, boys," said a gunner on Bidwell's battery, "see me take a chimney!" The flag of the boat and the chimney fell with the shot.

When the vessels were out of range, the victors looked about them. The fine form of their embrasures was gone; heaps of earth had been cast over their platforms. In a space of twenty-four feet they had picked up as many shot and shells. The air had been full of flying missiles. For an hour and a half the brave fellows had been rained upon; yet their losses had been trifling in numbers. Each gunner had selected a ship and followed her faithfully throughout the action, now and then uniting fire on the *Carondelet*. The Confederates had behaved with astonishing valor. Their victory sent a thrill of joy through the army. The assault on the outworks, the day before, had been a failure. With the repulse of the gun-boats the Confederates scored success number two, and the communication by the river remained open to Nashville. The winds that blew sleet and snow over Donelson that night were not so unendurable as they might have been.

The night of the 14th of February fell cold and dark, and under the pitiless sky the armies remained in position so near to each other that neither dared light fires. Overpowered with watching, fatigue, and the lassitude of spirits which always follows a strain upon the faculties of men like that which is the concomitant of battle, thousands on both sides lay down in the ditches and behind logs and whatever else would in the least shelter them from the cutting wind, and tried to sleep. Very few closed their eyes. Even the horses, after their manner, betrayed the suffering they were enduring.

That morning General Floyd had called a council of his chiefs of brigades and division. He expressed the opinion that the post was untenable, except with fifty thousand troops. He called attention to the heavy reënforcements of the Federals, and suggested an immediate attack upon their right wing to reopen land communication with Nashville, by way of Charlotte.

The proposal was agreed to unanimously. General Buckner proceeded to make dispositions to cover the retreat, in the event the sortie should be successful. Shortly after noon, when the movement should have begun, the order was countermanded at the instance of Pillow. Then came the battle with the gun-boats.

In the night the council was recalled, with general and regimental officers in attendance. The situation was again debated, and the same conclusion reached. Accordingly to the plan resolved upon, Pillow was to move at dawn with his whole division, and attack the right of the besiegers. General Buckner was to be relieved by troops in the forts, and with his command to support Pillow by assailing the right of the enemy's center. If he succeeded, he was to take post outside the intrenchments on the Wynne's Ferry road to cover the retreat. He was then to act as rear-guard. Thus early, leaders in Donelson were aware of the mistake into which they were plunged. Their resolution was wise and heroic. Let us see how they executed it.

Preparations for the attack occupied the night. The troops for the most part were taken out of the rifle-pits and massed over on the left to the number of ten thousand or more. The ground was covered with ice and snow; yet the greatest silence was observed. It seems incomprehensible that columns mixed of all arms, infantry, cavalry, and artillery, could have en-gaged in simultaneous movement, and not have been heard by some listener outside. One would think the jolting and rumble of the heavy gun-carriages would have told the story. But the character of the night must be remembered. The pickets of the Federals were struggling for life against the blast, and probably did not keep good watch.

Oglesby's brigade held McClernand's extreme right. Here and there the musicians were beginning to make the woods ring with reveille, and the numbed soldiers of the line were rising from their icy beds and shaking the snow from their frozen garments. As yet, however, not a company had "fallen in." Suddenly the pickets fired, and with the alarm on their lips rushed back upon their comrades. The woods on the instant became alive.

The regiments formed, officers mounted and took their places; words of command rose loud and eager. By the time Pillow's advance opened fire on Oglesby's

On 14 February, Confederate troops attempted to break through Union lines. Despite initial success, Brigadier Generals Gideon J. Pillow and John B. Floyd decided against the completion of the maneuver and ordered their troops to fall back to the entrenchments of Fort Donelson.

right, the point first struck, the latter was fairly formed to receive it. A rapid exchange of volleys ensued. The distance intervening between the works on one side and the bivouac on the other was so short that the action began before Pillow could effect a deployment. His brigades came up in a kind of echelon, left in front, and passed "by regiments left into line," one by one, however; the regiments quickly took their places, and advanced without halting. Oglesby's Illinoisians were now fully awake. They held their ground, returning in full measure the fire that they received. The Confederate Forrest rode around as if to get in their rear, and it was then give and take, infantry against infantry. The semi-echelon movement of the Confederates enabled them, after an interval, to strike W. H. L. Wallace's brigade, on Oglesby's left. Soon Wallace was engaged along his whole front, now prolonged by the addition to his command of Morrison's regiments. The first charge against him was repulsed; whereupon he advanced to the top of the rising ground behind which he had sheltered his troops in the night. A fresh assault followed, but, aided by a battery across the valley to his left, he repulsed the enemy a second time. His men were steadfast, and clung to the brow of the hill as if it were theirs by holy right. An hour passed, and yet another hour, without cessation of the fire. Meantime the woods rang with a monstrous clangor of musketry, as if a million men were beating empty barrels with iron hammers.

Buckner flung a portion of his division on McClernand's left, and supported the attack with his artillery. The enfilading fell chiefly on W. H. L. Wallace. McClernand, watchful and full of resources, sent batteries to meet Buckner's batteries. To that duty Taylor rushed with his Company B; and McAllister pushed his three 24-pounders into position and exhausted his ammunition in the duel. The roar never slackened. Men fell by the score, reddening the snow with their blood. The smoke, in pallid white clouds, clung to the underbrush and tree-tops as if to screen the combatants from each other. Close to the ground the flame of musketry and cannon tinted everything a lurid red. Limbs dropped from the trees on the heads below, and the thickets were shorn as by an army of cradlers. The division was under peremptory orders to hold its position to the last extremity, and Colonel Wallace was equal to the emergency.

It was now 10 o'clock, and over on the right Oglesby was beginning to fare badly. The pressure on his front grew stronger. The "rebel yell," afterward a familiar battle-cry on many fields, told of ground being gained against him. To add to his doubts, officers were riding to him with a sickening story that their commands were getting out of ammunition, and asking where they could go to a supply. All he could say was to take what was in the boxes of the dead and wounded. At last he realized that the end was come. His right companies began to give way, and as they retreated, holding up their empty cartridge-boxes, the enemy were emboldened, and swept more fiercely around his flank, until finally they appeared in his rear. He then gave the order to retire the division.

W. H. L. Wallace from his position looked off to his right and saw but one regiment of Oglesby's in place, maintaining the fight, and that was John A. Logan's 31st Illinois. Through the smoke he could see Logan riding in a gallop behind his line; through the roar in his front and the rising yell in his rear, he could hear Logan's voice in fierce entreaty to his "boys." Near the 31st stood W. H. L. Wallace's regiment, the 11th Illinois, under Lieutenant-Colonel Ransom. The gaps in the ranks of the two were closed up always toward the colors. The ground at their feet was strewn with their dead and wounded; at length the common misfortune overtook Logan. To keep men without cartridges under fire sweeping them front and flank would be cruel, if not impossible; and seeing it, he too gave the order to retire, and followed his decimated companies to the rear. The 11th then became the right of the brigade, and had to go in turn. Nevertheless, Ransom changed front to rear coolly, as if on parade, and joined in the general retirement. Forrest charged them and threw them into a brief conclusion. The greater portion clung to their colors, and made good their retreat. By 11 o'clock Pillow held the road to Charlotte and the whole of the position occupied at dawn by the First Division, and with it the dead and all the wounded who could not get away.

Pillow's part of the programme, arranged in the council of the night before, was accomplished. The country was once more open to Floyd. Why did he not avail himself of the dearly bought opportunity, and march his army out?

Without pausing to consider whether the Confederate general could now have escaped with his troops, it must be evident that he should have made the effort. Pillow had discharged his duty well. With the disappearance of W. H. L. Wallace's brigade, it only remained for the victor to deploy his regiments into column and march into the country. The road was his. Buckner was in position to protect Colonel Head's withdrawal from the trenches opposite General Smith on the right; that done, he was also in position to cover the retreat. Buckner had also faithfully performed his task.

On the Union side the situation at this critical time was favorable to the proposed retirement. My division in the center was weakened by the dispatch of one of my brigades to the assistance of General McClernand; in addition to which my orders were to hold my position. As a point of still greater importance, General Grant had gone on board the *St. Louis* at the request of Flag-Officer Foote, and he was there in consultation with that officer, presumably uninformed of the disaster which had befallen his right. It would take a certain time for him to return to the field and dispose his forces for pursuit. It may be said with strong assurance, consequently, that Floyd could have put his men fairly *en route* for Charlotte before the Federal commander could have interposed an obstruction to the movement. The real difficulty was in the hero of the morning, who now made haste to blight his laurels. General Pillow's vanity whistled itself into ludicrous exaltation. Imagining General Grant's whole army defeated and fleeing in rout for Fort Henry and the transports on the river, he deported himself accordingly. He began by ignoring Floyd. He rode to Buckner and accused him of shameful conduct. He sent an aide to the nearest telegraph station with a dispatch to Albert Sidney Johnston, then in command of the Department, asseverating, "on the honor of a soldier," that the day was theirs. Nor did he stop at that. The victory, to be available, required that the enemy should be followed with energy. Such was a habit of Napoleon. Without deigning even to consult his chief, he ordered Buckner to move out and attack the Federals. There was a gorge, up which a road ran toward our central position, or rather what had been our central position. Pointing to the gorge and the road, he told Buckner that was his way and bade him attack in force. There was nothing to do but obey; and when Buckner had begun the movement, the wise programme decided upon the evening before was wiped from the slate.

When Buckner reluctantly took the gorge road marked out for him by Pillow, the whole Confederate army, save the detachments on the works, was virtually in pursuit of McClernand, retiring by the Wynn's Ferry road— falling back, in fact, upon my position. My division was now to feel the weight of Pillow's hand; if they should fail, the fortunes of the day would depend upon the veteran Smith.

When General McClernand perceived the peril threatening him in the morning, he sent an officer to me with a request for assistance. This request I referred to General Grant, who was at the time in consultation with Foote. Upon the turning of Oglesby's flank, McClernand repeated his request, with such a representation of the situation that, assuming the responsibility, I ordered Colonel Cruft to report with his brigade to McClernand. Cruft set out promptly. Unfortunately a guide misdirected him, so that he became involved in the retreat, and was prevented from accomplishing his object.

I was in the rear of my single remaining brigade, in conversation with Captain Rawlins, of Grant's staff, when a great shouting was heard behind me on the Wynn's Ferry road, whereupon I sent an orderly to ascertain the cause. The man reported the road and woods full of soldiers apparently in rout. An officer then rode by at full speed, shouting, "All's lost! Save yourselves!" A hurried consultation was had with Rawlins, at the end of which the brigade was put in motion toward the enemy's works, on the very road by which Buckner was pursuing under Pillow's mischievous order. It happened also that Colonel W. H. L. Wallace had dropped into the same road with such of his command as staid by their colors. He came up riding and at a walk, his leg over the horn of his saddle. He was perfectly cool, and looked like a farmer from a hard day's plowing. "Good-morning," I said. "Good-morning," was the reply. "Are they pursuing you?" "Yes." "How far are they behind?" That instant the head of my command appeared on the road. The

colonel calculated, then answered: "You will have about time to form line of battle right here." "Thank you. Good-day." "Good-day."

At that point the road began to dip into the gorge; on the right and left there were woods, and in front a dense thicket. An order was dispatched to bring Battery A forward at full speed. Colonel John A. Thayer, commanding the brigade, formed it on the double-quick into line; the 1st Nebraska and the 58th Illinois on the right, and the 58th Ohio, with a detached company, on the left. The battery came up on the run and swung across the road, which had been left open for it. Hardly had it unlimbered, before the enemy appeared, and firing began. For ten minutes or thereabouts the scenes of the morning were reëacted. The Confederates struggled hard to perfect their deployments. The woods range with musketry and artillery. The brush on the slope of the hill was mowed away with bullets. A great cloud arose and shut out the woods and the narrow valley below. Colonel Thayer and his regiments behaved with great gallantry, and the assailants fell back in confusion and returned to the intrenchments. W. H. L. Wallace and Oglesby reformed their commands behind Thayer, supplied them with ammunition, and stood at rest waiting for orders. There was then a lull in the battle. Even the cannonading ceased, and everybody was asking, What next?

Just then General Grant rode up to where General McClernand and I were in conversation. He was almost unattended. In his hand there were some papers, which looked like telegrams. Wholly unexcited, he saluted and received the salutations of his subordinates. Proceeding at once to business, he directed them to retire their commands to the heights out of cannon range, and throw up works. Reënforcements were *en route*, he said, and it was advisable to await their coming. He was then informed of the mishap to the First Division, and that the road to Charlotte was open to the enemy.

In every great man's career there is a crisis exactly similar to that which now overtook General Grant, and it cannot be better described than as a crucial test of his nature. A mediocre person would have accepted the news as an argument for persistance in his resolution to enter upon a siege. Had General Grant done so, it is very probable his history would have been then and there concluded. His admirers and detractors are alike invited to study him at this precise juncture. It cannot be doubted that he saw with painful distinctness the effect of the disaster to his right wing. His face flushed slightly. With a sudden grip he crushed the papers in his hand. But in an instant these signs of disappointment or hesitation—as the reader pleases—cleared away. In his ordinary quiet voice he said, addressing himself to both officers, "Gentlemen, the position on the right must be retaken." With that he turned and galloped off.

Seeing in the road a provisional brigade, under Colonel Morgan L. Smith, consisting of the 11th Indiana and the 8th Missouri Infantry, going, by order of General C. F. Smith, to the aid of the First Division, I suggested that if General McClernand would order

Grant with his favorite mount **Cincinnati.** *The general's victory proved a great relief to the North which was embarrassed by the disastrous defeat at Bull Run a year earlier.*

Colonel Smith to report to me, I would attempt to recover the lost ground; and the order having been given, I reconnoitered the hill, determined upon a place of assault, and arranged my order of attack. I chose Colonel Smith's regiments to lead, and for that purpose conducted them to the crest of a hill opposite a steep bluff covered by the enemy. The two regiments had been formerly of my brigade. I knew they had been admirably drilled in the Zouave tactics, and my confidence in Smith and in George F. McGinnis, colonel of the 11th, was implicit. I was sure they would take their men to the top of the bluff. Colonel Cruft was put in line to support them on the right. Colonel Ross, with his regiments, the 175h and 49th, and the 46th, 57th, and 58th Illinois, were put as support on the left. Thayer's brigade was held in reserve. These dispositions filled the time till about 2 o'clock in the afternoon, when heavy cannonading, mixed with a long roll of musketry, broke out over on the left, whither it will be necessary to transfer the reader.

The veteran in command on the Union left had contented himself with allowing Buckner no rest, keeping up a continual sharp-shooting. Early in the morning of the 14th he made a demonstration of assault with three of his regiments, and though he purposely withdrew them, he kept the menace standing, to the great discomfort of his *vis-à-vis*. With the patience of an old soldier, he waited the pleasure of the general commanding, knowing that when the time came he would be called upon. During the battle of the gunboats he rode through his command and grimly joked with them. He who never permitted the slightest familiarity from a subordinate, could yet indulge in fatherly pleasantries with the ranks when he thought circumstances justified them. He never for a moment doubted the courage of volunteers; they were not regulars—that was all. If properly led, he believed they would storm the gates of his Satanic Majesty. Their hour of trial was now come.

From his brief and characteristic conference with McClernand and myself, General Grant rode to General C. F. Smith. What took place between them is not known, further than that he ordered an assault upon the outworks as a diversion in aid of the assault about to be delivered on the right. General Smith personally directed his chiefs of brigade to get their regiments ready. Colonel John Cook by his order increased the number of his skirmishers already engaged with the enemy.

Taking Lauman's brigade, General Smith began the advance. They were under fire instantly. The guns in the fort joined in with the infantry who were at the time in the rifle-pits, the great body of the Confederate right wing being with General Buckner. The defense was greatly favored by the ground, which subjected the assailants to a double fire from the begin-

A Federal picket on guard against a possible Confederate attack.

ning of the abatis. The men have said that "it looked too thick for a rabbit to get through." General Smith, on his horse, took position in the front and center of the line. Occasionally he turned in the saddle to see how the alignment was kept. For the most part, he held his face steadily toward the enemy. He was, of course, a conspicuous object for the sharp-shooters in the rifle-pits. The air around him twittered with minie-bullets. Erect as if on review, he rode on, timing the gait of his horse with the movement of his colors. A soldier said: "I was nearly scared to death, but I saw the old man's white mustache over his shoulder, and went on."

On to the abatis the regiments moved without hesitation, leaving a trail of dead and wounded behind. There the fire seemed to get trebly hot, and there some of the men halted, whereupon, seeing the hesitation, General Smith put his cap on the point of his sword, held it aloft, and called out, "No flinching now, my lads?—Here—this is the way! Come on!" He picked a path through the jagged limbs of the trees,

holding his cap all the time in sight; and the effect was magical. The men swarmed in after him, and got through in the best order they could—not all of them, alas! On the other side of the obstruction they took the semblance of re-formation and charged in after their chief, who found himself then between the two fires. Up the ascent he rode; up they followed. At the last moment the keepers of the rifle-pits clambered out and fled. The four regiments engaged in the feat—the 25th Indiana, and the 2d, 7th, and 14th Iowa—planted their colors on the breastwork. Later in the day, Buckner came back with his division; but all his efforts to dislodge Smith were vain.

We left my division about to attempt the recapture of the hill, which had been the scene of the combat between Pillow and McClernand. If only on account of the results which followed that assault, in connection with the heroic performance of General C. F. Smith, it is necessary to return to it.

Riding to my old regiments,—the 8th Missouri and the 11th Indiana,—I asked them if they were ready. They demanded the word of me. Waiting a moment for Morgan L. Smith to light a cigar, I called out, "Forward it is, then!" They were directly in front of the ascent to be climbed. Without stopping for his supports, Colonel Smith led them down into a broad hollow, and catching sight of the advance, Cruft and Ross also moved forward. As the two regiments began the climb, the 8th Missouri slightly in the lead, a line of fire ran along the brow of the height. The flank companies cheered while deploying as skirmishers. Their Zouave practice proved of excellent service to them. Now on the ground, creeping when the fire was hottest, running when it slackened, they gained ground with astonishing rapidity, and at the same time maintained a fire that was like a sparkling of the earth. For the most part the bullets aimed at them passed over their heads and took effect in the ranks behind them. Colonel Smith's cigar was shot off close to his lips. He took another and called for a match. A soldier ran and gave him one. "Thank you. Take your place now. We are almost up," he said, and, smoking, spurred his horse forward. A few yards from the crest of the height the regiments began loading and firing as they advanced. The defenders gave way. On the top there was a brief struggle, which was ended by Cruft and Ross with their supports.

The whole line then moved forward simultaneously, and never stopped until the Confederates were within the works. There had been no occasion to call on the reserves. The road to Charlotte was again effectually shut, and the battle-field of the morning, with the dead and wounded lying where they had fallen, was in possession of the Third Division, which stood halted within easy musket-range of the rifle-pits. It was then about half-past 3 o'clock in the afternoon. I was reconnoitering the works of the enemy preliminary to charging them, when Colonel Webster, of General Grant's staff, came to me and repeated the order to fall back out of cannon range and throw up breastworks. "The general does not know that we have the hill," I said. Webster replied: "I give you the order as he gave it to me." "Very well," said I, "give

him my compliments, and say that I have received the order." Webster smiled and rode away. The ground was not vacated, though the assault was deferred. In assuming the responsibility, I had no doubt of my ability to satisfy General Grant of the correctness of my course; and it was subsequently approved.

When night fell, the command bivouacked without fire or supper. Fatigue parties were told off to look after the wounded; and in the relief given there was no distinction made between friend and foe. The labor extended through the whole night, and the surgeons never rested. By sunset the conditions of the morning were all restored. The Union commander was free to order a general assault next day or resort to a formal siege.

A great discouragement fell upon the brave men inside the works that night. Besides suffering from wounds and bruises and the dreadful weather, they were aware that though they had done their best they were held in a close grip by a superior enemy. A council of general and field officers was held at headquarters, which resulted in a unanimous resolution that if the position in front of General Pillow had not been reoccupied by the Federals in strength, the army should effect its retreat. A reconnoissance was ordered to make the test. Colonel Forrest conducted it. He reported that the ground was not only reoccupied, but that the enemy were extended yet farther around the Confederate left. The council then held a final session.

General Simon B. Buckner, as the junior officer present, gave his opinion first; he thought he could not successfully resist the assault which would be made by daylight by a vastly superior force. But he further remarked, that as he understood the principal object of the defense of Donelson was to cover the movement of General Albert Sidney Johnston's army from Bowling Green to Nashville, if that movement was not completed he was of opinion that the defense should be continued at the risk of the destruction of the entire force. General Floyd replied that General Johnston's army had already reached Nashville, whereupon General Buckner said that "it would be wrong to subject the army to a virtual massacre, when no good could result from the sacrifice, and that the general officers owed it to their men, when further resistance was unvailing, to obtain the best terms of capitulation possible for them."

Both Generals Floyd and Pillow acquiesced in the opinion. Ordinarily the council would have ended at this point, and the commanding general would have addressed himself to the duty of obtaining terms. He would have called for pen, ink, and paper, and prepared a note for dispatch to the commanding general of the opposite force. But there were circumstances outside the mere military situation which at this juncture pressed themselves into consideration. As this was the first surrender of armed men banded together for war upon the general government, what would the Federal authorities do with the prisoners? This question was of application to all the gentlemen in the council. It was lost to view, however, when General Floyd announced his purpose to leave with two steamers which were to be down at daylight, and to take with him as many of his division as the steamers could carry away.

General Pillow then remarked that there were no two persons in the Confederacy whom the Yankees would rather capture than himself and General Floyd (who had been Buchanan's Secretary of War, and was under indictment at Washington). As to the propriety of his accompanying General Floyd, the latter said, coolly, that the question was one for every man to decide for himself. Buckner was of the same view, and added that as for himself he regarded it as his duty to stay with his men and share their fate, whatever it might be. Pillow persisted in leaving. Floyd then directed General Buckner to consider himself in command. Immediately after the council was concluded, General Floyd prepared for his departure. His first move was to have his brigade drawn up. The peculiarity of the step was that, with the exception of one, the 20th Mississippi regiment, his regiments were all Virginians. A short time before daylight the two steamboats arrived. Without loss of time the general hastened to the river, embarked with his Virginians, and at an early hour cast loose from the shore, and in good time, and safely, he reached Nashville. He never satisfactorily explained upon what principle he appropriated all the transportation on hand to the use of his particular command.

Colonel Forrest was present at the council, and when the final resolution was taken, he promptly announced that he neither could nor would surrender his command. The bold trooper had no qualms upon the subject. He assembled his men, all as hardy as himself, and after reporting once more at headquarters, he moved out and plunged into a slough formed by backwater from the river. An icy crust covered its surface, the wind blew fiercely, and the darkness was

unrelieved by a star. There was fearful floundering as the command followed him. At length he struck dry land, and was safe. He was next heard of at Nashville.

General Buckner, who throughout the affair bore himself with dignity, ordered the troops back to their positions and opened communications with General Grant, whose laconic demand of "unconditional surrender," in his reply to General Buckner's overtures, became at once a watchword of the war.

The Third Division was astir very early on the 16th of February. The regiments began to form and close up the intervals between them, the intention being to charge the breastworks south of Dover about breakfast-time. In the midst of the preparation a bugle was heard and a white flag was seen coming from the town toward the pickets. I sent my adjutant-general to meet the flag half-way and inquire its purpose. Answer was returned that General Buckner had capitulated during the night, and was now sending information of the fact to the commander of the troops in this quarter, that there might be no further bloodshed. The division was ordered to advance and take possession of the works and of all public property and prisoners. Leaving that agreeable duty to the brigade commanders, I joined the officer bearing the flag, and with my staff rode across the trench and into the town, till we came to the door of the old tavern already described, where I dismounted. The tavern was the headquarters of General Buckner, to whom I sent my name; and being an acquaintance, I was at once admitted.

I found General Buckner with his staff at breakfast. He met me with politeness and dignity. Turning to the officers at the table, he remarked: "General Wallace, it is not necessary to introduce you to these gentlemen; you are acquainted with them all." They arose, came forward one by one, and gave their hands in salutation. I was then invited to breakfast, which consisted of corn bread and coffee, the best the gallant host had in his kitchen. We sat at the table about an hour and a half, when General Grant arrived and took temporary possession of the tavern as his headquarters. Later in the morning the army marched in and completed the possession.

With no hope of relief in sight, the Confederates display a white flag demonstrating their capitulation after accepting Grant's terms of unconditional surrender.

One of the most daring cavalrymen of the Civil War, Nathan Bedford Forrest. A colonel commanding Floyd's cavalry at Fort Donelson, Forrest was unwilling to become a captive of the Yankees in the surrender of the garrison. Taking a route through Grant's lines, he made a successful escape with his troopers.

PEA RIDGE

While certainly not ranking among the better known battles of the Civil War, Pea Ridge was one of the greatest fights west of the Mississippi River. The action took place on 7-8 March 1862 between a Federal army of 11,000 under Brigadier General Samuel R. Curtis and Confederate forces numbering some 16,000 troops commanded by Major-General Earl Van Dorn. After this bitter struggle in Northern Arkansas, Van Dorn's army was forced to retreat and surrender Missouri forever to the Union.

The 8th Missouri Volunteer Regiment charges over the 18th U.S. Regulars to take up the fight against the Confederate line at Pea Ridge.

★★★

DABNEY H. MAURY
Bloody Arkansas

*Dabney Herndon Maury, who hailed from Virginia, attained the rank of colonel and served as chief of staff to Earl Van Dorn during the Pea Ridge Campaign.
After the war, he was noted for founding the Southern Historical Society. This*

abridged selection on his close relationship with Van Dorn and the battle of Pea Ridge, or Elk Horn Tavern, was originally published in the Southern Society Historical Papers *under the title "Recollections of Earl Van Dorn."*

General Earl Van Dorn was, in the opinion of the writer, the most remarkable man the State of Mississippi has ever known. My acquaintance with him began in Monterey, in the fall of 1846. He was aide-de-camp then to General Persifor F. Smith, and was one of the most attractive young fellows in the army. He used to ride a beautiful bay Andalusian horse, and as he came galloping along the lines, with his yellow hair waving in the wind and his bright face lighted with kindliness and courage, we all loved to see him. His figure was lithe and graceful; his stature did not exceed five feet six inches; but his clear blue eyes, his firm-set mouth, with white, strong teeth, his well-cut nose, with expanding nostrils, gave assurance of a man whom men could trust and follow. No young officer came out of the Mexican war with a reputation more enviable than his. After the close of that war he resumed his duties and position in the infantry regiment of which he was a lieutenant.

In 1854 the Second Cavalry was organized, and Van Dorn was promoted to be the major of the regiment. He conducted several of the most important and successful expeditions against the Comanches we have ever made, and in one of them was shot through the body, the point of the arrow just protruding through the skin. No surgeon was at hand. Van Dorn, reflecting that to withdraw the arrow would leave the barbed head in his body, thrust it on through, and left the surgeon little to do. When the States resumed their State sovereignty he took a bold and efficient part in securing to Texas, where he was serving, all of the war material within her borders. Early in the war he was ordered to join the army under General Joe Johnston at Manassas; whence soon after, in February, 1861, he was ordered to take command of the Trans-Mississippi Department.

I was associated with him in this command as chief of his staff and saw him daily for many months. He had conceived the bold project of capturing St. Louis and transferring the war into Illinois, and was actively engaged in preparing for this enterprise when

he was summoned by General Price to Boston mountain, where the forces of Price and McCulloch lay in great need of a common superior—for these two generals could not co-operate because of questions of rank. Therefore, Van Dorn promptly responded to Price's summons, and in a few hours was in the saddle and on his way to Van Buren. I went with him, and one aide-de-camp, an orderly and my servant man Jem made up our party. Van Dorn rode a fine thoroughbred black mare he had brought from Virginia. I was mounted on a sorrel I had bought in Pocahontas a few hours before we set out. Except my sorrel mare, Van Dorn's black mare was the hardest trotter in the world, and as we trotted fifty-five miles every day for five or six days, we had a very unusual opportunity of learning all that a hard trotter can do to a man in a long day's march. Had it not been that we slept every night in a feather bed that soothed our sore bones and served as a poultice to our galled saddle pieces, we would have been permanently disabled for cavalry service forever.

Chief of staff for Major General Earl Van Dorn, Colonel Dabney Herndon Maury. His services to the Confederacy at Pea Ridge won him a Major General rank shortly after the battle.

My boy Jem alone enjoyed that trip. He rode in the ambulance all day and slept *ad libitum* day and night; and except when he got a ducking by the upsetting of a canoe in Black river, he was as happy as ever he had been since the last herring season on the Potomac. The battle of Elkhorn disturbed Jem's equilibrium even more than the upsetting of the canoe. The excitement of imminent danger, which was never a pleasing emotion to Jem, was kept up at Elkhorn much longer than in Black river, and I could not find him for three days—not, indeed, until we accidentally met on the route of our retreat, when I must say he showed great delight at "meeting up" with me again, and took to himself no little credit for the skill with which he had conducted the movements of that ambulance for the past three days. It had contained all of our clothing and blankets and camp supplies, of no little value to hungry and wearied warriors. The blankets and clothing were all right, but we found nothing whatever for the inner man. Jem was cheerful and cordial and comfortable, but we never could ascertain where he had the ambulance from time to time the first shot was fired, until the moment we encountered him in full retreat, and with the last sound of the battle died out in the distance behind him.

Van Dorn had planned the battle of Elkhorn well; he had moved so rapidly from Boston mountain with the forces of Price and McCulloch combined that he caught the enemy unprepared, and with his division so far separated that but for the inevitable indiscipline of troops so hastily thrown together he would have destroyed the whole Federal army. By the loss of thirty minutes in reaching Bentonville we lost the cutting off of Siegel with seven thousand men, who were hurrying to join the main body on Sugar creek. But we pushed him hard all that day, and after he had closed upon the main body Van Dorn, leaving a small force to occupy the attention in front, threw his army, by a night march, quite around the Federal army and across their only road by which retreat to Missouri could be effected. He handled his forces well; always attacking, always pressing the enemy back. When he heard of the death in quick succession of the three principal commanders of his right wing—McCulloch, McIntosh and Hebert—and the consequent withdrawal from the attack of that whole wing, he only set his lips a little firmer; his blue eyes blazed brighter, and his nostrils looked wider, as he said: "Then we must press them the harder." And he did, too, and he had everything moving finely by sundown, and all the enemy's line before us in full retreat at a run, and falling back into their wagon trains; when, by misapprehension on the part of the commander with our advanced troops, the pursuit was arrested, our forces withdrawm from the attack to go into bivouac, and the enemy was permitted to quietly reorganize his army and prepare for a combined attack upon us in the morning. During the night we found that most of our batteries and regiments had exhausted their amunition, and the ordnance train, with all the reserve amunition, had been sent away, fifteen miles

back, on the road along which we had come, and the enemy lay between. There was nothing left for Van Dorn but to get his train on the road to Van Buren and his army off by the same route and to fight enough to secure them. This he did, and marched away unmolested.

Commander of the Confederate forces at Pea Ridge, Major General Earl Van Dorn.

Victor of the battle of Pea Ridge, or Elkhorn Tavern, Brigadier General Samuel R. Curtis.

After being driven back from their initial defensive position on the first day of the battle on 7 March 1862, General Curtis' Yankees victoriously counter-attack on the 8th.

Arrived at Van Buren, Van Dorn addressed himself to the completion of the reorganization of his army, thenceforth known as the Army of the West, and it was there he gave an illustration of true magnanimity—very rarely known in ambitious men—by the offer he made to move with all his forces to reinforce General Sidney Johnston at Corinth. By this he surrendered the great independent command of the Trans-Mississippi Department and all the plans he had formed for the sake of his views of the best interests of their common country, and became a subordinate commander of an army corps instead of the commander-in-chief of an army. He hoped to reach Johnston in time for the battle in Shiloh, and had he done so, would have given a very different result to that critical battle. But Shiloh had been fought and our army, under Beauregard, was occupying the works of Corinth when Van Dorn, with the Army of the West, sixteen thousand effectives, reached that point. We lay near Corinth more than six weeks, and three

Brigadier General Samuel R. Curtis' army battles Major General Earl Van Dorn's Confederates. Van Dorn had managed to sneak into his enemy's rear, but Curtis was able to turn his army around the Rebel attack.

times offered battle to Halleck, who, with one hundred thousand men, was cautiously advancing as if to attack us. Three times our army (forty thousand strong) marched out of its entrenchments and advanced to meet Halleck and give him battle, but every time he drew back and declined it. In every council Van Dorn's voice was for war. May 30, 1862, Beauregard evacuated his works in a masterly manner, and marched south unmolested to Tupelo, when he halted the army and held it ready for battle. In June Van Dorn was ordered to go to Vicksburg, which was threatened with attack, and was in poor condition for defence. He evinced here great energy and ability. He repulsed the enemy's fleet, put the place in a good condition of defence, occupied Port Hudson, and there erected such works as enabled us for a year longer to control the Mississippi river and its tributaries so as to keep open free intercourse with the trans-Mississippi, whence large supplies for the armies on this side were drawn. He organized an expedition against Baton Rouge during this time, which but for the cholera, which swept off half of the force, and the untimely breaking down of the ram Arkansas' engine when almost within range of that town, would have been a brilliant and complete success.

After this Van Dorn urged General Price, who had been left at Tupelo with the Army of the West when Bragg moved to Chattanooga, to unite all their available forces in Mississippi, carry Corinth by assault, and sweep the enemy out of West Tennessee. This, unfortunately, Price, under his instructions, could not then do. Our combined forces would then have exceeded twenty-five thousand effectives, and there is no doubt as to the results of the movement. Later, after Breckenridge had been detached with six thousand men and Price had lost about four thousand on the Iuka expedition (mainly stragglers), the attempt on Corinth was made. Its works had been greatly strengthened and its garrison greatly increased. Van Dorn attacked with his usual vigor and dash. His left and centre stormed the town, captured all the guns in their front and broke Rosecrans' centre. The division comprising our right wing remained inactive, so that the enemy, believing that our right was merely making a feint, detached Stanley with six thousand fresh men from his left and drove us out of the town.

Never was a general more disappointed than Van Dorn; but no man in all our army was so little shaken in his courage by the result as he was. I think his was the highest courage I have ever known. It rose above every disaster, and he never looked more gallant than when his broken army in utter disorder was streaming through the open woods which then environed Corinth and its formidable defences. However much depression all of us showed and felt, he alone remained unconquered, and if he could have gotten his forces together would have tried it again. But seeing that was impossible, he brought Lovell's Division, which not having assaulted was unbroken, to cover the rear, and moved back to Chewalla, seven miles west of Corinth, encouraging officers and men to reform their broken organizations as we marched long.

The commander of Curtis' Third Division, Brigadier General Alexander Asboth with his staff. Asboth, a Hungarian expatriate, was wounded at Pea Ridge, but later returned to active command to fight in western Florida.

SHILOH

While the Federal disaster of First Bull Run served as a harbinger that the Civil War would not be brief affair, Shiloh proved what the true cost of modern war would be. Forced out of Missouri, Kentucky, and losing Tennessee, the commander of Confederate forces in the West, Albert Sidney Johnston, concentrated the troops under his command to surprise Grant's isolated command at Pittsburgh Landing and Shiloh Church in southwestern Tennessee on 6 April 1862. Grant's army was able to hold the Confederates off until reinforcements arrived, and routed the attackers the next day. At least 13,047 Federals were lost while the Confederates suffered 10,699 casualties, a horrific toll by any standards. Among the Southern dead was one of the most promising Confederate commanders in the Western Theatre, Albert Sidney Johnston.

Members of the 5th Company of Washington Artillery.

U. S. GRANT

Shiloh

After the fall of Forts Henry and Donelson, U.S. Grant embarked on what would become a triumphant military career. However, shortly after these victories he was surprised by the Confederate attack on his encampment at Pittsburgh Landing. A major defeat here could have led to his removal from command. Another officer caught off guard by the

sudden assault was William Tecumseh Sherman who commanded a division in Grant's Army of the Tennessee. Had events turned differently, both officers probably would have been cashiered and their essential services lost to the Union cause. After the war, Grant authored his reminiscences entitled Personal Memories of U.S. Grant *from which this selection is taken.*

When I reassumed command on the 17th of March I found the army divided, about half being on the east bank of the Tennessee at Savannah, while one division was at Crump's landing on the west bank about four miles higher up, and the remainder at Pittsburg landing, five miles above Crump's. The enemy was in force at Corinth, the junction of the two most important railroads in the Mississippi valley—one connecting Memphis and the Mississippi River with the East, and the other leading south to all the cotton states. Still another railroad connects Corinth with Jackson, in west Tennessee. If we obtained possession of Corinth the enemy would have no railroad for the transportation of armies or supplies until that running east from Vicksburg was reached. It was the great strategic position at the West between the Tennessee and the Mississippi rivers and between Nashville and Vicksburg.

I at once put all the troops at Savannah in motion for Pittsburg landing, knowing that the enemy was fortifying at Corinth and collecting an army there under Johnston. It was my expectation to march against that army as soon as Buell, who had been ordered to reinforce me with the Army of the Ohio, should arrive; and the west bank of the river was the place to start from. Pittsburg is only about twenty miles from Corinth, and Hamburg landing, four miles further up the river, is a mile or two nearer. I had not been in command long before I selected Hamburg as the place to put the Army of the Ohio when it arrived. The roads from Pittsburg and Hamburg to Corinth converge some eight miles out. This disposition of the troops would have given additional roads to march over when the advance commenced, within supporting distance of each other.

Before I arrived at Savannah, Sherman, who had

The victorious leader of the Army of the Tennessee, U.S. "Sam" Grant. Albert S. Johnston's surprise attack on Grant at Shiloh proved a major test for the military prowess of the brigadier and future president from Ohio.

joined the Army of the Tennessee and been placed in command of a division, had made an expedition on steamers convoyed by gunboats to the neighborhood of Eastport, thirty miles south, for the purpose of destroying the railroad east of Corinth. The rains had been so heavy for some time before that the lowlands had become impassable swamps. Sherman debarked his troops and started out to accomplish the object of the expedition; but the river was rising so rapidly that the back-water up the small tributaries threatened to cut off the possibility of getting back to the boats, and the expedition had to return without reaching the railroad. The guns had to be hauled by hand through the water to get back to the boats.

On the 17th of March the army on the Tennessee River consisted of five divisions, commanded respectively by Generals C. F. Smith, McClernand, L. Wallace, Hurlbut and Sherman. General W. H. L. Wallace was temporarily in command of Smith's division, General Smith, as I have said, being confined to his bed. Reinforcements were arriving daily and as they came up they were organized, first into brigades, then into a division, and the command given to General Prentiss, who had been ordered to report to me. General Buell was on his way from Nashville with 40,000 veterans. On the 19th of March he was at Columbia, Tennessee, eighty-five miles from Pittsburg. When all reinforcements should have arrived I expected to take the initiative by marching on Corinth, and had no expectation of needing fortifications, though this subject was taken into consideration. McPherson, my only military engineer, was directed to lay out a line to intrench. He did so, but reported that it would have to be made in rear of the line of encampment as it then ran. The new line, while it would be nearer the river, was yet too far away from the Tennessee, or even from the creeks, to be easily supplied with water, and in case of attack these creeks would be in the hands of the enemy. The fact is, I regarded the campaign we were engaged in as an offensive one and had no idea that the enemy would leave strong intrenchments to take the initiative when he knew he would be attacked where he was if he remained. This view, however, did not prevent every precaution being taken and every effort made to keep advised of all movements of the enemy.

Johnston's cavalry meanwhile had been well out towards our front, and occasional encounters occurred between it and our outposts. On the 1st of April this cavalry became bold and approached our lines, showing that an advance of some kind was contemplated. On the 2d Johnston left Corinth in force to attack my army. On the 4th his cavalry dashed down and captured a small picket guard of six or seven men, stationed some five miles out from Pittsburg on the Corinth road. Colonel Buckland sent relief to the guard at once and soon followed in person with an entire regiment, and General Sherman followed Buckland taking the remainder of a brigade. The pursuit was kept up for some three miles beyond the point where the picket guard had been captured,

and after nightfall Sherman returned to camp and reported to me by letter what had occurred.

At this time a large body of the enemy was hovering to the west of us, along the line of the Mobile and Ohio railroad. My apprehension was much greater for the safety of Crump's landing than it was for Pittsburg. I had no apprehension that the enemy could really capture either place. But I feared it was possible that he might make a rapid dash upon Crump's and destroy our transports and stores, most of which were kept at that point, and then retreat before Wallace could be reinforced. Lew. Wallace's position I regarded as so well chosen that he was not removed.

At this time I generally spent the day at Pittsburg and returned to Savannah in the evening. I was intending to remove my headquarters to Pittsburg, but Buell was expected daily and would come in at Savannah. I remained at this point, therefore, a few days longer than I otherwise should have done, in order to meet him on his arrival. The skirmishing in our front, however, had been so continuous from about the 3d of April that I did not leave Pittsburg each night until an hour when I felt there would be no further danger before the morning.

On Friday the 4th, the day of Buckland's advance, I was very much injured by my horse falling with me, and on me, while I was trying to get to the front where firing had been heard. The night was one of impenetrable darkness, with rain pouring down in torrents; nothing was visible to the eye except as revealed by the frequent flashes of lightning. Under these circumstances I had to trust to the horse, without guidance, to keep the road. I had not gone far, however, when I met General W. H. L. Wallace and Colonel (afterwards General) McPherson coming from the direction of the front. They said all was quiet so far as the enemy was concerned. On the way back to the boat my horse's feet slipped from under him, and he fell with my leg under his body. The extreme softness of the ground, from the excessive rains of the few preceding days, no doubt saved me from a severe injury and protracted lameness. As it was, my ankle was very much injured, so much so that my boot had to be cut off. For two or three days after I was unable to walk except with crutches.

On the 5th General Nelson, with a division of Buell's army, arrived at Savannah and I ordered him to move up the east bank of the river, to be in a position where he could be ferried over to Crump's landing or Pittsburg as occasion required. I had learned that General Buell himself would be at Savannah the next day, and desired to meet me on his arrival. Affairs at Pittsburg landing had been such for several days that I did not want to be away during the day. I determined, therefore, to take a very early breakfast and ride out to meet Buell, and thus save time. He had arrived on the evening of the 5th, but had not advised me of the fact and I was not aware of it until some time after. While I was at breakfast, however, heavy firing was heard in the direction of Pittsburg landing, and I hastened there, sending a hurried note to Buell informing him of the reason why I could not meet him at Savannah. On the way up the river I directed the dispatch-boat to run in close to Crump's landing, so that I could communicate with General Lew. Wallace. I found him waiting on a boat apparently expecting to see me, and I directed him to get his troops in line ready to execute any orders he might receive. He replied that his troops were already under arms and prepared to move.

Up to that time I had felt by no means certain that Crump's landing might not be the point of attack. On reaching the front, however, about eight A.M., I found that the attack on Pittsburg was unmistakable, and that nothing more than a small guard, to protect our transports and stores, was needed at Crump's. Captain Baxter, a quartermaster on my staff, was accordingly directed to go back and order General Wallace to march immediately to Pittsburg by the road nearest the river. Captain Baxter made a memorandum of this

order. About one P.M., not hearing from Wallace and being much in need of reinforcements, I sent two more of my staff, Colonel McPherson and Captain Rowley, to bring him up with his division. They reported finding him marching towards Purdy, Bethel, or some point west from the river, and farther from Pittsburg by several miles than when he started. The road from his first position to Pittsburg landing was direct and near the river. Between the two points a bridge had been built across Snake Creek by our troops, at which Wallace's command had assisted, expressly to enable the troops at the two places to support each other in case of need. Wallace did not arrive in time to take part in the first day's fight. General Wallace has since claimed that the order delivered to him by Captain Baxter was simply to join the right of the army, and that the road over which he marched would have taken him to the road from Pittsburg to

Purdy where it crosses Owl Creek on the right of Sherman; but this is not where I had ordered him nor where I wanted him to go.

I never could see and do not now see why any order was necessary further than to direct him to come to Pittsburg landing, without specifying by what route. His was one of three veteran divisions that had been in battle, and its absence was severely felt. Later in the war General Wallace would not have made the mistake that he committed on the 6th of April, 1862. I presume his idea was that by taking the route he did he would be able to come around on the flank or rear of the enemy, and thus perform an act of heroism that would redound to the credit of his command, as well as to the benefit of his country.

Some two or three miles from Pittsburg landing was a log meeting-house called Shiloh. It stood on the ridge which divides the waters of Snake and Lick

creeks, the former emptying into the Tennessee just north of Pittsburg landing, and the latter south. This point was the key to our position and was held by Sherman. His division was at that time wholly raw, no part of it ever having been in an engagement; but I thought this deficiency was more than made up by the superiority of the commander. McClernand was on Sherman's left, with troops that had been engaged at forts Henry and Donelson and were therefore veterans so far as western troops had become such at that stage of the war. Next to McClernand came Prentiss

Hoosiers belonging to the 9th Indiana. Under the helm of Colonel William B. Hazen, the regiment bravely fought off a series of fierce attacks by Johnston's troops at Shiloh.

with a raw division, and on the extreme left, Stuart with one brigade of Sherman's division. Hurlbut was in rear of Prentiss, massed, and in reserve at the time of the onset. The division of General C. F. Smith was on the right, also in reserve. General Smith was still sick in bed at Savannah, but within hearing of our guns. His services would no doubt have been of inestimable value had his health permitted his presence. The command of his division devolved upon Brigadier-General W. H. L. Wallace, almost estimable and able officer; a veteran too, for he had served a year in the Mexican war and had been with his command at Henry and Donelson. Wallace was mortally wounded in the first day's engagement, and with the change of commanders thus necessarily effected in the heat of battle the efficiency of his division was much weakened.

The position of our troops made a continuous line from Lick Creek on the left to Owl Creek, a branch of Snake Creek, on the right, facing nearly south and possibly a little west. The water in all these streams was very high at the time and contributed to protect our flanks. The enemy was compelled, therefore, to attack directly in front. This he did with great vigor, inflicting heavy losses on the National side, but suffering much heavier on his own.

The Confederate assaults were made with such a disregard of losses on their own side that our line of tents soon fell into their hands. The ground on which the battle was fought was undulating, heavily timbered with scattered clearings, the woods giving some protection to the troops on both sides. There was also considerable underbrush. A number of attempts were made by the enemy to turn our right flank, where

Sherman was posted, but every effort was repulsed with heavy loss. But the front attack was kept up so vigorously that, to prevent the success of these attempts to get on our flanks, the National troops were compelled, several times, to take positions to the rear nearer Pittsburg landing. When the firing ceased at night the National line was all of a mile in rear of the position it had occupied in the morning.

In one of the backward moves, on the 6th, the division commanded by General Prentiss did not fall back with the others. This left his flanks exposed and enabled the enemy to capture him with about 2,200 of his officers and men. General Badeau gives four o'clock of the 6th as about the time this capture took place. He may be right as to the time, but my recollection is that the hour was later. General Prentiss himself gave the hour as half-past five. I was with him, as I was with each of the division commanders that day, several times, and my recollection is that the last time I was with him was about half-past four, when his division was standing up firmly and the General was as cool as if expecting victory. But no matter whether it was four or later, the story that he and his command were surprised and captured in their camps is without any foundation whatever. If it had been true, as currently reported at the time and yet believed by thousands of people, that Prentiss and his division had been captured in their beds, there would not have been an all-day struggle, with the loss of thousands killed and wounded on the Confederate side.

With the single exception of a few minutes after the capture of Prentiss, a continuous and unbroken line was maintained all day from Snake Creek or its

tributaries on the right to Lick Creek or the Tennessee on the left above Pittsburg. There was no hour during the day when there was not heavy firing and generally hard fighting at some point on the line, but seldom at all points at the same time. It was a case of Southern dash against Northern pluck and endurance. Three of the five divisions engaged on Sunday were entirely raw, and many of the men had only received their arms on the way from their States to the field. Many of them had arrived but a day or two before and were hardly able to load their muskets according to the manual. Their officers were equally ignorant of their duties. Under these circumstances it is not astonishing that many of the regiments broke at the first fire. In two cases, as I now remember, colonels led their regiments from the field on first hearing the whistle of the enemy's bullets. In these cases the colonels were constitutional cowards, unfit for any military position; but not so the officers and men led out of danger by them. Better troops never went upon a battle-field than many of these, officers and emn, afterwards proved themselves to be, who fled panic-stricken at the first whistle of bullets and shell at Shiloh.

During the whole of Sunday I was continuously engaged in passing from one part of the field to another, giving directions to division commanders. In thus moving along the line, however, I never deemed it important to stay long with Sherman. Although his troops were then under fire for the first time, their commander, by his constant presence with them, inspired a confidence in officers and men that enabled them to render services on that bloody battle-field worthy of the best of veterans. McClernand was next to Sherman, and the hardest fighting was in front of these two divisions. McClernand told me on that day, the 6th, that he profited much by having so able a commander supporting him. A casualty to Sherman that would have taken him from the field that day would have been a sad one for the troops engaged at Shiloh. And how near we came to this! On the 6th Sherman was shot twice, once in the hand, once in the shoulder, the ball cutting his coat and making a slight wound, and a third ball passed through his hat. In addition to this he had several horses shot during the day.

The nature of this battle was such that cavalry could not be used in front; I therefore formed ours into a line in rear, to stop stragglers—of whom there were many. When there would be enough of them to make a show, and after they had recovered from their fright, they would be sent to reinforce some part of the line which needed support, without regard to their companies, regiments or brigades.

On one occasion during the day I rode back as far as the river and met General Buell, who had just arrived; I do not remember the hour, but at that time there probably were as many as four or five thousand stragglers lying under cover of the river bluff, panic-stricken, most of whom would have been shot where they lay, without resistance, before they would have taken muskets and marched to the front to protect

A formidable array of field pieces from a siege battery mark the final position of Grant's line near Pittsburg Landing.

themselves. This meeting between General Buell and myself was on the dispatch-boat used to run between the landing and Savannah. It was brief, and related specially to his getting his troops over the river. As we left the boat together, Buell's attention was attracted by the men lying under cover of the river bank. I saw him berating them and trying to shame them into joining their regiments. He even threatened them with shells from the gunboats near by. But it was all to no effect. Most of these men afterward proved themselves as gallant as any of those who saved the battle from which they had deserted. I have no doubt that this sight impressed General Buell with the idea that a line of retreat would be a good thing just them. If he had come in by the front instead of through the stragglers in the rear, he would have thought and felt differently. Could he have come through the Confederate rear, he would have witnessed there a scene similar to that at our own. The distant rear of an army engaged in battle is not the best place from which to judge correctly what is going on in front. Later in the war, while occupying the country between the Tennessee and the Mississippi, I learned that the panic in the Confederate lines had not differed much from that within our own. Some of the country people estimated the stragglers from Johnston's army as high as 20,000. Of course this was an exaggeration.

The situation at the close of Sunday was as follows: along the top of the bluff just south of the log-house which stood at Pittsburg landing, Colonel J. D. Webster, of my staff, had arranged twenty or more pieces of artillery facing south or up the river. This line of artillery was on the crest of a hill overlooking a deep ravine opening into the Tennessee. Hurlbut with his division intact was on the right of this artillery, extending west and possibly a little north. McClernand came next in the general line, looking more to the west. His division was complete in its organization and ready for any duty. Sherman came next, his right extending to Snake Creek. His command, like the other two, was complete in its organization and ready, like its chief, for any service it might be called upon to render. All three divisions were, as a matter of course, more or less shattered and depleted in numbers from the terrible battle of the day. The division of W. H. L. Wallace, as much from the disorder arising from changes of division and brigade commanders, under heavy fire, as from any other cause, had lost its organization and did not occupy a place in the line as a division. Prentiss' command was gone as a division, many of its members having been killed, wounded or captured; but it had rendered valiant services before its final dispersal, and had contributed a good share to the defence of Shiloh.

The right of my line rested near the bank of Snake Creek, a short distance above the bridge which had been built by the troops for the purpose of connecting Crump's landing and Pittsburg landing. Sherman had posted some troops in a log-house and out-buildings which overlooked both the bridge over which Wallace was expected and the creek above that point. In this last position Sherman was frequently attacked before night, but held the point until he voluntarily abandoned it to advance in order to make room for Lew. Wallace, who came up after dark.

There was, as I have said, a deep ravine in front of our left. The Tennessee River was very high and there was water to a considerable depth in the ravine. Here the enemy made a last desperate effort to turn our flank, but was repelled. The gunboats *Tyler* and *Lexington*, Gwin and Shirk commanding, with the artillery under Webster, aided the army and effectually checked their further progress. Before any of Buell's troops had reached the west bank of the Tennessee, firing had almost entirely ceased; anything like an attempt on the part of the enemy to advance had absolutely ceased. There was some artillery firing from an unseen enemy, some of his shells passing beyond us; but I do not remember that there was the whistle of a single musket-ball heard. As his troops arrived in the dusk General Buell marched several of his regiments part way down the face of the hill where they fired briskly for some minutes, but I do not think a single man engaged in this firing received an injury. The attack had spent its force.

General Lew. Wallace, with 5,000 effective men, arrived after firing had ceased for the day, and was placed on the right. Thus night came, Wallace came, and the advance of Nelson's division came; but none—unless night—in time to be of material service to the gallant men who saved Shiloh on that first day against large odds. Buell's loss on the 6th of April was two men killed and one wounded, all members of the 36th Indiana infantry. The Army of the Tennessee lost on that day at least 7,000 men. The presence of two or three regiments of Buell's army on the west bank before firing ceased had not the slightest effect in preventing the capture of Pittsburg landing.

So confident was I before firing had ceased on the 6th that the next day would bring victory to our arms if we could only take the initiative, that I visited every commander in person before any reinforcements had reached the field. I directed them to throw out heavy lines of skirmishers in the morning as soon as they could see, and push them forward until they found the enemy, following with their entire divisions in supporting distance, and to engage the enemy as soon as found. To Sherman I told the story of the assault at Fort Donelson, and said that the same tactics would win at Shiloh. Victory was assured when Wallace arrived, even if there had been no other support. I was glad, however, to see the reinforcements of Buell and credit them with doing all there was for them to do. During the night of the 6th the remainder of Nelson's division, Buell's army, crossed the river and were ready to advance in the morning, forming the left wing. Two other divisions, Crittenden's and McCook's, came up the river from Savannah in the transports and were on the west bank early on the 7th. Buell commanded them in person. My command was thus nearly doubled in numbers and efficiency.

During the night rain fell in torrents and our troops were exposed to the storm without shelter. I made my headquarters under a tree a few hundred

Some of the steamboats that proved Grant's salvation in the form of desperately needed reinforcements from Buell's Army of the Ohio.

Buell's troops on the way to join Grant in his time of need. With the arrival of the Army of the Ohio, the chances for a Confederate victory at Shiloh were almost nil.

yards back from the river bank. My ankle was so much swollen from the fall of my horse the Friday night preceding, and the bruise was so painful, that I could get no rest. The drenching rain would have precluded the possibility of sleep without this additional cause. Some time after midnight, growing restive under the storm and the continuous pain, I moved back to the log-house under the bank. This had been taken as a hospital, and all night wounded men were being brought in, their wounds dressed, a leg or an arm amputated as the case might require, and everything being done to save life or alleviate suffering. The sight was more unendurable than encountering the enemy's fire, and I returned to my tree in the rain.

The advance on the morning of the 7th developed the enemy in the camps occupied by our troops before the battle began, more than a mile back from the most advanced position of the Confederates on the day before. It is known now that they had not yet learned of the arrival of Buell's command. Possibly they fell back so far to get shelter of our tents during the rain, and also to get away from the shells that were dropped upon them by the gunboats every fifteen minutes during the night.

The position of the Union troops on the morning of the 7th was as follows: General Lew. Wallace on the right; Sherman on his left; then McClernand and then Hurlbut. Nelson, of Buell's army, was on our extreme left, next to the river. Crittenden was next in line after Nelson and on his right; McCook followed and formed the extreme right of Buell's command. My old command thus formed the right wing, while the troops directly under Buell constituted the left wing of the army. These relative positions were retained during the entire day, or until the enemy was driven from the field.

In a very short time the battle became general all along the line. This day everything was favorable to the Union side. The enemy was driven back all day, as we had been the day before, until finally he beat a precipitate retreat. The last point held by him was near the road leading from the landing to Corinth, on the left of Sherman and right of McClernand. About three o'clock being near that point and seeing that the enemy was giving way everywhere else, I gathered up a couple of regiments, or parts of regiments, from troops near by, formed them in line of battle and marched them forward, going in front myself to prevent premature or long-range firing. At this point there was a clearing between us and the enemy favorable for charging, although exposed. I knew the enemy were ready to break and only wanted a little encouragement from us to go quickly and join their friends who had started earlier. After marching to within musket-range I stopped and let the troops pass. The command, *Charge,* was given, and was executed with loud cheers and with a run; when the last of the enemy broke.

During this second day of the battle I had been moving from right to left and back, to see for myself the progress made. In the early part of the afternoon, while riding with Colonel McPherson and Major Hawkins, then my chief commissary, we got beyond the left of our troops. We were moving along the northern edge of a clearing, very leisurely, toward the river above the landing. There did not appear to be an enemy to our right, until suddenly a battery with musketry opened upon us from the edge of the woods on the other side of the clearing. The shells and balls whistled about our ears very fast for about a minute. I do not think it took us longer than that to get out of range and out of sight. In the sudden start we made, Major Hawkins lost his hat. He did not stop to pick it up. When we arrived at a perfectly safe position we halted to take an account of damages. McPherson's horse was panting as if ready to drop. On examination it was found that a ball had struck him forward of the flank just back of the saddle, and had gone entirely through. In a few minutes the poor beast dropped dead; he had given no sign of injury until we came to a stop. A ball had struck the metal scabbard of my sword, just below the hilt, and broken it nearly off; before the battle was over it had broken off entirely. There were three of us: one had lost a horse, killed; one a hat and one a sword-scabbard. All were thankful that it was no worse.

After the rain of the night before and the frequent and heavy rains for some days previous, the roads were almost impassable. The enemy carrying his artillery and supply trains over them in his retreat, made them still worse for troops following. I wanted to pursue, but had not the heart to order the men who had fought desperately for two days, lying in the mud and rain whenever not fighting, and I did not feel disposed to positively order Buell, or any part of his command, to pursue. Although the senior in rank at the time I had been so only a few weeks. Buell was, and had been for some time past, a department commander, while I commanded only a district. I did not meet Buell in person until too late to get troops ready and pursue with effect; but had I seen him at the moment of the last charge I should have at least requested him to follow.

I rode forward several miles the day after the battle, and found that the enemy had dropped much, if not all, of their provisions, some ammunition and the extra wheels of their caissons, lightening their loads to enable them to get off their guns. About five miles out we found their field hospital abandoned. An immediate pursuit must have resulted in the capture of a considerable number of prisoners and probably some guns.

Shiloh was the severest battle fought at the West during the war, and but few in the East equalled it for hard, determined fighting. I saw an open field, in our possession on the second day, over which the Confederates had made repeated charges the day before, so covered with dead that it would have been possible to walk across the clearing, in any direction, stepping on dead bodies, without a foot touching the ground. On our side National and Confederate troops were mingled together in about equal proportions; but on the remainder of the field nearly all were Confederates. On one part, which had evidently not been ploughed for several years, probably because the land was poor, bushes had grown up, some to the height of eight or ten feet. There was not one of these left standing unpierced by bullets. The smaller ones were all cut down.

Contrary to all my experience up to that time, and to the experience of the army I was then commanding, we were on the defensive. We were without intrenchments or defensive advantages of any sort, and more than half the army engaged the first day was without experience or even drill as soldiers. The officers with them, except the division commanders and possibly two or three of the brigade commanders, were equally inexperienced in war. The result was a Union victory that gave the men who achieved it great confidence in themselves ever after.

The enemy fought bravely, but they had started out to defeat and destroy an army and capture a position. They failed in both, with very heavy loss in killed and wounded, and must have gone back discouraged and convinced that the "Yankee" was not an enemy to be despised.

After the battle I gave verbal instructions to division commanders to let the regiments send out parties to bury their own dead, and to detail parties, under commissioned officers from each division, to bury the Confederate dead in their respective fronts and to report the numbers so buried. The latter part of these instructions was not carried out by all; but they were by those sent from Sherman's division, and by some of the parties sent out by McClernand. The heaviest loss sustained by the enemy was in front of these two divisions.

The criticism has often been made that the Union troops should have been intrenched at Shiloh. Up to that time the pick and spade had been but little resorted to at the West. I had, however, taken this subject under consideration soon after re-assuming command in the field, and, as already stated, my only military engineer reported unfavorably. Besides this, the troops with me, officers and men, needed discipline and drill more than they did experience with the pick, shovel and axe.

Soldiers attend to the duties of clearing the battlefield of debris and carnage at Shiloh. While the bodies of dead soldiers are hastily buried, the carcasses of horses are burned in huge pyres.

LEADNDER STILLWELL

Shiloh—A Private's View

The battle of Shiloh or Pittsburgh Landing was similar to the eastern battle of First Bull Run in the fact that both armies were primarily composed of rookie soldiers who had yet to experience the realities of brutal warfare or discipline needed to undertake complex maneuvers in combat.

Among the ranks of inexperienced fighting men was Leander Stillwell, who was motivated to join the 61st Illinois Regiment after the events of First Bull Run. He later wrote of his experiences in the Federal Army in his book The Story of a Common Soldier.

Let the generals and historians, therefore, write of the movements of corps, divisions, and brigades. I have naught to tell but the simple story of what one private soldier saw of one of the bloodiest battles of the war.

The regiment to which I belonged was the 61st Illinois Infantry. It left its camp of instruction (a country town in southern Illinois) about the last of February, 1862. We were sent to Benton Barracks, near St. Louis, and remained there drilling (when the weather would permit) until March 25th. We left on that day for the front. It was a cloudy, drizzly, and most gloomy day, as we marched through the streets of St. Louis down to the levee, to embark on a transport that was to take us to our destination. The city was enveloped in that pall of coal smoke for which St. Louis is celebrated. It hung heavy and low and set us all to coughing. I think the colonel must have marched us down some by-street. It was narrow and dirty, with high buildings on either side. The line officers took the sidewalks, while the regiment, marching by the flank, tramped in silence down the middle of the street, slumping through the nasty, slimy mud. There was one thing very noticeable on this march through St. Louis, and that was the utter lack of interest taken in us by the inhabitants. From pictures I had seen in books at home, my idea was that when soldiers departed for war, beautiful ladies stood on balconies and waved snowy-white handkerchiefs at the troops, while the men stood on the sidewalks and corners and swung their hats and cheered.

There may have been regiments so favored, but ours was not one of them. Occasionally a fat, chunky-looking fellow, of a German cast of countenance, with a big pipe in his mouth, would stick his head out of a door or window, look at us a few seconds, and then disappear. No handkerchiefs nor hats were waved, we heard no cheers. My thoughts at the time were that the Union people there had all gone to war, or else the colonel was marching us through a "Secesh" part of town.

We marched to the levee and from there on board the big sidewheel steamer, Empress. The next evening she unfastened her moorings, swung her head out into the river, turned down stream, and we were off for the "seat of war." We arrived at Pittsburg Landing on March 31st. Pittsburg Landing, as its name indicates, was simply a landing place for steamboats. It is on the west bank of the Tennessee river, in a thickly wooded region about twenty miles northeast of Corinth. There was no town there then, nothing but "the log house on the hill" that the survivors of the battle of Shiloh will all remember. The banks of the Tennessee on the Pittsburg Landing side are steep and bluffy, rising about 100 feet above the level of the river. Shiloh church, that gave the battle its name, was a Methodist meeting house. It was a small, hewed log building with a clapboard roof, about two miles out from the landing on the main Corinth road. On our arrival we were assigned to the division of General B. M. Prentiss, and we at once marched out and went into camp. About half a mile from the landing the road forks, the main Corinth road goes to the right, past Shiloh church, the other goes to the left. These two roads come together again some miles out. General Prentiss' division was camped on this left-hand road at right angles to it. Our regiment went into camp almost on the extreme left of Prentiss' line. There was a brigade of Sherman's division under General Stuart still further to the left, about a mile, I think, in camp near a ford of Lick Creek, where the Hamburg and Purdy road crosses the creek; and between the left of Prentiss' and General Stuart's camp there were no troops. I know that, for during the few days intervening between our arrival and the battle I roamed all through those woods on our left, between us and Stuart, hunting for wild onions and "turkey peas."

The camp of our regiment was about two miles from the landing. The tents were pitched in the woods, and there was a little field of about twenty acres in our front. The camp faced nearly west, or possibly southwest.

I shall never forget how glad I was to get off that old steamboat and be on solid ground once more, in camp out in those old woods. My company had made the trip from St. Louis to Pittsburg Landing on the hurricane deck of the steamboat, and our fare on the route had been hardtack and raw fat meat, washed down with river water, as we had no chance to cook anything, and we had not then learned the trick of catching the surplus hot water ejected from the boilers and making coffee with it. But once on solid ground, with plenty of wood to make fires, that bill of fare was changed. I shall never again eat meat that will taste as good as the fried "sowbelly" did then, accompanied by "flapjacks" and plenty of good, strong coffee. We had not yet got settled down to the regular drills, guard duty was light, and things generally seemed to run "kind of loose." And then the climate was delightful. We had just left the bleak, frozen north, where all was cold and cheerless, and we found ourselves in a clime where the air was as soft and warm as it was in Illinois in the latter part of May. The green grass was springing from the ground, the "Johnny-jump-ups" were in blossom, the trees were bursting into leaf, and the woods were full of feathered songsters. There was a redbird that would come every morning about sunup and perch himself in the tall black-oak tree in our company street, and for perhaps an hour he would practice on his impatient,

Troops of Grant's Army of the Tennessee arrive at Pittsburg Landing unaware of the cruel surprise Albert Sidney Johnston had in store for them.

querulous note, that said, as plain as a bird could say, "Boys, boys! get up! get up! get up!" It became a standing remark among the boys that he was a Union redbird and had enlisted in our regiment to sound the reveille.

So the time passed pleasantly away until that eventful Sunday morning, April 6, 1862. According to the Tribune Almanac for that year, the sun rose that morning in Tennessee at 38 minutes past five o'clock. I had no watch, but I have always been of the opinion that the sun was fully an hour and a half high before the fighting began on our part of the line. We had "turned out" about sunup, answered to roll-call, and had cooked and eaten our breakfast. We had then gone to work, preparing for the regular Sunday morning inspection, which would take place at nine o'clock. The boys were scattered around the company streets and in front of the company parade grounds, engaged in polishing and brightening their muskets, and brushing up and cleaning their shoes, jackets, trousers, and clothing generally. It was a most beautiful morning. The sun was shining brightly through the trees, and there was not a cloud in the sky. It really seemed like Sunday in the country at home. During week days there was a continual stream of army wagons going to and from the landing, and the clucking of their wheels, the yells and oaths of the drivers, the cracking of whips, mingled with the braying of mules, the neighing of the horses, the commands of the officers engaged in drilling the men, the incessant hum and buzz of the camps, the blare of bugles, and the roll of drums,—all these made up a prodigious volume of sound that lasted from the coming-up to the going-down of the sun. But this morning was strangely still. The wagons were silent, the mules were peacefully munching their hay, and the army teamsters were

giving us a rest. I listened with delight to the plaintive, mournful tones of a turtle-dove in the woods close by, while on the dead limb of a tall tree right in the camp a woodpecker was sounding his "long roll" just as I had heard it beaten by his Northern brothers a thousand times on the trees in the Otter Creek bottom at home.

Suddenly, away off on the right, in the direction of Shiloh church, came a dull, heavy "Pum!" then another, and still another. Every man sprung to his feet as if struck by an electric shock, and we looked inquiringly into one another's faces. "What is that?" asked every one, but no one answered. Those heavy booms then came thicker and faster, and just a few seconds after we heard that first dull, ominous growl off to the southwest, came a low, sullen, continuous roar. There was no mistaking that sound. That was not a squad of pickets emptying their guns on being relieved from duty; it was the continuous roll of thousands of muskets, and told us that a battle was on.

What I have been describing just now occurred during a few seconds only, and with the roar of musketry the long roll began to beat in our camp. Then ensued a scene of desperate haste, the like of which I certainly had never seen before, nor ever saw again. I remember that in the midst of this terrible uproar and confusion, while the boys were buckling on their catridge boxes, and before even the companies had been formed, a mounted staff officer came galloping wildly down the line from the right. He checked and whirled his horse sharply around right in our company street, the iron-bound hoofs of his steed crashing among the tin plates lying in a little pile where my mess had eaten its breakfast that morning. The horse was flecked with foam and its eyes and nostrils were red as blood. The officer cast one hurried glance around him, and exclaimed: "My God! this regiment not in line yet! They have been fighting on the right over an hour!" And wheeling his horse, he disappeared in the direction of the colonel's tent.

I know now that history says the battle began about 4:30 that morning; that it was brought on by a reconnoitering party sent out early that morning by General Prentiss; that General Sherman's division on the right was early advised of the approach of the Rebel army, and got ready to meet them in ample time. I have read these things in books and am not disputing them, but am simply telling the story of an enlisted man on the left of Prentiss' line as to what he saw and knew of the condition of things at about seven o'clock that morning.

Well, the companies were formed, we marched out on the regimental parade ground, and the regiment was formed in line. The command was given: "Load at will; load!" We had anticipated this, however, as the most of us had instinctively loaded our guns before we had formed company. All this time the roar on the right was getting nearer and louder. Our old colonel rode up close to us, opposite the center of the regimental line, and called out, "Attention, battalion!" We fixed our eyes on him to hear what was coming. It turned out to be the old man's battle harangue.

Despite being hard pressed by the Confederate attack, Colonel Hugh B. Reed's 44th Indiana holds its ground in the Hornet's Nest. The tenacity of the Federals in this position blocked the Rebel advance until Grant could form a stronger defensive line near Pittsburg Landing.

*Brigadier General William T. Sherman's division
retreats in a panic from a brutal surprise attack by
Albert Sidney Johnston's Army of the Tennessee on
the morning of 6 April 1862.*

*Despite the shock of the initial Confederate attack
and a hard day of fighting in which the Federals narrowly avoided disaster, Grant's Yankees made their
final stand as darkness descended on the first day of
battle. With reinforcements from Don Carlos Buell
and Lew Wallace arriving on the field, U.S. Grant
had the means to turn the tide on the morrow.*

"Gentlemen," said he, in a voice that every man in the regiment heard, "remember your State, and do your duty today like brave men."

That was all. A year later in the war the old man doubtless would have addressed us as "soldiers," and not as "gentlemen," and he would have omitted his allusion to the "State," which smacked a little of Confederate notions. However, he was a Douglas Democrat, and his mind was probably running on Buena Vista, in the Mexican war, where, it is said, a Western regiment acted badly, and threw a cloud over the reputation for courage of the men of that State which required the thunders of the Civil War to disperse. Immediately after the colonel had given us his brief exhortation, the regiment was marched across the little field I have before mentioned, and we took our place in line of battle, the woods in front of us, and the open field in our rear. We "dressed on" the colors, ordered arms, and stood awaiting the attack. By this time the roar on the right had become terrific. The Rebel army was unfolding its front, and the battle was steadily advancing in our direction. We could begin to see the blue rings of smoke curling upward among the trees off to the right, and the pungent smell of burning gun-powder filled the air. As the roar came travelling down the line from the right it reminded me (only it was a million times louder) of the sweep of a thunder-shower in summer-time over the hard ground of a stubble-field.

And there we stood, in the edge of the woods, so still, waiting for the storm to break on us. I know mighty well what I was thinking about then. My mind's eye was fixed on a little log cabin, far away to the north, in the backwoods of western Illinois. I could see my father sitting on the porch, reading the little local newspaper brought from the post-office the evening before. There was my mother getting my little brothers ready for Sunday-school; the old dog lying asleep in the sun; the hens cackling about the barn; all these things and a hundred other tender recollections rushed into my mind. I am not ashamed to say now that I would willingly have given a general quit-claim deed for every jot and tittle of military glory falling to me, past, present, and to come, if I only could have been miraculously and instantaneously set down in the yard of that peaceful little home, a thousand miles away from the haunts of fighting men.

The time we thus stood, waiting the attack, could not have exceeded five minutes. Suddenly, obliquely to our right, there was a long, wavy flash of bright light, then another, and another! It was the sunlight shining on gun barrels and bayonets—and—there they were at last! A long brown line, with muskets at a right shoulder shift, in excellent order, right through the woods they came.

We began firing at once. From one end of the regiment to the other leaped a sheet of red flame, and the roar that went up from the edge of that old field doubtless advised General Prentiss of the fact that the Rebels had at last struck the extreme left of his line. We had fired but two or three rounds when, for some reason,—I never knew what,—we were ordered to fall back across the field, and did so. The whole line, so far as I could see to the right, went back. We halted on the other side of the field, in the edge of the woods, in front of our tents, and again began firing. The Rebels,

Confederate and Federal battlelines slug it out in the Peach Orchard, not far from where General Albert Sidney Johnston died from his mortal wound.

of course, had moved up and occupied the line we had just abandoned. And here we did our first hard fighting during the day. Our officers said, after the battle was over, that we held this line an hour and ten minutes. How long it was I do not know. I "took no note of time."

We retreated from this position as our officers afterward said, because the troops on our right had given way, and we were flanked. Possibly those boys on our right would give the same excuse for their leaving, and probably truly, too. Still, I think we did not fall back a minute too soon. As I rose from the comfortable log from behind which a bunch of us had been firing, I saw men in gray and brown clothes, with trailed muskets, running through the camp on our right, and I saw something else, too, that sent a chill all through me. It was a kind of flag I had never seen before. It was a gaudy sort of thing, with red bars. It flashed over me in a second that that thing was a Rebel flag. It was not more than sixty yards to the right. The smoke around it was low and dense and kept me from seeing the man who was carrying it, but I plainly saw the banner. It was going fast, with a jerky motion, which told me that the bearer was on a double-quick. About that time we left. We observed no kind of order in leaving; the main thing was to get out of there as quick as we could. I ran down our company street, and in passing the big Sibley tent of our mess I thought of my knapsack with all my traps and belongings, including that precious little packet of letters from home. I said to myself, "I will save my knapsack, anyhow;" but one quick backward glance over my left shoulder made me change my mind, and I went on. I never saw my knapsack or any of its contents afterwards.

Our broken forces halted and re-formed about half a mile to the rear of our camp on the summit of a gentle ridge, covered with thick brush. I recognized our regiment by the little gray pony the old colonel rode, and hurried to my place in the ranks. Standing there with our faces once more to the front, I saw a seemingly endless column of men in blue, marching by the flank, who were filing off to the right through the woods, and I heard our old German adjutant, Cramer, say to the colonel, "Dose are de troops of Sheneral Hurlbut. He is forming a new line dere in de bush." I exclaimed to myself from the bottom of my heart, "Bully for General Hurlbut and the new line in the bush! Maybe we'll whip 'em yet." I shall never forget my feelings about this time. I was astonished at our first retreat in the morning across the field back to our camp, but it occurred to me that maybe that was only "strategy" and all done on purpose; but when we had to give up our camp, and actually turn our backs and run half a mile, it seemed to me that we were forever disgraced, and I kept thinking to myself: "What will they say about this at home?"

I was very dry for a drink, and as we were doing nothing just then, I slipped out of ranks and ran down to the little hollow in our rear, in search of water. Finding a little pool, I threw myself on the ground and took a copious draught. As I rose to my feet, I observed an officer about a rod above me also quenching his thirst, holding his horse meanwhile by the bridle. As he rose I saw it was our old adjutant. At no other time would I have dared accost him unless in the line of duty, but the situation made me bold. "Adjutant," I said, "What does this mean—our having to run this way? Ain't we whipped?" He blew the water from his mustache, and quickly answered in a careless way: "Oh, no; dat is all ride. We yoost fall back to form on the reserve. Sheneral Buell vas now crossing der river mit 50,000 men, and vill be here pooty quick; and Sheneral Lew Vallace is coming from Crump's Landing mit 15,000 more. Ve vips 'em; ve vips 'em. Go to your gompany." Back I went on the run, with a heart as light as a feather. As I took my place in the ranks beside my chum, Jack Medford, I said to him: "Jack, I've just had a talk with the old adjutant, down at the branch where I've been to get a drink. He says Buell is crossing the river with 75,000 men and a whole world of cannon, and that some other general is coming up from Crump's Landing with 25,000 more men. He says we fell back here on purpose, and that we're going to whip the Secesh, just sure. Ain't that just perfectly bully?" I had improved some on the adjutant's figures, as the news was so glorious I thought a little variance of 25,000 or 30,000 men would make no difference in the end. But as the long hours wore on that day, and still Buell and Wallace did not come, my faith in the adjutant's veracity became considerably shaken.

It was at this point that my regiment was detached from Prentiss' division and served with it no more that day. We were sent some distance to the right to support a battery, the name of which I never learned.* It was occupying the summit of a slope, and was actively engaged when we reached it. We were put in position about twenty rods in the rear of the battery, and ordered to lie flat on the ground. The ground sloped gently down in our direction, so that by hugging it close, the rebel shot and shell went over us.

It was here, at about ten o'clock in the morning, that I first saw Grant that day. He was on horseback, of course, accompanied by his staff, and was evidently making a personal examination of his lines. He went by us in a gallop, riding between us and the battery, at the head of his staff. The battery was then hotly engaged; shot and shell were whizzing overhead, and cutting off the limbs of trees, but Grant rode through the storm with perfect indifference, seemingly paying no more attention to the missiles than if they had been paper wads.

We remained in support of this battery until about 2 o'clock in the afternoon. We were then put in motion by the right flank, filed to the left, crossed the left-hand Corinth road; then we were thrown into the line by the command: "By the left flank, march." We crossed a little ravine and up a slope, and relieved a regiment on the left of Hurlbut's line. This line was desperately engaged, and had been at this point, as we afterwards learned, for fully four hours. I remember as we went up the slope and began firing, about the first thing that met my gaze was what out West we would call a "windrow" of dead men in blue; some doubled up face downward, others with their white faces upturned to the sky, brave boys who had been shot to death in "holding the line." We were then relieved by another regiment. We filled out cartridge boxes again and went back to the support of our battery. The boys laid down and talked in low tones. Many of our comrades alive and well an hour ago, we had left dead on that bloody ridge. And still the battle raged. From right to left, everywhere, it was one never-ending, terrible roar, with no prospect of stopping.

Somewhere between 4 and 5 o'clock, as near as I can tell, everything became ominously quiet. Our battery ceased firing; the gunners leaned against the pieces and talked and laughed. Suddenly a staff officer rode up and said something in a low tone to the commander of the battery, then rode to our colonel and said something to him. The battery horses were at once brought up from a ravine in the rear, and the battery limbered up and moved off through the woods diagonally to the left and rear. We were put in motion by the flank and followed it. Everything kept so still, the loudest noise I heard was the clucking of the wheels of the gun-carriages and caissons as they wound through the woods. We emerged from the woods and entered a little old field. I then saw to our right and front lines of men in blue moving in the same direction we were, and it was evident that we were falling back. All at once, on the right, the left, and from our recent front, came one tremendous roar, and the bullets fell like hail. The lines took the double-quick towards the rear. For awhile the attempt was made to fall back in order, and then everything

went to pieces. My heart failed me utterly. I thought the day was lost. A confused mass of men and guns, caissons, army wagons, ambulances, and all the debris of a beaten army surged and crowded along the narrow dirt road to the landing, while that pitiless storm of leaden hail came crashing on us from the rear. It was undoubtedly at this crisis in our affairs that the division of General Prentiss was captured.

I will digress here for a minute to speak of a little incident connected with this disastrous feature of the day that has always impressed me as a pathetic instance of the patriotism and unselfish devotion to the cause that was by no means uncommon among the rank and file of the Union armies.

There was in my company a middle-aged German named Charles Oberdieck. According to the company descriptive book, he was a native of the then kingdom of Hanover, now a province of Prussia. He was a typical German, flaxen-haired, blue-eyed, quiet and taciturn, of limited and meager education, but a model soldier, who accepted without question and obeyed without a murmur the orders of his military superiors. Prior to the war he had made his living by chopping cord-wood in the high, timbered hills over the mouth of the Illinois river, or by working as a common laborer in the country on the farms at $14 a month. He was unmarried, his parents were dead, and he had no other immediate relative surviving, either in his fatherland or in the country of his adoption. He and I enlisted from the same neighborhood. I had known him in civil life at home, and hence he was disposed to be more communicative with me than with the other boys of the company. A day or two after

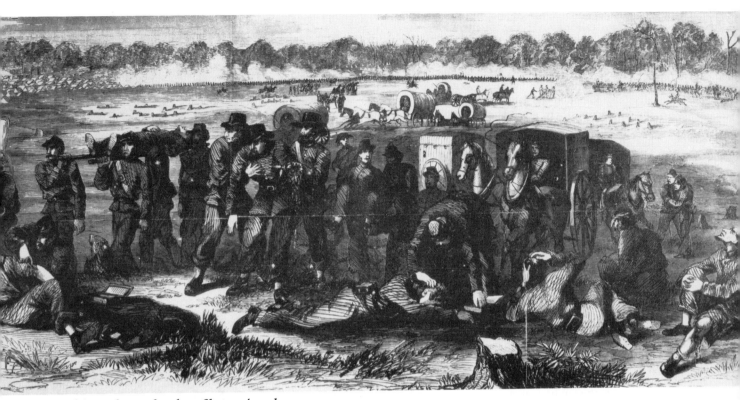

Casualties and stragglers from Sherman's and McClernand's divisions in the Federal rear as their comrades come under heavy pressure from Polk's and Hardee's men. During the battle, many soldiers attempted to escape combat by escorting a wounded compatriot to the rear.

Below:
Confused by Grant's orders to aid the troops fighting at Shiloh, Lew Wallace slowly approached the battlefield while the rest of the army buckled under the pressure from Johnston's attack.

the battle he and I were sitting in the shade of a tree, in camp, talking over the incidents of the fight. "Charley," I said to him, "How did you feel along about four o'clock Sunday afternoon when they broke our lines, we were falling back in disorder, and it looked like the whole business was gone up generally?" He knocked the ashes from his pipe and, turning his face quickly towards me, said: "I yoost tells you how I feels. I no care anydings about Charley; he haf no wife nor children, fadder nor mudder, brudder nor sister; if Charley get killed, it makes no difference; dere vas nobody to cry for him, so I dinks nudding about myselfs; but I tells you, I yoost den feels bad for de Cause!"

Noble, simple-hearted old Charley! It was the imminent danger only to the Cause that made his heart sink in that seemingly fateful hour. When we heard in the malignant and triumphant roar of the Rebel cannon in our rear what might be the death-knell of the last great experiment of civilized men to establish among the nations of the world a united republic, freed from the curse of pampered kings and selfish, grasping aristocrats—it was in that moment, in his simple language, that the peril to the Cause was the supreme and only consideration.

It must have been when we were less than half a mile from the landing on our disorderly retreat before mentioned, that we saw standing in line of battle, at ordered arms, extending from both sides of the road until lost to sight in the woods, a long, well-ordered line of men in blue. What did that mean? and where had they come from? I was walking by the side of Enoch Wallace, the orderly sergeant of my company. He was a man of nerve and courage, and by word and deed had done more that day to hold us green and untried boys in ranks and firmly to our duty than any other man in the company. But even he, in the face of this seemingly appalling state of things, had evidently lost heart. I said to him: "Enoch, what are those men there for?" He answered in a low tone: "I guess they are put there to hold the Rebels in check till the army can get across the river." And doubtless that was the thought of every intelligent soldier in our beaten column. And yet it goes to show how little the common soldier knew of the actual situation. We did not know then that this line was the last line of battle of the "Fighting Fourth Division" under General Hurlbut; that on its right was the division of McClernand, the Fort Donelson boys; that on its right, at right angles to it, and, as it were; the refused wing of the army, was glorious old Sherman, hanging on with a bulldog grip to the road across Snake Creek from Crump's Landing by which Lew Wallace was coming with 5,000 men. In other words, we still had an unbroken line confronting the enemy, made up of men who were not yet ready, by any manner of means, to give up that they were whipped. Nor did we know then that our retreating mass consisted only of some regiments of Hurlbut's division, and some other isolated commands, who had not been duly notified of the recession of Hurlbut and of his falling back to form a new line, and thereby came very near sharing the fate of

Wounded soldiers are collected in wagons to be transported to hospitals. In the two days of fighting at Shiloh, Johnston's army took over 10,500 casualties while more than 13,000 Yankees were listed as killed, wounded, or missing.

Prentiss' men and being marched to the rear as prisoners of war. Speaking for myself, it was twenty years after the battle before I found these things out, yet they are true, just as much so as the fact that the sun rose yesterday morning. Well, we filed through Hurlbut's line, halted, re-formed, and faced to the front once more. We were put in place a short distance in the rear of Hurlbut, as a support to some heavy guns. It must have been about five o'clock now. Suddenly, on the extreme left, and just a little above the landing, came a deafening explosion that fairly shook the ground beneath our feet, followed by others in quick and regular succession. The look of wonder and inquiry that the soldiers' faces wore for a moment disappeared for one of joy and exultation as it flashed across our minds that the gunboats had at last joined hands in the dance, and were pitching big twenty-pound Parrott shells up the ravine in front of Hurlbut, to the terror and discomfiture of our adversaries.

The last place my regiment assumed was close to the road coming up from the landing. As we were lying there I heard the strains of martial music and saw a body of men marching by the flank up the road. I slipped out of ranks and walked out to the side of the road to see what troops they were. Their band was playing "Dixie's Land," and playing it well. The men were marching at a quick step, carrying their guns, cartridge-boxes, haversacks, canteens, and blanket-rolls. I saw that they had not been in the fight, for there was no powder-smoke on their faces. "What regiment is this?" I asked of a young sergeant marching on the flank. Back came the answer in a quick, cheery tone, "The 36th Indiana, the advance guard of Buell's army."

I did not, on hearing this, throw my cap into the air and yell. That would have given those Indiana fellows a chance to chaff and guy me, and possibly make sarcastic remarks, which I did not care to provoke. I gave one big, gasping swallow and stood still, but the blood thumped in the veins of my throat and my heart fairly pounded against my little infantry jacket in the joyous rapture of this glorious intelligence. Soldiers need not be told of the thrill of unspeakable exultation they all have felt at the sight of armed friends in danger's darkest hour. Speaking for myself alone, I can only say, in the most heart-felt sincerity, that in all my obscure military career, never to me was the sight of reinforcing legions so precious and so welcome as on that Sunday evening when the rays of the descending sun were flashed back from the bayonets of Buell's advance column as it deployed on the bluffs of Pittsburg Landing.

My account of the battle is about done. So far as I saw or heard, very little fighting was done that evening after Buell's advance crossed the river. The sun must have been fully an hour high when anything like regular and continuous firing had entirely ceased.

What the result would have been if Beauregard had massed his troops on our left and forced the fighting late Sunday evening would be a matter of opinion, and a common soldier's opinion would not be considered worth much.

My regiment was held in reserve the next day, and was not engaged. I have, therefore, no personal experience of that day to relate. After the battle of Shiloh, it fell to my lot to play my humble part in several other fierce conflicts of arms, but Shiloh was my maiden fight. It was there I first saw a gun fired in anger, heard the whistle of a bullet, or saw a man die a violent death, and my experiences, thoughts, impressions, and sensations on that bloody Sunday will abide with me as long as I live.

WILLIAM G. STEVENSON
Behind Confederate Lines

One of the more interesting accounts of the Civil War belongs to William G. Stevenson in his Thirteen Months in the Rebel Army. *A transplanted Northerner living in Arkansas, Stevenson narrowly escaped being lynched for his Yankee background by enlisting in Jeff Davis' Invincibles. By the time of Shiloh, this reluctant Johnny Reb had risen to the*

rank of lieutenant and aide-de-camp to Brigadier General John C. Breckenridge. Following the battle, Stevenson was able to effect an escape into Federal territory where he wrote Thirteen Months *to convince the North of the deadly earnest with which the Southerners were willing to fight for their cause.*

General Breckenridge, about the 1st of April, let me know that he would soon wish me to act on his staff as special *aid-de-camp*, and advised me to instruct the next officers in command what to do in my absence.

But, before proceeding further, let us return to the one for another, until each had sped away; and turning to me, he said, "You will act as a special *aid-de-camp*." This announcement I received with especial gratification, as it would relieve me of all actual fighting against the Old Flag, and give me an opportunity to see far more of the progress of the battle which was to ensue than if I were confined to the ranks. The special danger of the mission to which I was called made no impression upon me. I can not recall any

time when I had a fear of falling, and I had none then. From that hour until the close of the battle on Monday, I was near General Breckenridge, or conveying dispatches to others from him; hence my narrative of the scenes of the next three days will be mainly of what occurred in General Breckenridge's division, and what I saw while traversing the field of action, which I crossed and recrossed twelve times.

On Friday, at eight P.M., we commenced to move toward Shiloh, in silence, and with great circumspection, the army on different, but converging roads. We made eight miles, and reached Monterey, a little more than seven miles from Shiloh, at five o'clock on Saturday morning. Here the different divisions formed a junction, and marched forward prepared for action, though not immediately expecting it. We proceeded with extreme caution until within three and a half miles of Grant's pickets, and until our scouts had determined their situation. We could get no nearer without bringing on an engagement; and as General Beauregard had great confidence that the reinforcements would arrive by morning, the afternoon of Saturday was spent in making all necessary disposition of the forces for an early and combined attack on Sunday morning.

While it is no part of my duty, in this narrative, to criticise military movements, and especially those of the Union forces, I may state that the total absence of cavalry pickets from General Grant's army was a matter of perfect amazement to the Rebel officers. There were absolutely none on Grant's left, where General Breckenridge's division was meeting him, so that we were able to come up within hearing of their drums entirely unperceived.

The Southern generals always kept cavalry pickets out for miles, even when no enemy was supposed to be within a day's march of them. The infantry pickets of Grant's forces were not above three-fourths of a mile from his advance camps, and they were too few to make any resistance. With these facts all made known to our headquarters on Saturday evening, our army was arranged for battle with the certainty of a surprise, and almost the assurance of a victory. Every regiment was carefully and doubly guarded, so that no man might glide away from our ranks and put the Union forces on their guard. This I noted particularly, as I was studying plans of escape that night, that I might put the loyal forces on their guard against the fearful avalanche ready to be hurled upon them. I already saw that they would stand no fair chance for victory, taken completely at unawares. But the orders were imperative to allow no man to leave the ranks, and to shoot the first who should attempt it on any pretence. Then of the nature of the ground between the opposing forces I knew nothing, except that it was said to be crossed and seamed by swamps, in many places almost impassable by daylight, much more so at night. If, then, I should attempt to desert, I must run the gauntlet of our own double guard, risk the chance of making the three or four miles through woods and swamps in deep darkness, and the more hazardous chance, on reaching the Federal lines, of being shot by their pickets. I was therefore compelled to relinquish the hope of escape that night—a sad necessity, for if I had succeeded, it might have saved many Union lives.

About eight o'clock P.M. a council of war was held among the principal generals, and the plan of battle arranged. In an open space, with a dim fire in the midst, and a drum on which to write, you could see grouped around their "little Napoleon," as Beauregard was sometimes fondly called, ten or twelve generals, the flickering light playing over their eager faces, while they listened to his plans and made suggestions as to the conduct of the fight. He soon warmed with his subject, and throwing off his cloak to give free play

Perhaps the most promising Confederate general in the West, General Albert Sidney Johnston. His untimely death proved to be a major blow to the Confederacy.

to his arms, he walked about in the group, gesticulating rapidly, and jerking out his sentences with a strong French accent. All listened attentively, and the dim light just revealing their countenances showed their different emotions of confidence or distrust in his plans. General Sidney Johnson stood apart from the rest, with his tall straight form standing out like a specter against the dim sky, and the illusion was fully sustained by the light-gray military cloak which he folded around him. His face was pale, but wore a determined expression, and at times he drew nearer the center of the ring and said a few words, which were listened to with great attention. It may be he had some foreboding of the fate he was to meet on the morrow, for he did not seem to take much part in the discussion. General Breckenridge lay stretched out on a blanket near the fire, and occasionally sat upright and added a few words of counsel. General Bragg spoke frequently and with earnestness. General Polk sat on a camp-stool at the outside of the circle, and held his head between his hands, seeming buried in thought. Others reclined or sat in various positions. What a grand study for a Rembrandt was this, to see these men, who held the lives of many thousands in their power, planning how best to invoke the angel

Azrael to hurl his darts with the breaking of morning light.

For two hours the council lasted, and as it broke up, and the generals were ready to return to their respective commands, I heard General Beauregard say,—raising his hand and pointing in the direction of the Federal camps, whose drums we could plainly hear,—"Gentlemen, we sleep in the enemy's camp to-morrow night."

The Confederate generals had minute information of General Grant's position and numbers. This knowledge was obtained through spies and informers, some of whom had lived in that part of the country and knew every foot of the ground.

Yet that was a dreary night to prepare for the dreadful battle of to-morrow. The men were already weary, hungry, and cold. No fires were allowed, except in holes in the ground, over which the soldiers bent with their blankets round their shoulders, striving to catch and concentrate the little heat that struggled up through the bleak April air. Many a poor fellow wrote his last sentence in his note-book that night by the dim light of these smothered fires, and sat and talked in undertones of home, wife, and mother, sister or

sweetheart. Promises were made to take care of each other, if wounded, or send word home, if slain; keepsakes were looked at again for the last time, and silent prayers were offered by men unused to look above. What an awful thing is war! Here lay, almost within cannon-shot of one another, eighty or ninety thousand men—brothers of the same race and nation, many of them blood relations; thousands of them believing in the same Saviour, and worshipping the same God, their prayers meeting that night at the throne of Heavenly Grace;—yet waiting for the light of the holy Sabbath that they may see how most surely to destroy one another! And yet the masses of these have no ill feeling. it is human butchery, at the bidding of archconspirators. Upon them be all the blood shed! A fearful guilt is theirs!

What sleep the men could get on the cold, damp ground, with little protection or fire, they secured

Officers of the Washington Artillery. Their guns played a major role in forcing the Federals to fall back towards the Tennessee River.

during the early part of Saturday night. On Sunday morning, the 6th of April, we were under arms and ready to move by three o'clock.

General Hardee, one of the bravest men in the Confederate service, led the advance and center, and made the attack. Had I not been called to staff duty, I should have been in the advance with my company. Glad was I that I was not called to fire upon the unsuspecting soldiers of my Northern home. As the day dawned we could hear the musketry, first in dropping shots, then volley after volley, as the battle grew hotter. A little after daylight we passed General Beauregard and staff, who were then over a mile in rear of the troops engaged. He addressed each brigade as it passed, assuring them of a glorious victory, telling them to fight with perfect confidence, as he had 80,000 men available, who should come into action as fast as needed; and wherever reinforcements were wanted, Beauregard would be there. This boast of 80,000 men the officers knew to be false, as he had not a man over 45,000; but as he expected 30,000 under Price and Van Dorn he counted them in, and added 10,000 more to strengthen confidence. But neither he nor any other Confederate general asks any defence for such statements. "Military necessity" will justify any course they choose to take in advancing their cause. After we passed Beauregard, a few minutes of "double quick" brought our division to Grant's advance pickets, who had been surprised and cut down by Hardee's cavalry. This was the first time many of the soldiers had seen men killed in battle, and they stepped carefully around the dead bodies, and seemed to shudder at the sight. General Breckenridge observing it, said quickly, "Never mind this, boys; press on!" Before night, those who remained walked over dead bodies in heaps without a shudder. We soon reached

Rookie Confederates received their baptism by fire in the bloody struggle near Pittsburg Landing.

an open field, about eighty rods wide, on the further side of which we could see the camps, and the smoke of battle just beyond. We here made a sharp *détour* to the right, and ascended a broken range of hills, pressing on for nearly a mile. Here we took position just in front of General Albert Sidney Johnson and staff, and awaited orders. General Breckenridge rode up to General Johnson, and after conversing in a low tone for a few minutes, Johnson said, so that many heard it, "I will lead *your* brigade into the fight to-day; for I intend to show these Tennesseans and Kentuckians that I am no coward." Poor general! you were not allowed the privilege. We then advanced in line of battle, and General Statham's brigade was engaged first. "Boys," said Breckenridge, "we must take that battery which is shelling Statham. Will you do it?" A wild shout of "Ay, ay, sir," and "Forward to take that battery," was the word; but before we reached the ground it was withdrawn. We now advanced, cautiously, and soon entered the camp of the Seventy-first Ohio Volunteers. By this time, ten o'clock A.M., the battle seemed to be raging along the whole line.

A part of the original plan of battle was to have a space several hundred yards wide between Breckenridge's left and Hardee's right, and thus invite Grant's men into a trap. They refusing to be entrapped, and keeping their front unbroken, Breckenridge sent me to General Johnson for new instructions. When I had come within about ten rods of Johnson's staff, a shell burst in the air about equidistant from myself and the staff. The missiles of death seemed to fill the air in every direction, and almost before the fragments had found their resting-place, I reined up my horse and saluted. General Johnson, who was in front of his staff, had turned away his horse and was leaning a little forward, pressing his right knee against the saddle. In a moment, and before the dispatch was delivered, the staff discovered that their leader was wounded, and hastened to his assistance. A piece of the shell, whose fragments had flown so thick around me as I came up, had struck his thigh half way between his hip and knee, and cut a wide path through, severing the femoral artery. Had he been instantly taken from his horse and a tourniquet applied, he might perhaps have been saved. When reproached by Governor Harris, chief of staff and his brother-in-law, for concealing his wound while his life-blood was ebbing away, he replied, with true nobility of soul, "My life is nothing to the success of this charge; had I exclaimed I was wounded

when the troops were passing, it might have created a panic and defeat." In ten minutes after he was lifted from his horse he ceased to breathe. Thus died one of the bravest generals in the Rebel army. My dispatch was taken by Colonel Wickliffe and handed to Harris, who directed me to take it to General Beauregard. When he had read it, he asked—

"Why did you not take this to General Johnson?"

"I did, sir."

"Did he tell you to bring it to me?"

"General Johnson is dead, sir."

"How do you know?"

"I saw him die ten minutes ago."

"How was he killed?"

I told him. He then dictated two dispatches, one to Governor Harris and one to General Breckenridge, telling them to conceal the death of Johnson, and bidding me not to speak of it to any one. So far as the report of his death was circulated the officers denied it, some affirming that it was Governor Johnson of Kentucky who was killed, others admitting that General A. S. Johnson was slightly wounded. The army knew not of his death till they reached Corinth.

When I returned to General Breckenridge's staff they had advanced half a mile, and were furiously

Youths at war. Young Confederates take time to relax before their first real experience of full-fledged warfare.

engaged within half-musket range with both small-arms and artillery. About noon General Bowen's brigade—Breckenridge's left—was forced to fall back for ammunition and to reform, their place being supplied by two regiments of Louisiana troops. Here, from two to four P.M., was the hardest fighting in the battle. Breckenridge's own brigade losing nearly one-fourth within two hours. The fire of the Union troops was low and very effective. A battery here did fearful execution among the Rebels with shell, grape, and canister. A wounded gunner belonging to this battery told me the shells were fired with one-second fuses. Our men were ordered to lie down and load, and yet many were killed in this position, so accurate was the fire of the Federal troops. I saw five men killed by the explosion of one shell.

About three o'clock I was sent to the rear with dispatches of the progress of the battle, and asking reinforcements. When about half way to Beauregard's staff, riding at full gallop, my first serious accident occurred, my life being saved by but a hair's breadth.

As my horse rose in a long leap, his fore-feet in the air and his head about as high as my shoulder, a cannon-ball struck him above the eye and carried away the upper part of his head. Of course the momentum carried his lifeless body some ten feet ahead, and hurled me some distance further,—saber, pistols, and all. I gathered myself up, and to my surprise was not hurt in the least. One second later, the ball would have struck me and spared the horse. Thankful for my life, I threw off my saber and my tight uniform-coat, gave my pistols to a cavalryman near by, and started in search of another horse. General Breckenridge had told me in the morning, if my horse was killed to take the first unemployed one I could find. I knew where some of the infantry field-officers had tied their horses in a ravine in the rear, and while seeking them,

Officers of the 9th Mississippi Company B, the Home Guards of Marshall County.

I met a scene which lives in my memory as if it were but yesterday.

I had just filled my canteen at a spring, and as I turned from it my eye met the uplifted gate of a Federal officer, I think a colonel of an Illinois regiment, who was lying desperately wounded, shot through the body and both legs, his dead horse lying on one of his shattered limbs. A cannon-ball had passed through his horse and both of his own knees. He looked pleadingly for a drink, but hesitated to ask it of an enemy, as he supposed me to be. I came up to him, and said, "You seem to be badly wounded, sir; will you have some water?"

"Oh yes," said he; "but I feared to ask you for it."

"Why?"

"Because I expected no favor of an enemy."

Two other men coming by, I called them to aid in removing the dead horse from his wounded limb. They did so, and then passed on; but I seemed bound to him as by a spell. His manly face and soldierly bearing, when suffering so terribly, charmed me. I changed his position, adjusted his head, arranged his mangled legs in an easy posture, supporting them by leaves stuffed under the blanket on which we had laid him. In the mean time he took out his watch and money, and requested me to hand him his pistols from the saddle-holsters, and urged me to take them, as some one might rob him, and I was the only one who had shown him kindness. I declined, and wrapping them up in a blanket, placed them under his head, telling him the fortunes of war might yet bring his own troops to his side. He seemed overcome, and said, "My friend, why this kindness to an enemy?"

As I gave him another draught of water, I said, *"I am not the enemy I seem;"* and pressing his hand, I walked quickly on.

He could not live long, but I hope his friends found him as they swept back over the ground the next day.

I soon found a splendid horse, and rode to General Beauregard for orders, and reached my own general about four o'clock P.M. I found that the Federal troops had fallen back more than a mile, but were still fiercely contending for the ground. The Rebels were confident of victory, and pressed them at every point. I had scarce time to mark the condition of things however, until I was again dispatched to the commander-in-chief. I had but fairly started, when I was struck on the right side by a piece of a shell almost spent, which yet came near ending my earthly career. My first feeling after the shock was one of giddiness and blindness, then of partial recovery, then of deathly sickness. I succeeded in getting off rather than falling from my horse, near the root of a tree, where I fainted and lay insensible for nearly an hour. At length, I recovered so far as to be able to remount my horse, whose bridle I had somehow held all the time, though unconsciously. I had ridden but a few rods when a musket-ball passed through the neck of this, my second horse, but, to my surprise, he did not fall immediately. A tremor ran through his frame which I felt, convincing me that he was mortally wounded. I dismounted, and stood watching him. He soon sank on his knees, and then slowly lay down on his side. As his lifeblood ebbed away, his eye glazed, and making a last futile effort to rise, he fell back again and died with a groan almost like the last agony of a human being. The pain of my side and my knee, which was never entirely free from pain, grew worse, and I saw that unless I found surgical attendance and rest, I would soon be exhausted. In making my way to the general hospital which was established on the ground where the battle commenced, I met one of Forrest's cavalry, wounded in the foot, and very weak from loss of blood. With my handkerchief and a short stick, I made a simple tourniquet, which stopped the bleeding, when I accompanied him to the hospital. After the dressing of my wound, which was an extensive

The 9th Mississippi, lacking proper military uniforms, drill in the months before their participation at Shiloh. During the battle, their charge against elements of Prentiss' division was instrumental in the capitulation of the Federals in the famed Hornets' Nest.

bruise, about five inches in diameter, I took the cav-alryman's horse, and started back to my command. When I had reached the camp of the 71st Ohio Volun-teers, my strength failed, and after getting something to eat for myself and horse, and a bucket of water to bathe my side during the night, I tied my horse near the door of a tent, and crept in to try to sleep. But the shells from the gunboats, which made night hideous, the groans of the wounded, and the pleadings of the dying, for a time prevented. Weariness at length over-came me, and sleep followed more refreshing and sound than I hoped for under the circumstances.

The sharp rattle of musketry awakened me early, announcing the opening of the second day's battle. But before I speak of Monday the 7th, I will state why the Confederates ceased to fight at half-past five P.M., on Sabbath evening, when they had another hour of daylight. They had already driven back the Federal forces more than three miles along their whole line, had taken 4000 prisoners, including most of General Prentiss's brigade, had captured about seventy pieces of artillery, according to their statement, had taken an immense baggage-train, with vast quantities of com-missary, quartermaster's, and medical stores, and had driven Grant's forces under the shelter of their gun-boats. Had the battle ended here, the victory would have been most triumphant for the Rebels. Generals Bragg and Breckenridge urged that the battle should go on, that Grant's force was terribly cut up and de-moralized, and another hour would take them all pris-oners, or drive them into the river, and that then the transport fleet of more than a hundred boats, would be at the control of the Confederates, who could assume the offensive, and in five days take Louisville. Other officers argued that half of their own troops were disabled or scattered, that it would risk the victory already gained to push the remainder of Grant's forces, which now turned at bay, might make a des-perate stand. They estimated their own loss at ten or twelve thousand men, and knew that many, thinking the battle was over, had left their commands and were loading themselves with plunder, from the pockets of the dead and the knapsacks lying over the field or found in the Federal camps. Some expressed strong confidence that Price and Van Dorn would arrive dur-ing the night, and the victory would be easily com-pleted on the morrow.

While this argument lasted, the men were resting, the hour passed away, and night spread her sable pall over the scene.

The night was spent in removing the wounded, and as much of the captured stores and artillery as pos-sible; but horses and wagons were scarce, and most of the stores and some wounded were left. The Con-federates carried off thirty-six pieces of artillery, which were not retaken. Hospitals were established on the road leading to Corinth, and most of the wounded of the first day received every attention pos-sible under the circumstances; though the advance had been made so suddenly, that insufficient atten-tion had been given to providing medical stores and surgical instruments. The scattered regiments were

Encampment of the Fighting 9th, the 9th Mississippi. The commander of the regiment, Lieutenant Colonel William Rankin, was mortally wounded during Shiloh.

gathered, reorganized, and put, as far as possible, in order for battle, and Beauregard ordered a large cavalry force to stretch themselves out in a line a short dis-tance in rear of the army, to turn back all stragglers, and gave them instructions to shoot any unwounded man retreating. This was rigidly enforced, and some who attempted to escape were shot. Orders were is-sued to shoot any one found plundering the dead or wounded. Stragglers were forced into the nearest regi-ment, and every thing done that could be to insure success.

From the foregoing account it will be seen that the following telegram, sent by Beauregard to Richmond, is not far from literally true:

General S. Cooper, Adjutant-general,—We have this morning attacked the enemy in strong position in front of Pittsburg, and after a severe battle of ten hours, thanks to Almighty God, gained a complete victory, driving the enemy from every position.
"The loss on both sides is heavy, including our commander-in-chief, General Albert Sidney Johnson, who fell gallantly leading his troops into the thickest of the fight.

The morning of Monday, April 7th, was dark and gloomy; the men were weary and stiffened by the exertions of the previous day, and from the chilling effects of the rain which fell during the night. The dead of both armies lay strewed over the field by hundreds, and many of the desperately wounded were still groaning out their lives in fearful agony. At five A.M. I was in the saddle, though scarcely able to mount, from the pain in knee and side; and in making my way to General Beauregard's staff, my head reeled and my heart grew sick at the scenes through which I passed. I record but one. In crossing a small ravine, my horse hesitated to step over the stream, and I glanced down to detect the cause. The slight rain during the night had washed the leaves out of a narrow channel down the gully some six inches wide, leaving the hard clay exposed. Down this pathway ran sluggishly a band of blood nearly an inch thick, filling the channel. For a minute I looked and reflected, how many human lives are flowing past me, and who shall account for such butchery! Striking my rowels into the horse to escape from the horrible sight, he plunged his foot into the stream of blood, and threw the already thickening mass in ropy folds upon the dead leaves on the bank! The only relief to my feelings was the reflection that I had not shred one drop of that blood.

I took my position on General B.'s staff at six o'clock in the morning, and remained near him most of the day. The Federal forces had already commenced the attack, and the tide of battle soon turned. Grant's reinforcements had come up during the night, but Beauregard's had not, and early in the day it became evident that we were fighting against fearful odds. Beauregard sent forward 3000 of his best troops, held as a reserve during the first day. They did all that so small a number could do, but it was of no avail. Step by step they drove us back, while every foot of ground was yielded only after a determined resistance. The battle raged mainly on our left, General Breckenridge's division doing but little fighting this day, compared with the first day. General Grant seemed determined to outflank our left, and occupy the road behind us, and as the Confederates had not men enough to hold the camps they had taken, and check this flank movement, retreat became necessary. About nine A.M. I rode to General Beauregard for orders; when returning, I heard the report that General Buell had been killed and his body taken toward Corinth. This report that the Federal commander, as many supposed Buell to be, was killed, and his body taken, revived the flagging hopes of the Confederates. Of the fluctuations of the battle from nine A.M. till three P.M. I can say but little as it was mainly confined to our center and left. During this time the Rebel forces had fallen back to the position occupied by

Grant's advance Sabbath morning. The loyal troops had regained all the ground lost, and whatever of artillery and stores the Rebels had been unable to convey to the rear, and were now pressing us at every point.

Just before the retreat, occurred one of the most remarkable incidents of the battle; few more wonderful are on record. General Hindman, than whom no more fearless, dashing, or brave man is found in the Rebel service, was leading his men in a fearful struggle for the possession of a favorable position, when a shell from the Federal batteries, striking his horse in the breast and passing into his body, exploded. The horse was blown to fragments, and the rider, with his saddle, lifted some ten feet in the air. His staff did not doubt that their general was killed, and some one cried out, "General Hindman is blown to pieces." Scarcely was the cry uttered, when Hindman sprang to his feet and shouted, "Shut up there, I am worth two dead men yet. Get me another horse." To the amazement of every one, he was but little bruised. His heavy and strong cavalry saddle, and probably the bursting of the shell downward, saved him. In a minute he was on a new horse and rallying his men for another dash. A man of less flexible and steel-like frame would probably have been so jarred and stunned by the shock as to be unable to rise; he, though covered with blood and dust, kept his saddle during the remainder of the day, and performed prodigies of valor. But no heroism of officers or men could avail to stay the advance of the Federal troops.

While attempting to capture a mounted Confederate officer, a surprised Yankee captures only the hairpiece of his adversary.

After failing to reach the battlefield in time to fight on 6 April 1862, the troops of Lew Wallace's division drive the Rebels from the field at Shiloh.

At three o'clock P.M. the Confederates decided on a retreat to Corinth; and General Breckenridge, strengthened by three regiments of cavalry,—Forrest's, Adams', and the Texas Rangers, raising his effective force to 12,000 men,—received orders to protect the rear. By four P.M. the Confederates were in full retreat. The main body of the army passed silently and swiftly along the road toward Corinth, our division bringing up the rear, determined to make a desperate stand if pursued. At this time the Union forces might have closed in upon our retreating columns and cut off Breckenridge's division, and perhaps captured it. A Federal battery threw some shells, as a feeler, across the road on which we were retreating, between our division and the main body, but no reply was made to them, as this would have betrayed our position. We passed on with little opposition or loss, and by five o'clock had reached a point one and a half miles nearer Corinth than the point of attack Sabbath morning.

The combined might of Buell and Grant drive the Confederates from the field on the second day of battle, 7 April 1862. The Army of Tennessee, under the command of P.G.T. Beauregard defiantly, but hopelessly, attempt to hold their gains of the previous day, only to retreat from the field in defeat.

Up to this time the pursuit seemed feeble, and the Confederates were surprised that the victorious Federals made no more of their advantage. Nor is it yet understood why the pursuit was not pressed. A rapid and persistent pursuit would have created a complete rout of the now broken, weary, and dispirited Rebels. Two hours more of such fighting as Buell's fresh men could have made, would have demoralized and destroyed Beauregard's army. For some reason this was not done, and night closed the battle.

About five o'clock I requested permission to ride on toward Corinth, as I was faint and weary, and from the pain in my side and knee, would not be able to keep the saddle much longer. This was granted, and I made a *détour from* the road on which the army was retreating, that I might travel faster and get ahead of the main body. In his ride of twelve miles alongside of the routed army, I saw more of human agony and woe than I trust I will ever again be called on to witness. The retreating host wound along a narrow and almost impassable road, extending some seven or eight miles in length. Here was a long line of wagons loaded with wounded, piled in like bags of grain, groaning and cursing, while the mules plunged on in mud and water belly-deep, the water sometimes coming into

the wagons. Next came a straggling regiment of infantry pressing on past the train of wagons, then a stretcher borne upon the shoulders of four men, carrying a wounded officer, then soldiers staggering along, with an arm broken and hanging down, or other fearful wounds which were enough to destroy life. And to add to the horrors of the scene, the elements of heaven marshaled their forces,—a fitting accompaniment of the tempest of human desolation and passion which was raging. A cold, drizzling rain commenced about nightfall, and soon came harder and faster, then turned to pitiless blinding hail. This storm raged with unrelenting violence for three hours. I passed long wagon trains filled with wounded and dying soldiers, without even a blanket to shield them from the driving sleet and hail, which fell in stones as large as partridge eggs, until it lay on the ground two inches deep.

Some three hundred men died during that awful retreat, and their bodies were thrown out to make room for others who, although wounded, had struggled on through the storm, hoping to find shelter, rest, and medical care.

By eight o'clock at night I had passed the whole retreating column, and was now in advance, hoping to reach Corinth, still four miles ahead. But my powers of endurance, though remarkable, were exhausted, and I dismounted at a deserted cabin by the wayside, scarce able to drag myself to the doorway. Here a surgeon was tending some wounded men who had been sent off the field at an early hour of the first day. To his question, "Are you wounded?" I replied that my wound was slight, and that I needed refreshment and sleep more than surgical aid. Procuring two hard crackers and a cup of rye coffee, I made a better meal than I had eaten in three days, and then lay down in a vacant room and slept.

When I awoke it was broad daylight, and the room was crowded full of wounded and dying men, so thickly packed that I could hardly stir. I was not in the same place where I had lain down; but of my change of place, and of the dreadful scenes which had occurred during the night, I had not the slightest knowledge.

As I became fully awake and sat up, the surgeon turned to me, and said, "Well, you are alive at last. I thought nothing but an earthquake would wake you.

The "Napoleon in Gray," Pierre Gustave Toutant Beauregard. After supervising the bombardment of Fort Sumter, Beauregard became a subordinate to Albert Sidney Johnston. Originally against Johnston's attack on Grant at Pittsburg Landing, he took command of the Army of Tennessee after his commander's death.

We have moved you about like a log, and you never groaned or showed any signs of life. Men have trampled on you, dying men have groaned all around you, and yet you slept as soundly as a babe in its cradle. Where is your wound?"

How I endured the horrors of that night, rather how I was entirely unconscious of them and slept refreshingly through them, is to me a mystery. But so it was, and it seemed to be the turning-point of my knee-wound, as it has never troubled me so much since.

I now rode on to Corinth, where I changed clothes, had a bath and breakfast, and found a hospital and a surgeon. He decided that I was unfit for duty, and must take my place among the invalids. After dressing my wounds he advised rest. I slept again for six hours, and woke in the afternoon almost a well man, as I thought.

Thus ended my courier service, and I then resolved that no earthly power should ever force me into another battle against the Government under which I was born; and I have kept my resolution.

General Beauregard's official dispatch of the second day's battle, given below, was a very neat attempt to cover up defeat. It expresses the general opinion of the people in the South as to the battle of Pittsburg Landing.

To the Secretary of War, Richmond:

We have gained a great and glorious victory. Eight to ten thousand prisoners, and thirty-six pieces of cannon. Buell reinforced Grant, and we retired to our intrenchments at Corinth, which we can hold. Loss heavy on both sides.

WILL S. HAYS

Drummer Boy of Shiloh

This tearful lyric describing the untimely demise of a saintly youth in the carnage of Shiloh serves as a good example of the romantic writing of mid-nineteenth century America.

"Look down upon the battlefield,
Oh Thou, Our Heavenly Friend,
Have mercy on our sinful souls."
The soldiers cried, "Amen."
There gathered 'round a little group,
Each brave man knelt and cried.
They listened to the drummer boy,
Who prayed before he died.

"Oh, Mother," said the dying boy,
"Look down from heaven on me.
Receive me to thy fond embrace,
Oh, take me home to thee.
I've loved my country as my God,
To serve them both I've tried!"
He smiled, shook hands—death seized the boy,
Who prayed before he died.

Each soldier wept then like a child.
Stout hearts were they and brave.
They wrapped him in his country's flag
And laid him in the grave.
They placed by him the Bible,
A rededicated guide
To those that mourn the drummer boy
Who prayed before he died.

Ye angels 'round the throne of grace,
Look down upon the braves,
Who fought and died on Shiloh's plain,
Now slumbering in their graves.
How many homes made desolate,
How many hearts have sighed.
How many like that drummer boy,
Who prayed before he died.

Drummer boys serving with the Federal army.

Chapter IV

KENTUCKY INVADED

Despite the victories at Fort Henry, Fort Donelson, Pea Ridge and Shiloh, the Federals never launched a knockout blow against the demoralized Confederate forces facing them in the West. As the Yankees bided their time, Braxton Bragg and Kirby Smith headed their armies north to gallivant around Kentucky in the late summer of 1862 at about the same time Lee was engaging in his Maryland Campaign in the East. Commanding the Confederate Army of the West, Major General Sterling Price decided to assist his comrades in Kentucky by attempting to invade the Volunteer State, but he was defeated in Mississippi at Iuka on 19 September and Corinth on 3-4 October 1862 by Major General William Rosecrans commanding the Union Army of the Mississippi. Meanwhile, forced to pursue Generals Bragg and Smith, Major General Don Carlos Buell took his Army of the Ohio north to do battle where he engaged the former in the indecisive battle of Perryville, Kentucky, on 8 October 1862. Despite inflicting heavy losses on the Federals, Bragg was forced to abandon his invasion and fall back to Tennessee with Smith.

★★★

S. P. BARRON

The Iuka-Corinth Campaign

The battles of both Iuka and Corinth marked two of the few times the Confederacy was on the offensive against the Yankees even though they wielded superior numbers. The Confederates *failed to pull out a victory when they most desperately needed one. S. P. Barron, a member of the 3rd Texas Cavalry, related the events of these tragic battles in his book* The Lone Star Defenders.

In the early days of June our command halted and went into camp near Tupelo, Miss., where it remained for several weeks. Here, as I was physically unfit for service, I voluntarily abandoned my place at General Cabell's headquarters and returned to my own regiment. Obtaining, without difficulty, a thirty days' furlough, I called on Dr. Shaw for medicine, but he informed me that he had nothing but opium, which would do me no good. But he added, "You need a tonic; if you could only get some whisky, that would soon set you up." Mounting my horse I went down into Pontotoc County, and, finding a good-looking farmhouse away from the public roads, I engaged

board with Dr. Dunn, the proprietor, for myself and horse for thirty days. Mr. Dunn told me of a distillery away down somewhere below the town of Pontotoc, and finding a convalescent in the neighborhood I sent him on my horse to look for it, with the result that he brought me back four canteens of "tonic."

Now Mr. Dunn's family consisted of that clever elderly gentleman, his wife, and a handsome, intelligent daughter, presumably about twenty years of age. I soon realized that I had been very fortunate in the selection of a boarding house and that my lot for the next thirty days had been cast in a pleasant place, for every necessary attention was cheerfully shown me by each member of the family. They had lost a son and brother, who had wasted away with consumption, and in my dilapidated and emaciated condition they said I favored him, so they were constantly reminded of a loved one who had gone to his grave in about the same manner I seemed to be going, and they felt almost as if they were ministering to the wants of one of the family. They lived in a comfortable house, and everything I saw indicated a happy, well-to-do family. Their table, spread three times a day, was all that could be desired. We had corn bread, fresh milk and butter, fresh eggs, last year's yam potatoes, a plentiful supply of garden vegetables and other good things, everything brought on the table being well prepared. At first I had little or no appetite, but thanks to Miss Dunn's treatment, it soon began to improve. She, using the "tonic," gave me an egg-nog just before each meal, and blackberries being plentiful, she gave me

After presiding over the Confederate defeat at Pea Ridge, Major General Earl Van Dorn tried his hand at besting Major General William S. "Rosey" Rosecrans at Corinth.

blackberries in every form, including pies and cordial, all of which, for one in my condition, was the best possible treatment.

So I improved and gained strength, not rapidly, but steadily, and though the thirty days was not as much time as I needed for a complete convalescence, it was all I had asked for. Mr. Dunn manifested a great deal of interest in my welfare; he did not think I could recover my health in the service, and urged me most earnestly to go back to camp, get a discharge, and go to Cooper's Well, a health resort down in Mississippi, and I was almost compelled to promise him I would do so, when in truth I had no such intention. The thirty days having expired, I bade farewell to these good people who had taken in a stranger and so kindly cared for him, and returned to camp, not strong or well by any means, but improved, especially in the matter of an appetite.

Going up to regimental headquarters upon my return to the command I let out my horse for his board,

Attempting to assist Braxton Bragg's invasion of Kentucky, Major General Sterling Price's Army of the West engaged the Federal Army of the Mississippi in a sharp fight at Iuka, Mississippi, on 19 September 1862.

procured a rifle and at once reported to our company commander for duty. The strictest military discipline was maintained by General Louis Hebert in every particular, and one day's duty was very much like the duties of every other day, with a variation for Sunday. Of course the same men did not have the same duties to perform every day, as guard duty and fatigue duty were regulated by details made from the alphabetical rolls of the companies, but the same round of duties came every day in the week. At reveile we must promptly rise, dress, and hurry out into line for roll call; then breakfast. After breakfast guard-mounting for the ensuing twenty-four hours, these guards walking their posts day and night, two hours on and four hours off. Before noon there were two hours' drill for all men not on guard or some other special duty; then dinner. In the afternoon it was clean up camps, clean guns, dress parade at sundown; then supper to bed at taps. On Sunday no drill, but, instead, we had to go out for a review, which was worse, as the men had to don all their armor, the officers button up their uniforms to the chin, buckle on their swords, and all march about two miles away through the dust and heat to an old field, march around a circle at least a mile in circumference, and back to camps. All that, including the halting and waiting, usually took up the time until about noon.

With the understanding and agreement that I

would be excused from the drill ground when I broke down, and when on guard be allowed to rest when I had walked my post as long as I could, I went on duty as a well man. For quite a while I was compelled to leave the drill ground before the expiration of the two hours, and when I found I could not walk my post through the two hours some one of my comrades usually took my place. It was necessary for me to muster all my courage to do this kind of soldiering, but the exertion demanded of me and the exercise so improved my condition that soon I no longer had to be excused from any part of my duties. We had men in the command afflicted with chronic diarrhea who, yielding to the enervating influence of the disease, would lie down and die, and that was what I determined to avoid if I could.

Among other bugle calls we had "the sick call." Soon after breakfast every morning this, the most doleful of all the calls, was sounded, when the sick would march up and line themselves in front of the surgeon's tent for medical advice and treatment. Our surgeon, Dr. Dan Shaw, was a character worthy of being affectionately remembered by all the members

Corinth, Mississippi, an important rail terminus vital to both Confederate and Union war efforts.

of the Third Texas Cavalry. He was a fine physician, and I had fallen in love with him while he was a private soldier because he so generously exerted his best skill in assisting Dr. McDugald to save my life at Carthage, Mo. He was a plain, unassuming, jolly old fellow, brave, patriotic, and full of good impulses. He was the man who indignantly declined an appointment as surgeon soon after the battle of Oak Hills, preferring to remain a private in "Company B, Greer's Texas regiment," to being surgeon of an Arkansas regiment.

Knowing that he had no medicine except opium, I would go up some mornings, through curiosity, to hear his prescriptions for the various ailments that he had to encounter. He would walk out with an old jackknife in his hand, and conveniently located just behind him could be seen a lump of opium as big as a cannonball. Beginning at the head of the line he would say to the first one: "Well, sir, what is the matter with *you?*" "I don't know, doctor; I've got a pain in my head, or I had a chill last night." "Let me see your tongue. How's your bowels?" He would then turn around and vigorously attack the lump of opium with his knife, and roll out from two to four pills to the man, remarking to each of his waiting patients: "There, take one of these every two hours." Thus he would go, down the line to the end, and in it all there was little variation—none to speak of except in the answers of the individuals, the number of pills, or the manner of taking. And what else could he do? He had told me frankly that he had nothing in his tent that would do me any good, but these men had to have medicine.

For water at Tupelo we dug wells, each company a well, using a sweep to draw it. In this hilly portion of the State good water could be obtained by digging

from twenty to twenty-five feet.

From the time of the reorganization at Corinth up to the middle of July Company C had lost a number of men. Some, as McDugald and Dillard, were commissioned officers, and did not re-enlist; some were discharged on applications, and others under the conscription law then in force, a law exempting all men under eighteen and over forty-five years of age. Among those discharged I remember the two Ackers, Croft, I. K. Frazer, Tom Hogg, Tom Johnson, W. A. Newton, William Pennington, and R. G. Thompson, all of whom returned to Texas except William Pennington, who remained with us a considerable time, notwithstanding his discharge. In the regimental officers several changes had been made. After the death of Major Barker, Captain Jiles S. Boggess, of Company B, from Henderson, was promoted to major; Colonel R. H. Cumby resigned, and Lieutenant-Colonel Mabry was made colonel. J. S. Boggess, Lieutenant-Colonel, and Captain A. B. Stone, of Company A, from Marshall, promoted to major. About the first of August we moved up the railroad to Saltillo, about fifteen miles north of Tupelo, established camps, dug wells, and remained about three weeks. Here the Fortieth (?) or Mississippi regiment joined the brigade. This was a new regiment, just out from home, and it seemed to us, from the amount of luggage they had, that they had brought about all their household goods along. This regiment is remembered for these distinct peculiarities. Aside from the weight and bulk of its baggage they had the tallest man and the largest boy

During the Confederate attack on Battery Robinett, guns stationed at Robinson (at the far left) had a clear field of view to lay down a terrible enfilade fire on the attacking Confederate left.

in the army, and the colonel used a camel to carry his private baggage. The tall man was rather slender, and looked to be seven feet high; the boy was sixteen or eighteen years old, and weighed more than three hundred pounds.

The brigage now consisted of the Third Texas, Whitfield's Texas Legion, the Third Louisiana, the Fourteenth and Seventeenth Arkansaas, and the Fortieth Mississippi.* The army here, commanded by General Price, was composed of two divisions commanded by Generals Little and D. H. Maury. Many of the troops that came out of Corinth with General Beauregard had gone with General Bragg into Kentucky. At the end of three weeks wemoved farther up the railroad to Baldwin. Here we dug more wells, and it was my fortune to be on the second day's detail that dug our company well. The first detail went down some eight feet, about as deep as they could throw the earth out. The next morning four of us, including C. C. Watkins and myself, the two weakest men, physically, in the company, were detailed to continue the digging. We arranged means for drawing the earth out, and began work, two at the time, one to dig and one to draw. At quitting time in the evening we had it down twenty-one feet, and had plenty of water. But we were not to remain long at Baldwin, as preparations for moving on Iuka were soon begun. As commissary supplies were gathered in for the approaching campaign there were stored in the freight department of the depot. One R. M. Tevis, of Galveston, was acting as commissary of subsistence, and Charlie Dunn, of Shreveport, was his assistant. They occupied a small room, the station agent's office, in the building during the day. A good many fatigue men were usually about the place during the day, to handle the stuff that was brought in.

One day, while I was on the platform, a country wagon drove up. Tevis and Dunn seemed to have expected its arrival, as they were soon out looking after the unloading. Among the rest was a barrel, a well-hooped, forty-gallon barrel, and instead of being sent in with the other stores it was hurriedly rolled into the private office of the commissary. This proved to be a barrel of peach brandy. Now, peach brandy was "contraband." The character and contents of the barrel were shrewdly guessed by the bystanders as it was hurried into its hiding-place, and its locality, after it had been stowed away, was clearly observed and mental note made thereof. The depot building was located at the north end of a cut and was elevated fully three feet above the ground, platforms and all. The Third Texas was camped along on the east side of the cut, say one hundred yards below the depot. The supplies were guarded day and night, the guards walking their beats, around on the platform. The next morning the guards were seen pacing the beats all right enough, but in the bottom of that barrel was an auger hole, and there was an auger hole through the depot floor, but there was not a gill of brandy in the barrel. At dress parade that morning it was unnecessary to call in an expert to determine that the brandy, when it leaked out, had come down the railroad cut. The two gentlemen most vitally interested in this occurrence dared not make complaint, but bore their sad bereavement in profound silence, and no one else ever mentioned it.

The City of Corinth, Mississippi, during P.G.T. Beauregard's evacuation of the town in the spring of 1862.

This brief stay at Baldwin terminated our summer vacation and our study of Hardie's infantry tactics. The constant all-summer drilling and the strict discipline we had been subjected to had rendered our dismounted cavalry the most efficient troops in the army, as they were good in either infantry or cavalry service, as was afterwards abundantly proved.

All things being ready, the march to Iuka was begun under General Price, with his two divisions. Up to this time the only infantry marching I had done, beyond drillling and reviews, was the two moves, Tupelo to Sattillo and Sattillo to Baldwin. As we were furnished transportation for cooking utensils only, the men had to carry all their worldly effects themselves and the knapsack must contain all clothing, combs, brushes, writing material and all else the soldier had or wished to carry, in addition to his gun, his cartridge box with forty rounds of ammunition, his cap box, haversack, and canteen. The weather was extremely hot, and the roads dry and fearfully dusty. While I had been on full duty for some time I was very lean, physically weak, and far from being well, and starting out to make a march of several days, loaded down as I was, I had some misgivings as to my ability to make it; but I did not hesitate to try. As the object of the expedition was to move on Iuka and capture the force there before General Grant could reinforce them from Corinth, a few miles west of that place, the troops were moved rapidly as practicable, the trains being left behind to follow on at their leisure. Unfortunately for me, I was on guard duty the last night before reaching our destination, and as we moved on soon after midnight I got no sleep.

Next morning after daylight, being within six or seven miles of Iuka, the Third Texas and Third Louisiana were placed in front, with orders to march at quick time into Iuka. Now, literally, this means thirty inches at a step and 116 steps per minute; practiclly it meant for us to get over that piece of road as rapidly as our tired legs could carry us. To keep up with this march was the supreme effort of the expedition on my part. I do not think I could have kept up if Lieutenant Germany had not relieved me of my gun for three or four miles of the distance. We found the town clear of troops, but had come so near surprising them that they had to abandon all their commissary stores, as they did not have time to either remove or destroy them. At the end of the march my strength was exhausted, and my vitality nearly so. The excitement being at an end, I collapsed, as it were, and as soon as we went into camp I fell down on the ground in the shade of a tree where I slept in kind of stupor until nearly midnight.

We remained about a week in and around Iuka, in line of battle nearly all the time, expecting an attack by forces from Corinth; and as it was uncertain by which one of three roads they would come, we were hurried out on first one road and then another. One afternoon we were hurriedly moved out a mile or two on what proved to be a false alarm, and were allowed to return to camps. On returning we found a poor soldier lying in our company camp with a fearful hole

in his head, where a buck and ball cartridge had gone through it. A musket was lying near him, and we could only suppose he was behind in starting on the march, and had killed himself accidentally.

On the night of September 18 we marched out about four miles on the Corinth road, leading west, and lay in line of battle until about 4 P.M. the next day, when a courier came in great haste, with the information that the enemy was advancing on the Bay Springs road from the south, with only a company of our cavalry in front of them. We had then to double quick back about three miles in order to get into the road they were on. We found them among the hills about one and a half miles from the town, a strong force of infantry, with nine or ten pieces of artillery, and occupying a strong position of their own selection. We formed on another hill in plain view of them, a little valley intervening between the two lines. Our fighting force consisted of General Little's division of two brigades, Hebert's, and a brigade of Alabama and Mississippi troops commanded by Colonel John D. Martin, and the Clark battery of four guns, Hebert's brigade in front of their center, with two of Martin's regiments on our right and two on our left. We began a skirmish fire, and kept it up until our battery was in position, when we began a rapid fire with canister shot. We then advanced in double line of battle, slowly at first, down the hill on which we had formed, across the little valley and began the ascent of the hill on which the enemy was posted, General W. S. Rosecrans in command. As we ascended the hill we came in range of our own artillery, and the guns had to be silenced. The entire Federal artillery fire was soon turned on us, using grape and canister shot, and as their battery was directly in front of the Third Texas, their grape shot and musketry fire soon began to play havoc with our people, four of our men, the two files just to my right, being killed. We charged the battery, and with desperate fighting took nine pieces and one caisson. The horses hitched to the caisson tried to run off, but we shot them down and took it, the brave defenders standing nobly to their posts until they were nearly all shot down around their guns,—one poor fellow being found lying near his gun, with his ramrod grasped in both hands, as if he were in the act of ramming down a cartridge when he was killed. The infantry fought stubbornly, but after we captured their guns we drove them back step by step, about six hundred yards, when darkness put an end to a battle that had lasted a little more than two and a half hours, the lines being within two hundred yards of each other.

I cannot give the number of Federal troops engaged in the battle, but General Rosecrans, in giving his casualties, enumerates eighteen regiments of infantry, three of cavalry, one detached company, and four batteries of artillery. The cavalry was not in the engagement, and I think he had but two batteries enagaged. One of these, the Eleventh Ohio Light Battery, lost its guns and fifty-four men. The total Federal loss, reported, was 790, including killed, wounded, and missing. Hebert's brigade, that did the main fighting, was

The commander of Price's First Division, Brigadier General Lewis Henry Little, was killed when a minie ball pierced his skull in the battle of Iuka.

composed of six regiments, reporting 1774 for duty, and lost 63 killed, 305 wounded, and 40 missing; total, 408. Colonel Martin had four regiments (1405 men), and lost 22 killed and 95 wounded; total, 117. We had two batteries with us, the Clark battery and the St. Louis battery, but they only fired a few shots. The Third Texas had 388 men, and lost 22 killed and 74 wounded; total, 96. Company C lost W. P. Bowers, Carter Caldwell, W. P. Crawley, and W. T. Harris killed; and J. J. Felps severely wounded. Crawley had a belt of gold around his waist, but only four or five of us knew this, and I presume, of course, it was buried with him. General Maury's division was not engaged. General Henry Little, our division commander, was killed. Lieutenant Odell, of the Third Texas, who was acting regimental commissary, and who was mounted on my horse, was killed, and the horse was also killed. Colonels Mabry and Whitfield, and, I believe, all our other colonels were wounded. The captured artillery was drawn by hand into town that night, where the guns were left next morning, after being spiked, as we had no spare horses to pull them away. Spiking guns means that round steel files were driven hard into the touch-holes, giving the enemy the trouble of drilling these out before the guns can be of any use again.

As General Ord was marching rapidly with a strong force from Corinth to reinforce General Rosecrans, General Price concluded to retreat. Putting the trains in the road some time before daylight, early in the morning the troops marched out southward, leaving our wounded men in Iuka and sending a detail back to bury the dead. As General Hebert's brigade had stood the brunt of the battle the evening before, we were put in front and, to clear the road for the other toops, we had to move at double quick time for six miles. This used me up, and I obtained permission

to go as I pleased, which enabled me to outgo the command and to rest occasionally while they were coming up. We made a march of twenty-five miles that day on our way back to Baldwin. But oh, how my feet were blistered! They felt as if I had my shoes filled with hot embers. Late in the afternoon, when I was away ahead of the command I came to Bay Springs. This little village stands on a bluff of a wide, deep creek, and is crossed by a long, high bridge. At this time, when the creek was low, the bridge was at least twenty-five feet above the mud and water below. I climbed down under the bluff, just below the bridge, to a spring, where I slaked my thirst, bathed my burning feet and sat there resting and watching the wagons cross the bridge. Presently a six-mule team, pulling a wagon heavily loaded with ammunition in boxes, was driven onto the bridge, and as it was moving slowly along one of the hind wheels, the right one, ran so close to the edge that the end of the bridge flooring crumbled off and let the wheel down. Gradually this wheel kept sliding until the other hind wheel was off. This let the ammunition go to the bottom of the creek, followed by the wagon bed. Soon off came one fore wheel. This pulled off the other one, then the wagon tongue tripped the offwheel mule and he dangled by the side of the bridge, and soon pulled the saddle mule off, and this process gradually went on, until the last mule started, and as he fell off his hamestring caught on the end of the bridge flooring, and for an instant the whole outfit of wagon and six mules hung by the hamestring, when it broke and down the wagon and the six mules atop of it. The driver had seen the danger in time to make his escape.

We soon arrived at Baldwin, our starting point. Our wounded left at Iuka fell into the hands of the enemy and were kindly treated and well cared for. The good women of the town and surrounding country came to their rescue nobly, and they received every necessary attention.

Captain Dunn, of Company F, was one of our badly wounded men, one of his legs having been broken by a grape shot. Captain Dunn was a unique character. He was a lawyer by profession, a very bright fellow, and lived at Athens, Tex. The first I ever knew of him he came to Rusk just before the war, to deliver an address to a Sunday-school convention. He was a very small man. In fact, so diminutive in stature that he was almost a dwarf. He was a brave, gallant soldier, a companionable, pleasant associate, and much of a wag. He was a great lover of fun, so much so that he would sacrifice comfort and convenience and risk his reputation in order to perpetrate a joke.

The ladiees who came to nurse and care for our wounded soldiers at Iuka were like other women in one particular respect, at least,—they were desirous to know whether the soldiers were married or single, religious or otherwise, and if religious, their church relationship, denominational preferences and so on, and would converse with the boys with a view of learning these particulars. The usual questions were put to Captain Dunn by one of these self-sacrificing attendants. He made no effort to deny that he was

Charles S. Hamilton, leader of Rosecrans' Third Division. After running afoul of U.S. Grant, the opportunistic Hamilton resigned his commission in April of 1863.

Without loss of time in preliminaries, the spokeswoman of the committee said: "Captain Dunn, we have heard that you are a Mormon and have come to you, as a committee, to learn the truth of the matter. Are you a Mormon?" "Yes, madam," said Captain Dunn. "Have you more than one wife?" "Yes," said Captain Dunn, "I have four wives." "Captain Dunn, don't you think it awful wrong? Don't you think it's monstrous to be a Mormon?" "No, madam," said Dunn, "that's my religion, the religion I was brought up in from childhood. All of my regiment are Mormons. All of them that are married have two or more wives. The colonel has six; some have four, and some five, just as they may feel able to take care of them." A meeting of the ladies was then called, an indignation meeting, and indignation was expressed in unmeasured terms. The very idea! that they had scraped lint, torn their best garments into bandages, had cooked and brought soups and all the delicacies they could prepare to the hospital—done all they could, even to the offering up their prayers, for a detestable Mormon, with four wives! It was unanimously resolved that it could be done no longer. From that good hour, in passing through the hospital ministering to the wants of all the other wounded, they gave Dunn not even as much as a look, to say nothing of smiles, cups of cold water, soups, cakes, pies, and other more substantial comforts.

This neglect of Captain Dunn was eventually noticed by the other soldiers, talked of, and regretted by them and its cause inquired into. They earnestly interceded with the ladies in his behalf, and urged them that whatever Captain Dunn's faults might be, he was a brave Confederate soldier, and had been severely wounde ind an attempt to defend their homes, that he was suffering greatly from his wounds; that if he was a Mormon he was a human being, and for humanity's sake he deserved some attention and sympathy, and should not be allowed to die through neglect. This argument finally prevailed, the resolution was rescinded, and the captain fared well for the rest of the time, even better than he had before the matter came up.

One day one of the ladies asked Captain Dunn how it happened that he got his leg so badly crushed. In the most serious manner he said to her: "Well, madam, I am captain of a company, and when we got into the battle the Yankees began shooting cannonballs at us, and to protect my men I got out in front of them and would catch the cannonballs as they came and throw them back at the Yankees; but when the battle grew real hot they came so fast I couldn't catch all of them, and one of them broke my leg."

As soon as our men thought they were able to travel they were paroled and allowed to go free. When Captain Dunn was paroled he went to Texas for a rest, until he supposed he might be exchanged. On his return, he was traveling through Arkansas when a woman on the train asked him where he was going? He replied, "Madam, I am going to Richmond in the interest of the women of Texas. I am going to make an effort to induce the Confederate congress, in view of the great number of men that are being killed in the

married and, with some hesitation, frankly acknowledged that he was a member of the church of the Latter Day Saints, usually called Mormons, which was enough information for one interview. With the exclamation, "Why, you a Mormon!" the woman retired. In whispers she soon imparted to all the other ladies who visited the hospital the astounding information that one of the Texas soldiers was a Mormon. They were incredulous, but after being vehemently assured by the interviewer that she had it from his own lips, some believed it was true, while others believed it was a joke or a mistake. To settle the question they appointed a committee of discreet ladies to ascertain the truth of the matter, and the committee promptly waited upon Captain Dunn.

war, to pass a law providing that every man, after the war ends, shall have two wives."

When paroling our people their paroles were filled out by a Federal officer and presented to them for their signatures. The majority of the men cared little about the form, but only of the fact that they were to be allowed to go free until they were exchanged. But when they came to Colonel Mabry he read the parole over very carefully. He was described as H. P. Mabry, a colonel in the "so-called Confederate States Army." Mabry shook his head and said, "Sir, can you not leave out that 'so-called'?" He was informed that it could not be done. "Then," said the colonel, "I will not sign it." "In that case," said the officer, "you will have to go to prison." "Well," Mabry replied, "I will go to prison and stay there until I rot before I will sign a parole with that 'so-called Confederate States' in it."

Captain Lee, of the Third Texas, was of the same way of thinking, and they both went to prison and remained there until they were exchanged, being sent to some prison in Illinois. Some months after they were exchanged and came back to us we captured some prisoners one day. One of them inquired if the Third Texas was there, and was told that it was. "Then," said he, "take me to Colonel Mabry or Captain Lee, and I'll be all right." This man was a "copperhead" whose acquaintance they had made while in prison. He didn't want to serve in the army against us, but had been drafted in, and was glad of an opportunity of changing his uniform.

At Baldwin about two days was spent in preparation for a march to Ripley, there to join General Van Dorn's command for a move on Corinth. I was on fatigue duty while at Baldwin, and had no time to recuperate after the hard campaign to Iuka and back, having been on guard duty the night before arriving at Ripley. We camped at that town one night and started next morning, September 29, 1862, for Corinth, General Van Dorn in command. On that morning I found myself with a fever, and feeling unequal to a regular march I obtained permission to march at will, and found Lieutenant R. L. Hood and F. M. Dodson in the same condition and having a like permit. We joined our forces and moved up the hot, dusty road about six miles. Being weary, foot-sore, and sick, we turned into the woods, lay down and went to sleep under some oak trees and did not wake until the beef cattle were passing us in the afternoon. This meant that we had slept until the army was ahead of us—cavalry, infantry, artillery, and wagon train. We moved on until night without overtaking our command. Nearing the village of Ruckersville it occurred to me that many years ago this had been the post office of Peter Cotten, my mother's brother. Stopping at a house to make inquiries, I learned that Willis Cook, his son-in-law, lived only three-quarters of a mile west of the village. We turned in that direction, and soon found the place without difficulty. My call at the gate was answered by my uncle at the front door. I recognized his voice, although I had not heard it since I was a small boy. Going into the house I made myself known to him and his daughter, Mrs. Crook, and received a cordial welcome, such a welcome as made me and my com-

rades feel perfectly at home. My good cousin, Tabitha, whose husband, Willis Crook, was in the cavalry service, and in the army then on its way to Corinth, soon had a splendid supper ready for us and in due time offered us a nice bed. We begged out of occupying the beds, however, and with their permission stretched our weary limbs under a shade tree in the yard and enjoyed a good night's sleep.

Next morning one or two of the party had chills, and we rested for the day. We soon learned that a Federal cavalry command had dropped in behind our army, and so we were cut off. Had we gone on in the morning we would probably have been captured during the day. Learning how we could find parallel roads leading in the direction we wished to go, late in the evening we started, traveled a few miles and slept in the woods. The next morning we moved on until ten o'clock, and meeting a ten-year-old boy on a pony in a lane, we asked him if he knew where we could get something to eat. He said there was a potato patch right over there in the field. We asked him to whom it belonged, and he answered: "It belongs to my uncle; but he is layng out in the brush to keep out of the army;" and told us that his uncle lived up on the hill a short distance ahead of us. We did not go into the potato patch, but went up to the uncle's house. The house was a fairly good one, and in the front were two good-sized rooms with a wide, open hall. As we marched up to the rail fence in front of the house a woman came out into the hall, and we could see that the very looks of us aggravated and annoyed her. By way of getting acquainted with her, Dodson said: "Madam, have you got any water?" In a sharp, cracked voice, she answered: "I reckon I have. If I hain't, I would be in a mighty bad fix!" Having it understood that Dodson was to do the talking, we marched in and helped ourselves to a drink of water each, from a bucket setting on a shelf in the hall. During the next few minutes silence of the most profound sort prevailed. We stood there as if waiting to be invited to sit down and rest, but instead of inviting us to seats she stood scowling on us as if she was wishing us in Davy Jones' locker or some similar place. Hood and myself finally moved a little towards the front of the hall, and the following dialogue took place between Dodson and the woman: Dodson: "Madam, we are soldiers and are tired and hungry. We have been marching hard, and last night we slept in the woods and haven't had anything to eat. Could we get a little something here?" "No, you can't. I don't feed none of your sort. You are just goin' about over the country eatin' up what people's got, and a-doin' no good." "Why, madam, we are fighting for the country." "Yes, you are fightin' to keep the niggers from bein' freed, and they've just as much right to be free as you have." "Oh, no madam; the Bible says they shall be slaves as long as they live." "The Bible don't say no sech a thing." "Oh, yes, it does," said Dodson, gently; "let me have your Bible and I'll show it to you." "I hain't got no Bible." "Madam, where is your husband?" "That's none of your business, sir!" "Is he about the house, madam?" "No, he ain't." "Is he in the army, madam?" "No, he ain't. If you *must* know, he's gone

Opposing forces at the battle of Iuka engage in a sanguinary contest of courage, endurance, and musketry. Major General Sterling Price recalled in his official report that Iuka was fought "with a severity I have never seen surpassed."

A shell from a Yankee cannon explodes amongst Earl Van Dorn's Confederates in their desperate charge against the Federal fortifications at Battery Robinett.

off to keep from bein' tuk to Ripley and sold for twenty-five dollars." "Why, madam, is he a nigger?" "No, he ain't a nigger; he's just as white as you air, sir." "Well, madam, I didn't know that they sold white men in Mississippi." "No, you don't know what your own people's a-doin'." During the conversation I kept my eye on the lowest place in the fence. What she said about being sold for twenty-five dollars was in allusion to a reward of that amount offered by the conscript authorities for able-bodied men who were hiding in the brush to keep out of the army.

That night we lodged with a good old Confederate who treated us the best he could. Next morning Dodson bought a pony from him, which we used as a pack-horse to carry our luggage. We then moved much easier. Late in the evening we crossed Hatchie River on the bridge over which the army had passed on its way to Corinth. Here we found Adam's Brigade and Whitfield's Legion guarding the bridge, that it might be used in the event of the army's being compelled to retreat. This bridge was only a short distance south of the Memphis and Charleston Railroad, and a few miles west of Corinth. We took the railroad and followed it nearly all night, turning off to sleep a little while before daylight. Early in the morning we struck across into the main-traveled road, and pushed on in an effort to rejoin our command. Aobut nine or ten o'clock we came to a house, and determined to try for some breakfast, as we were quite hungry. We afterwards learned that a poor old couple occupied the house. Walking up to the front door we asked the old lady if we could get some breakfast, telling her we had been out all night and were hungry, and so on, the usual talk. She very readily said, yes, if we would wait until she could prepare it. She then invited us to come in and be seated, and said she would have the meal ready in a few minutes.

In a little while she came back and invited us in to breakfast in a little side room used for a kitchen and dining-room. As we started in I was in front, and as we entered the little dining-room and came in sight of the table she began to apologize because she was unable to give us anything more. I glanced at the table and saw a small, thin hoe-cake of corn bread and a few small slices of bacon, "only this and nothing more." I asked her if that was all she had. She answered that it was. Then I said, "Where are you going to get more when that is gone?" She did not know. Not doubting the truth of her statements, I said: "Madam, while we are hungry and do not know when we will get anything to eat, we could not take all you have. While we are just as thankful to you as if you had given us a bountiful breakfast, we are soldiers, and can manage to get something to eat somewhere, and will leave this for you and your husband," and we bade her good-by without sitting down to the table or tasting her scanty offering.

This poor old woman, who must have been sixty or more years old, had said, without a murmur and without hesitation or excuse, that she would prepare us some breakfast, and gone about it as cheerfully as if she had had an abundance, cooking us all the provisions she had, and only regretted she could not do more for us,—this, too, when not knowing where she would get any more for herself.

After leaving this humble abode we soon began to meet troops, ambulances, and so on, and from them we learned that our army was falling back. Instead of going farther we stopped on the road side and waited for our command. Noticing a squad of soldiers out some distance from the road engaged apparently about something unusual, my curiosity led me out to where they were. To my surprise I found they were Madison County, Alabama, men, most of whom I knew. They were burying a poor fellow by the name of Murry, whom I had known for years, and who lived out near Maysville. They had rolled him up in his blanket and were letting him down into a shallow grave when I approached, and they told me that some of the boys that I knew were wounded—in a wagon just across the road. I soon found my old friends, John M. Hunter and Peter Beasley, of Huntsville, Ala., in a common rough road-wagon. Poor Hunter! he was being hauled over the long, rough road only that he might die among his friends, which he did in a few days. Beasley was not dangerously wounded.

We soon after joined our command and marched westward toward Hatchie bridge. But long before we got there Generals Ord and Hurlbut had come down from Bolivar, Tenn., with a heavy force of fresh troops, had driven our guards away, and were in undisputed possession of the crossing. Whitfield's Legion had been on the west side and had been so closely crowded, with such a heavy fire concentrated on the bridge, that they had to take to the water to make their escape.

Here was a problem confronting General Van Dorn, a problem which must be speedily solved, otherwise a dire calamity awaited his whole army. These two divisions of fresh troops were in front of an army of tired, hungry, worn-out Confederates, with General Grant's victorious army only a few miles in our rear. What was called the boneyard road ran some miles south of us and crossed the river on a bridge at Crum's Mill; but this bridge, as a precautionary measure, had just

been burned, and even now its framework was still aflame. The route we were on led west from Corinth parallel with, and but a little south of, the Memphis and Charleston Railroad, crossing Hatchie only a short distance south of Pocahontas. After crossing the river we would turn south on the main Ripley road, and this road ran parallel with the river, passing not far, three or four miles perhaps, west of Crum's Mill, so that a force might move rapidly from Corinth, on the boneyard road, cross at Crum's Mill and strike us in the flank and possibly capture our trains. Hence the precaution of burning this bridge. Everything of our army, whether on wheels, on foot, or on horseback, was now between Ord and Hurlbut in front and Grant and Rosecrans in the rear, without a crossing on Hatchie. The trains were parked, with a view, as I was told at the time, to burning them, leaving the troops to get out as they could, and we already had visions of swimming the stream. Personally I was wondering how much of my luggage I could get over with, and whether or not I could make it with a dry gun and cartridge box. General Price, in this dilemma, undertook to get the trains out, and he succeeded notably.

We had a pretty heavy skirmish with the forces at the bridge, with infantry and artillery, but only to divert attention from the trains as they moved out to gain the boneyard road. General Price went to the mill

The savagery of war is vividly depicted in this sketch of the Confederate troops killed at the battle of Corinth. In the course of the fight, Van Dorn's Army of the West suffered 4800 casualties while Rosecrans lost almost half that number.

and, pulling down the gable end, cast it on the mill dam, and thus made a temporary bridge over which the trains and artillery were driven. Then that gallant old man, who had just proved himself to be as much at home acting as chief wagon master as when commanding his army corps, sat on his horse at the end of his unique bridge nearly all night, hurrying the wagons and artillery across. On the west bank of the stream he kept a bonfire alight, which threw a flickering glare across the bridge. As each teamster drove on to the east end of the queer bridge, he would slow up his team and peer through the dim light for the proper and safe route. Just as he would slow up one could hear the loud, distinct voice of "Old Pap" shouting: "Drive up there! Drive up! Drive up! Drive up!" And thus it continued until every wheel had rolled across to the west side of the Hatchie.

After we left the vicinity of the bridge and after the skirmishing ceased, there was no time for order in marching, unless it was with the rear guard; no time to wait for the trains to stretch out into the road and to follow it then in twos. We fell into the road pell-mell, and moved in any style we wished to, in among the wagons, or any way just so we moved along and kept out of the way of those behind us. During the afternoon, in the middle of the road, I stumbled upon a small pile of corn meal, half a gallon, maybe, that had sifted out of a commissary wagon, and gathered part of it into my haversack, mixed with a little dirt. I crossed the bridge away along, I suppose, about 11 P.M., after which I stopped and watched General Price's maneuvers and the crossing of the wagons until after midnight.

In the meantime I hunted around and found an old castaway tin cup, dipped up some river water and made up some dough, and then spreading it out on a board, I laid it on General Price's fire until it was partially cooked. Surely it was the most delicious piece of bread I have ever tasted, even to this day.

When a good portion of the Third Texas had come up we moved on into the Ripley road and were sent northward for a mile or two, where we lay in line of battle in ambush, near the road until the trains had all passed.

After daylight we moved on towards Ripley, being again permitted to march at will, as we had marched the night before. Approaching Ruckersville my heart turned again toward my good cousin, Tabitha Crook. Taking little David Allen with me, I made haste to find her home. Arriving there a short time before dinner I said to her, "Cousin, I am powerful hungry." "Oh, yes," she said, "I know you are, Willis came by home last night, nearly starved to death." Soon we were invited into her dining-room and sat down to a dinner fit for a king. Here I met her brother, George Cotten, whom I had never seen before. After dinner Mrs. Crook insisted that we rest awhile, which we did, and presently she brought in our haversacks filled up, pressed down, and running over with the most palatable cooked rations, such as fine, light biscuits, baked sweet potatoes, and such things, and my mess rejoiced that night that I had good kins-people in that particular part of Mississippi, as our camp rations that night were beef without bread.

We then moved on to Holly Springs and rested for somedays, after a fatiguing and disastrous campaign, which cost us the loss of many brave soldiers, and lost General Van Dorn his command, as he was superseded by General J. C. Pemberton.

The battle of Corinth was fought October 3 and 4, 1862. I do not know the number of troops engaged, but our loss was heavy. According to General Van Dorn our loss was: Killed, 594; wounded, 2162; missing, 2102. Total, 4858. The enemy reported: Killed, 355; wounded, 2841; missing, 319. Total, 3515. But if General Rosecrans stated the truth, our loss was much greater than General Van Dorn gave, as he (General R.) stated that they buried 1423 of our dead, which I think is erroneous. Company C lost our captain, James A. Jones, mortally wounded; John B. Long and L. F. Grisham, captured. As Captain Jones could not be carried off the field, Long remained with him and was taken prisoner, being allowed to remain with Captain Jones until he died. They were sent to Louisville, Ky., and then to Memphis, Tenn., where Captain Jones lingered for three months or more. After his death, Long, aided by some good women of Memphis, made his escape and returned to us.

It was at the battle of Corinth that the gallant William P. Rogers, colonel of the Second Texas Infantry, fell in such a manner, and under such circumstances, as to win the admiration of both friend and foe. Even General Rosecrans, in his official report, complimented him very highly. The Federals buried him with military honors. It was at Corinth, too, that Colonel L. S. Ross, with the aid of his superb regiment, the Sixth Texas Cavalry, won his brigadier-general's commission.

The evening before reaching Holly Springs we had what in Texas would be called a wet norther. Crawling in a gin-house I slept on the cotton seed, and when we reached Holly Springs I had flux, with which I suffered very severely for several days, as the surgeon had no medicine that would relieve me in the least. In a few days we moved south to Lumpkin's Mill, where we met our horses and were remounted, the Third, Sixth, Ninth and Whitfield's Legion composing the cavalry brigade, which organization was never changed. The army was soon falling back again, and continued to do so until it reached Grenada, on the south bank of Yalabusha River.

Right:
Casualty of the Confederate attack of the Federal fortifications at Corinth, a member of the 2nd Texas lies where he was killed in the assault on Battery Robinett. Further off to the left is the body of the Commander of the 2nd Texas, Colonel W.P. Rogers.

$$\star\star\star$$

LLOYD BRYNER
A Yankee in Mississippi

The general who was to lead his bluecoats to two successive victories over Price's Confederates was Major-General William S. "Rosey" Rosecrans. His solid fighting ability, while criticized by Grant, won the attention of President Abraham Lincoln who gave Rosecrans the leadership of the

Army of the Cumberland on 23 October 1863. Serving in "Old Rosey's" ranks at both Iuka and Corinth was Lloyd Bryner of the 47th Illinois. His account of the battle is taken from his stirring work Bugle Echoes.

Upon Col. Bryner's departure, William A. Thrush, who had been made Lieutenant-Colonel after the death of Miles, assumed command of the regiment. The band which, ever since the departure from Peoria, had been a source of pride and pleasure to the regiment, was ordered discharged. The expense of the government were enormous and all unnecessary impediments were being dispensed with. Bugles, drums and fifes could sound the calls and brass bands were allowed henceforth only to brigade headquarters and fighters and marchers like Mower had no use for them even there.

For almost three weeks the regiment remained at Rienzi, breaking camp August 18th, 1862, and once

more starting on a seemingly endless tramp. Eighteen miles this day through a village, they say it is Jacinto; at the end of the day another village on a railroad, which some say is the Memphis and Charleston, and the village Burnsville. The soldier doesn't know until the war is over, when he looks it up on the map, and then knows it is so. Memory of such marches is a horrid nightmare. Stifling dust those August days, parched throats and aching eyes seared by sun and irritated by sand, the smell of sweaty leather from burdening knapsack—weighting cartridge box and haversack—gun barrels that are hot and bayonets whose glint is an irritation, the water in the canteen hot and brackish, though the cloth cover is kept well

wet; when a stream is reached, a rush from the ranks, water hastily dipped and dashed in the face, canteen refilled and countless steps again to the camp at night unless, and it often happened, necessity required an all-night march, when the only bivouac fires were God's stars, and the tramp, tramp, tramp, went steadily on, fifty minutes of marching and ten minutes of rest, and so the boys of the "Eagle Brigade" marched for four years and five months.

From Burnsville to Iuka was another eight miles, twelve miles to Bear Creek and another twelve to Cane Creek, Alabama; good camp there and good to remember, plantations large, darkies a-plenty to point out supplies, hens, eggs, sweet potatoes, hams. A soldier's lot is not so bad after all. There are shading pines in Alabama and clear springs, by which to camp at night, and ten miles with the smell of pines and a spring was found at Tuscumbia, near the Tennessee River.

Soldiering is not all heroic. One stops to put shoulder to wheel of mired wagon or gun at times, roads must be cut through woods, enemy's stores are seized and must be loaded upon wagon or railroad trains. It was confiscated cotton at Tuscumbia and the 47th was detailed to do the loading upon cars. Cotton was valuable and the North would welcome it.

September 8th the regiment took the back track towards Corinth again and camped at Cane Creek;

Victor of Iuka and Corinth, Major General William S. Rosecrans, known as "Old Rosy" to his troops.

Brigadier General Stephen A. Hurlbut's division of the Army of the Tennessee tramps through the muck and mire during the Federal advance on city of Corinth, Mississippi.

The scourge of Mississippi—a Federal foraging party "requisitions" its needs from the citizens of the South.

twenty-four miles to Bussard's Roost, the "Johnnies" pressing the rear guard and killing one cavalryman. On the 10th they camped at Iuka, reached Burnsville on the 11th and on the 12th were again at the old camp at Clear Creek, which they had left in June. Price captured Iuka almost immediately after the regiment had left there. Other than guerilla operations there had been but little of active operations from June until September.

Determining to crush Price, Grant at once put two columns in motion under Generals E. O. C. Ord and W. S. Rosecrans to accomplish this purpose. Ord was to attack in front while Rosecrans was to attack on flank and in rear. Ord had 5,000 men and additional troops were given him by a division under Gen. Ross. Rosecrans had Generals C. S. Hamilton's and D. S. Stanley's divisions, about 9,000 strong. With

Members of the 11th Ohio Battery watch the flowing ranks of blue of Major General Williams S. Rosecrans' Army.

Hamilton's division in the advance the "Eagle Brigade" with Stanley's division left Camp Clear Creek on the night of the 18th with three days' cooked rations and 100 rounds of ammunition for each man and marching through a drenching rain only reached San Jacinto, twenty miles south of Iuka, the following evening, having been detained by falling in rear of Ross through fault of the guide. Hamilton had pushed forward, listening for the sound of Ord's guns, and found a line of battle two miles from Iuka on densely wooded heights. The ground was in terrible condition, unknown to the Union troops and with no room for development. Hamilton's skirmishers were driven back and a desperate battle ensued. On the crest of the hill stood the 11th Ohio battery. Hamilton fought three times his own force led by Price in person—the battle became furious. In front, up the road, came the enemy's heavy columns. From the battery upon the hill a deadly fire was poured into the advancing foe. The Confederate musketry concentrating upon the devoted battery soon killed or disabled most of the horses. The wounded animals ran shrieking, mad with pain and fear. On came the line of gray, only to be hurled back in disorder. "The Eagle Brigade" came into action on the double quick, the 47th on the left of the 11th Missouri, the 5th Minnesota on the right and the Wisconsin 8th in support. A whole brigade of Texans born down upon the 48th Indiana, which was forced to give about one hundred yards, when it was met and supported by the 4th Minnesota and held its position until relieved by the 47th Illinois. Three times the guns on the crest of the hill were charged by the Confederates, the cannoniers were bayoneted at the guns; seventy-two dying at their posts. In the last desperate attempt two Mississippi brigades were sent to the work. As the first brigade came from the woods, bearing down upon the 11th Missouri and when within one hundred paces a Confederate officer

sprang forward and shouted, "Don't fire upon your friends, the 37th Mississippi." He was answered by a withering volley, which drove them back in confusion. The Second Confederate brigade followed, darkness had come on, the smoke of battle hung so heavy that objects could scarcely be seen at five paces. On came the brave Mississippians but as vainly beat the waves against the rocks as these Confederate heroes against the Illinois boys of the 11th Missouri. They were received at the point of the bayonet from which they were fired, officers discharged their pistols in the very faces of their foes and the battle closed. The 47th Illinois and 39th Ohio held the front, slightly in front of the advanced regiments, which were withdrawn to replenish their ammunition. It was now night and the battle which had raged for several hours was over.

The next morning the enemy was gone. The 47th Illinois lost one killed, five wounded and Major Cromwell captured. After the battle 162 Confederate dead were found, collected for burial, in the rear of their hospital, covered with tarpaulins. The entire Union loss was nearly 800 killed, wounded and missing; the Confederates losing over 1,400, amongst whom were General Little and Colonel Stanton, killed. One thousand six hundred and twenty-nine stand of arms, 13,000 rounds of ammunition and quantities of stores fell into the hands of the Union troops. The usual laudations in general orders followed, of which every regiment in the "Eagle Brigade" received its due share. Iuka was ordered placed upon the colors of the 47th following "Island Ten," "New Madrid" and "Farmington."

Pursuing the enemy, who retreated toward Ripley, there was everywhere found that saddest of sights, the desolated path of a defeated army in flight. The Confederates had been obliged to leave their dead unburied, their wounded to the mercies of the victors. Demoralized and dispirited, discipline had relaxed, and the line of retreat was marked by acts of vandalism. A Confederate soldier wrote: "Corn fields were laid waste, potato patches robbed, barn yards and smoke-houses despoiled, hogs killed and all kinds of outrages, perpetrated in broad daylight and in full view of our officers." It was through such scenes the pursuit was continued to Crippled Deer, thirty miles, where finding it useless to continue further, the brigade returned by way of Jacinto to Rienzi, where it remained a few days watching the movements of Price and Van Dorn, who were concentrating their forces at Ripley, Mississippi, and preparing for advance against Corinth. The combined forces of the Confederates numbered about forty thousand men, while Rosecrans had but about twenty thousand, twelve thousand of whom were strongly entrenched at Corinth and the balance serving upon outpost duty.

Late in September, Price and Van Dorn moved forward and encamped on the night of October 2d, within ten miles of Corinth. At 3 o'clock in the morning, Ocotber 1st, 1862, the bugles rang revielle and soon around a thousand fires men were busy preparing rations for a three days' march, which was to commence at daylight. An old campaigner's housekeeping is simple and orderly and sunrise found all in readiness. Assembly sounded, knapsack, haversack and accoutrements adjusted, rifles at a "right shoulder" and the column moved. At ten o'clock the Hatchie River, twelve miles distant, was reached. Here was the crossing of the Ripley and Rienzi Road and here the enemy were to be met and held, should they attempt the crossing. Arms were stacked and the time employed until five o'clock for the most part in digging up and cooking sweet potatoes from a five acre field of Confederate sand. When the halt was made Captain Harmon Andrews of Company "G" was detailed to place pickets and was absent for several hours. Returning late in the afternoon, he reported to General Mower that after placing his pickets he had gone forward several miles, where he saw the Confederate army moving rapidly and in force towards Corinth. After remaining in hiding and watching the enemy until he had counted eighteen batteries, he hurried back to camp and made his report, and at five o'clock imperative orders were issued to march to Kossuth, fifteen miles, that night. The boys knew that battle was impending and cheerfully they marched at "quick step" beneath the sun's sultry rays, in blinding sandy dust and almost without water. Until about nine P. M. all kept well up and then the heat and dust and swift pace began to tell. One by one the boys dropped out, unable to continue further. A rear guard was detailed to keep up the stragglers. With blistered feet and lolling tongues, men threw themselves beneath the trees along the roadside. Less than half the brigade was up when Kossuth was reached at midnight. Some of the companies numbered less than a dozen men. Those who reached their destination threw themselves down in the furrows of an old corn field, too weary to build fires or seek refreshment. Stragglers came up all through the night and early morning.

The morning of the 2d heard eight o'clock, breakfast call and saw a change of weather. The sun was veiled by clouds and heat replaced by rain. Mud took the place of dust. There were no tents and through it all was the inimitable, indomitable cheerfulness of the American soldier. You dwellers in palatial homes, who sleep upon high-trade spring mattresses, have no idea how comfortable a bunk of fence rails properly placed upon the ground with swamp grass for a mattress is after such a march upon such a night. The boys had these and slept soundly; many—and one a brave young colonel—for the last time upon this earth. Some of the 47th added fresh pork to their supper menu of hard tack and coffee, having captured a drove of Confederate "razor back" hogs. There was but little sleep that night, for some none at all, for no matter how weary the soldier, guard and picket duty must be done. At one o'clock in the morning, the brigade was aroused; two days' rations hastily prepared—easily enough when you have only to choose between pickled pork raw and pickled pork fried with your "hard tack." The "hard tack" (army bread) was not unlike water wafers and when fresh, good; when

Taking time out between battles, soldiers partake in games of chance. Oftentimes before going into a battle, soldiers discarded their playing cards and dice to conceal such vices from family and the Lord should they fall on the field of battle.

Federal quarters at Corinth, Mississippi.

mouldy, intolerable; when only wormy, if hungry enough, you are not fastidious. Coffee was issued whole, and ground in a quart cup with the butt end of a bayonet. Brown sugar was supplied and these usually constituted marching rations. Place these rations in a canvas haversack, let it rain all day, soaking the haversack through, and at night hunger might possibly prove preferable to supper.

At three o'clock Mower had his men moving and at nine o'clock was within two miles of Corinth, at the outer line of the old Confederate entrenchments. Halting and stacking arms, coffee was prepared and at twelve o'clock the line of march was again resumed and the column moved two miles further toward the left of the already contending Union lines. The Confederates had commenced the attack upon Oliver's Brigade early in the morning and had driven him back. McArthur was sent to his support, but still the Confederate lines came on and pressed the Union line back still further. McKean and Davies had been sent to the aid of Oliver and McArthur, but the Confederats were resolved to capture Corinth with its immense quantities of stores and munitions. In a

desperate charge upon the Union lines, two guns were captured. The continuous roll of musketry and the thundering artillery informed the "Eagle Brigade" of the desperate character of the conflict in which they were about to engage. The battle had raged since early dawn and fortune had thus far favored the enemy. Their whole force was now pressing heavily upon the Union center, which was being steadily driven back. The "Union Brigade," under Davies, was being flanked and McKean's position was growing untenable. Mounted orderly after mounted orderly came riding back from McKean with appeals for help. Hurried orders came to immediately advance. Utterly worn from the thirty-four miles' march of the preceding twenty-four hours, the brigade moved forward with alacrity but not sufficiently rapid for the impatient Stanley, who constantly urged them to greater speed. To these urgent demands Colonel Thrush replied, "The men are already almost utterly exhausted; to move them faster will render them unfit for action." The calls for help became more and more pressing and frequent. Faster and faster came riding orderlies, excitement grew, aching limps and blistered feet were

forgotten; the boys were now on the run; cheer followed cheer as they swung into line.

Passing Fort Robinett, they moved to the right of the "Union Brigade." For fifteen minutes the 47th had been under a scattering fire, but as they took position the fire from the Confederate lines became so fierce it seemed as though a magazine had exploded in their very faces. From both sides the volleys were rapid and terrific. The "Union Brigade" gave way and the left flank of the 47th became exposed. A moment more the regiment would be surrounded and prisoners, but Thrush and Stanley were there. "Fix bayonets," rang out the command from Thrush. "Charge bayonets," forward, charge," and with a rush and a cheer the Confederate line was swept back. God, how the boys fell! Thrush was killed, shot through the heart. A gentle noble soul had gone to God. He fell in the very moment of victory while cheering on his men. The 47th had lost their leader, and Captain John D. McClure took command. Adjutant Rush Chambers, calling to his men to stand fast, ran to the right wing and assumed command there, while Captain Harmon Andrews took charge of the left. Again the battle took a turn and for a while seemed to hang in even scale. The left was still exposed and without support. The men were falling like autumn leaves. Another charge—the enemy again driven back. As they reached their reserves the fight became more stubborn. Brave Captain David DeWolf was dead. Captain Harman Andrews and Lieutenant Edward Tobey wounded—Andrews a prisoner, and McClure alone in command. A portion of the enemy had gained the rear of the line—the 47th was almost without officers, and one-half the men had fallen. The survivors were terribly worn from their severe march and lack of water. A retreat was ordered. Slowly they retired, facing the foe and keeping up a steady fire.

It was now five o'clock and the men had been under a hail of lead for over two hours. The enemy

Members of Rosecrans' Army of the Mississippi at Corinth. While the Army of the Potomac met numerous defeats, the Yankees out West enjoyed a string of victories against their Confederate foe.

were exultant and threw the whole left wing of their army against this one brigade. An avalanche of gray in ranks of serried steel—on they came. Slowly the old "Eagle Brigade" fell back; steadily pouring their fire into that line of glittering steel—and yet fell back.

Price had said he would rather capture "Old Abe" than a dozen battle flags and that to the Confederate who succeeded would be granted "free pillage" in Corinth. There he was before them and seemingly within their grasp.

There were brave hearts beneath those coats of gray and they beat with exultant hope as on they pressed, firing faster and faster, the flame from the guns almost scorching the faces of the boys in Union blue. The eagle was delirious in the delight of the strange wild storm, his wings were beating and he gave screams of frantic joy. Suddenly he was seen to spring aloft and soar away over the heads of the combatants; a halt of the lines as they paused upon both sides to watch the eagle's flight and then the sharpshooters in gray began to fire at the circling bird as he rose higher and higher with exultant cries. The smoke

suddenly cleared and the eagle saw the gleam of the colors below and with magnificent swoop returned to his perch beside the Union flag.

The battle raged again with fury intensified and again the brigade was swept slowly back. They reached the ridge where Thrush had fallen. Stanley called to the men to hold their ground; fiercer the fire and more deadly that the heroic brigade poured into the foe. Not another inch was yielded and the enemy exhausted and defeated retired to the shadow of the woods. One-half of the 47th had fallen, dead or suffering from ghastly wounds.

So closed the day, October 3d, 1862. Night fell; the roar of artillery and sharp crack of musketry replaced by the cries of the wounded, the hoof beats of horses as orderlies rode hither and thither carrying reports

Ghastly fatalities of the Confederate attack on Corinth.

and orders for the morrow; rumbling of ambulances bearing wounded to the hospitals; the heavy tramp of marching troops taking position; the measured tread of sentries and, piercing the gloom, an occasional uncanny scream from the woods proclaimed the vulture seeking prey. Around the bivouac fires of the 47th sat the boys—all that was left of them—sad but not dispirited. Their brave young Colonel lay at the Tishomingo Hotel in Corinth, dead. Out under the stars, somewhere upon the field, lay De Wolf and an hundred others. Andrews wounded was a prisoner and ten were missing, captured or dead, who would ever know? And tomorrow, well tomorrow, they would fight again.

At one o'clock in the morning, Saturday, October 4th, the regiment was aroused and moved, from the support of Fort Robinette to the support of Fort Williams. Sharpshooters were detailed to watch the movements of the enemy and all night long the crack of rifles told of their faithful vigil. The light of the stars had not yet faded when at four o'clock the Confederates opened fire upon the town from a battery of twelve pounder guns posted in the woods to the west of Robinette. Lieutenant Robinette made no reply for twenty minutes; carefully training his guns to meet the expected attack. Dawn was fast approaching. Companies "E" and "B" of the 47th, under Puterbaugh and Kinnear were upon the skirmish line and opened the fight. Shells were bursting over the heads of the Union troops. One ball passed through the Tishomingo House, killing one of the wounded. Robinette's parrot guns were now speaking; their range was perfect and the enemy were soon obliged to shift their position. Near sunrise all was silent except the occasional angry snarl of a sharpshooter's rifle. Soon after Van Dorn attacked the Union left.

Mower had ridden forward to the skirmish line—no lover more impatient for his mistress than Mower for war's troubles. The 5th Minnesota half-breeds (Hubbard's Indians) with the prudence of the white man and the sagacity of the Indian were ideal skirmishers and a portion of them were upon the skirmish line with the 47th and here was likely to be trouble to Mower's taste. As the enemy advanced the skirmish line was driven back. Mower's horse was shot under him and he was made a prisoner. On came the Confederate lines only to be met by a cross fire from the Union batteries. The fight raged for a half hour when Van Dorn was sent whirling back. A rider, bare-headed, spurring his horse at furious pace, burst from the woods through the line of gray straight for the Union lines. From the wood blazed an hundred rifles. The rider reeled for a moment in his saddle, then righted himself and spurred onward. He had been shot in the neck. As he neared the lines he was recognized; it was Mower. In the confusion of retreat he had seized the horse of a Confederate officer and, springing into the saddle, made for the National lines. Cheer followed cheer along the whole line. The "Eagle Brigade" was wild with joy.

Charge and counter charge followed—feints to conceal the real point of attack while the Confederates were shifting their forces. Orderlies were dashing in every direction; ammunition being distributed; belts tightened and cartridge boxes adjusted; nervous oaths from men unused to utter them—just to show they were not afraid; stern lips from which came no sound; a stillness that spoke aloud; the furies of hell were preparing for wild orgie on that second day at Corinth.

The storm burst at about nine o'clock. After a heavy cannonading, the Confederate forces advanced rapidly in wedge formation and drove straight for Davies. Grape and cannister tore terrible lanes through the Confederate ranks, the gaps closed and the magnificent forces of gray swept onward. Seven Union batteries were in action, but the determined men of Arkansas, Texas and Mississippi never faltered. On they came over the fallen timbers. A field battery followed their advancing line to within three hundred yards of Robinette, when a timely shell from Battery Williams killed several of the gunners and horses and the guns were abandoned.

The Confederates captured Fort Powell on Davies' right and fully twenty men reached Rosecrans' headquarters. There was work here for a portion of the "Eagle Brigade," and the 5th Minnesota went to it gallantly. Cheering and cheered they went in with a rush and pressed the enemy back. Fort Powell was retaken by the 56th Illinois, while Hamilton's guns poured in a steady fire, making fearful havoc in the retreating columns that were compelled to seek cover in the woods.

Meanwhile Lovell made a terrific attack upon Fort Robinette. Within lay prone, Fuller's Ohio Brigade, the 27th Ohio, and Mower's own regiment, the 11th Missouri, in support. Upon the advancing lines the 47th were pouring a deadly enfilading fire with telling effect, the guns of Robinette were double charged and the redoubt was a circle of flame. Magnificently mounted and bearing the Confederate colors aloft, Colonel Rogers of Texas led the line of gray, led them to the very edge of the ditch which he was in the act of leaping when the Ohio Brigade arose and delivered a murderous fire, before which the Confederates recoiled and the heroic Rogers fell; the fighting was magnificent and at the very muzzle of the guns. The line of gray was shattered and trembling, but still undaunted they advanced to the assault.

The 11th Missouri and 27th Ohio poured in a storm of bullets and advanced at a charge. The 47th, beyond the line of the enemy's fire, were pouring lead into the foe as rapidly as they could load and fire. And now the entire line sweeps to the charge and the day is won. It is eighty rods to the woods and forty "grim dogs of war" are let loose to tear at their heels, and hundreds fall. In front of Fort Robinette the Confederate dead lay piled from three to seven deep; for an hundred feet the bodies lay so close it was almost impossible to walk between them. The Confederate loss in killed, wounded and prisoners was over 9,000. The Union loss in the two days' battle and in the pursuit which followed was 2,363, of which number the "Eagle Brigade" lost 644, or more than one-quarter of the entire loss.

STEVEN C. FOSTER

"My Old Kentucky Home"

Though his songs pre-dated the Civil War, Stephen Forster's melodies such as "Swannee River" and "Old Kentucky Home" were sung by soldiers and civilians of the North and South alike.

The sun shines bright in the old Kentucky home;
  'Tis summer, and everyone is gay,
The corn-top's ripe and the meadow's in the
  bloom,
  While the birds make music all the day.
The young folks roll on the little cabin floor,
  All merry, all happy and bright;
By-'n-by hard times comes a-knocking at the
  door:—
  Then my old Kentucky home, good-night!

Chorus—
Weep no more, my lady,
Oh! weep no more today!
We will sing one song for the old Kentucky home,
For the old Kentucky home, far away.

PATRICK S. GILMORE

"When Johnny Comes Marchin' Home"

Probably the most famous song from the Civil War is not even associated with that great conflict. Patrick Gilmore's rousing "When Johnny Comes Marching Home" has more often than not been associated with later struggles such as World War One. There is no cause for wonder why this tune was frequently sung by those soldiers mustered out of service.

When Johnny comes marching home again,
  Hurrah! Hurrah!
We'll give him a hearty welcome then,
  Hurrah! Hurrah!
The men will cheer, the boys will shout,
The ladies they will all turn out.

Chorus—
  And we'll all feel gay,
When Johnny comes marching home.
The old church-bell will peal with joy,
  Hurrah! Hurrah!
To welcome home our darling boy,
  Hurrah! Hurrah!
The village lads and lasses say
With roses they will strew the way.

VICKSBURG

By fall of 1862, the Federals controlled most of the Mississippi River save for a comparatively small 150 mile stretch guarded by a garrison at Port Hudson, Louisiana, to the south and the fortified city of Vicksburg, Mississippi, to the north. If the Yankees ever managed to take Vicksburg, the entire range of the Father of Waters would be under Federal control, opening the river to Northern commerce, military movements, and cleaving the Confederacy in two. Beginning in the late October of 1862, U.S. Grant, commanding the Army of the Tennessee, embarked on numerous attempts to storm the Southern citadel of Vicksburg only to meet frustration and failure. Finally, by spring of 1863, Grant had crossed the Mississippi below Vicksburg and inaugurated his brilliant campaign that ended in the successful siege and capture of the city and opened the Mississippi for the Union.

★★★

JOSEPH WHEELER

The Perryville Campaign

A native of Augusta, Georgia, Joseph Wheeler rose quickly through Confederate ranks from lieutenant in the artillery to colonel commanding a cavalry brigade in Bragg's army during the Perryville campaign. During the later stages of the war, he led mounted operations against Sherman's lines of supply and communi-cations during the advance on Atlanta and the successive march to the sea. Following the Civil War, he returned to military service as Major General of the Volunteers in the Spanish American War. His account of Bragg's and Smith's ill-fated invasion of Kentucky is taken from Battles and Leaders of the Civil War.

General Bragg succeeded General Beauregard in command of the Confederate troops at Tupelo, Miss., about fifty miles south of Corinth, on June 27th, 1862. The field returns of June 9th, a week after our army reached Tupelo, reported it at 45,080. This return included the Army of Mississippi, reënforced by the troops brought from Arkansas by Generals Price and Van Dorn, together with detachments gathered from various localities. About two thousand cavalry not included in this return also belonged to the army. This was the maximum force General Bragg could expect to concentrate at that point. General Halleck, immediately confronting Bragg with the armies of Grant, Pope, and Buell, had in and about Corinth a force of 128,315 men, of which the field return of June 1st showed 108,538 present for duty. A division reporting 8682 for duty, under the Federal General George W. Morgan, was at Cumberland Gap; a division with 6411 for duty, under General Ormsby M. Mitchel, was in north Alabama, and there brigades were located at Nashville, Murfreesboro', and other points in middle Tennessee. Buell soon started *en route* to north Alabama, General Halleck remaining at or near Corinth with seventy thousand men for duty, a force strong enough to hold Corinth and west Tennessee, while Buell could menace or even invade Alabama or north Georgia.

The changed condition of the opposing armies during four months should now be considered. In January, 1862, the confederates had held all of Tennessee and most of Kentucky, and the Mississippi River from Columbus to the delta. Now, after a series of Confederate reverses, both States were virtually under the control of the armies under General Halleck, and the Federal flotilla sailed unmolested from St. Louis to Vicksburg. The Federal right was thrown forward into Mississippi. Its center occupied north Alabama, and its left was pressing the Confederates to the southern border of east Tennessee.

One of the masterminds behind the Confederate invasion of Kentucky during the late spring and fall of 1862, Braxton Bragg.

The Confederate problem was to devise some plan to turn the tide of disaster and recover at least a portion of our lost territory. Our soldiers had expected a battle at Corinth, in which they felt confident of as decisive a victory as was won by them on the first day of Shiloh; and the withdrawal to Tupelo had at last forced upon them a conviction that the numerical preponderance of the enemy was such that they could not expect to cope successfully with the combined armies then commanded by General Halleck.

Already the army had suffered much from sickness, and we could hardly expect any improvement while it remained idle in the locality where it had halted after its retreat from Corinth. An advance into west Tennessee would not afford protection to Alabama or Georgia. An advance into middle Tennessee by crossing the river at Florence, Decatur, or any neighboring point, would have the disadvantage of placing the Confederates between the armies of Grant and Buell under circumstances enabling these two commanders to throw their forces simultaneously upon General Bragg, who could not, in this event, depend upon any material coöperation from the army in east Tennessee under General Kirby Smith. There was another line for an aggressive movement. A rapid march through Alabama to Chattanooga would save that city, protect Georgia from invasion, and open the way into Tennessee and Kentucky, without the disadvantage of an intervening force between the column commanded by Bragg and that under the orders of General Kirby Smith. This movement was determined upon and resulted in what is called the Kentucky Campaign of 1862.

Major-General E. Kirby Smith had reached Knoxville March 8th, 1862, and assumed command of the Confederate troops in east Tennessee. The returns for June reported his entire force at 11,768 infantry, 1055 cavalry, and 635 artillery. The occupation of Cumberland Gap, June 18th, by a Federal division, and the approach of Buell's forces toward Chattanooga seriously threatened his department. General Bragg recognized the inadequacy of General Smith's force, and in June 27th he transferred the division commanded by Major-General John P. McCown from Tupelo to Chattanooga. Forrest and John H. Morgan had already been sent into middle Tennessee and Kentucky, and the operations of these enterprising officers materially lessened the pressure upon General Smith. Correspondence between Generals Bragg and Smith resulted in an order, dated July 21st, transferring the entire Army of Mississippi to Chattanooga. To mislead the enemy and to prevent an advance upon Tupelo, Bragg had, on the 19th, sent Colonel Joseph Wheeler with a brigade of cavalry into west Tennessee, and Brigadier-General Frank C. Armstrong with a like force into north Alabama. Wheeler's operations in west Tennessee may be briefly summarized as a rapid march from Holly Springs, Mississippi, to Bolivar, Tennessee; an attack upon the outposts at that place; the destruction of bridges on the line of communications of the troops at Bolivar and Jackson; a number of slight affair with the enemy's cavalry, and the burning of quantity of cotton in transit to the North.

One week was thus occupied behind the enemy's lines, the main object of the movement being to create the impression of a general advance. On July 31st Bragg and Kirby Smith met at Chattanooga, and a joint movement into middle Tennessee was determined upon, Price and Van Dorn being left to confront Grant in northern Mississippi. On August 5th Bragg sent two of his brigades (Cleburne's and Preston

Major General Don Carlos Buell, a prominent commander in the Union war effort in the West before Bragg's invasion of Kentucky cost him his command.

Smith's) to General Smith at Knoxville. General C. L. Stevenson, with nearly nine thousand men, was ordered to watch the Federal General G. W. Morgan, who occupied Cumberland Gap. General Smith started on the 14th *en route* to Rogers's Gap, with 4 brigades, 6000 strong. The brigades of Preston Smith and B. J. Hill were commanded by General P. R. Cleburne and the brigades of McCray and McNair were under command of General T. J. Churchill. General Henry Heth, with a force nearly 4000 strong, was ordered to march direct to Barboursville by way of Big Creek Gap, and the army was preceded by 900 cavalry under Colonel John S. Scott. General Smith had at first contemplated cutting of the supplies of the garrison at Cumberland Gap, but learning that they were well provisioned, and seeing the difficulty of supplying his own troops in the poor and barren region of south-eastern Kentucky, he determined to push rapidly on to the rich blue-grass country in the central part of the State. This determination had been communicated to General Bragg, and a march toward Lexington was commenced.

On the evening of the 29th, having reached Madison County, Kentucky, Colonel Scott found the enemy about half way between the small village of Kingston and the town of Richmond. The force displayed and resistance offered indicated that they were resolved to contest any farther advance of the Confederates. Although his troops were quite weary and

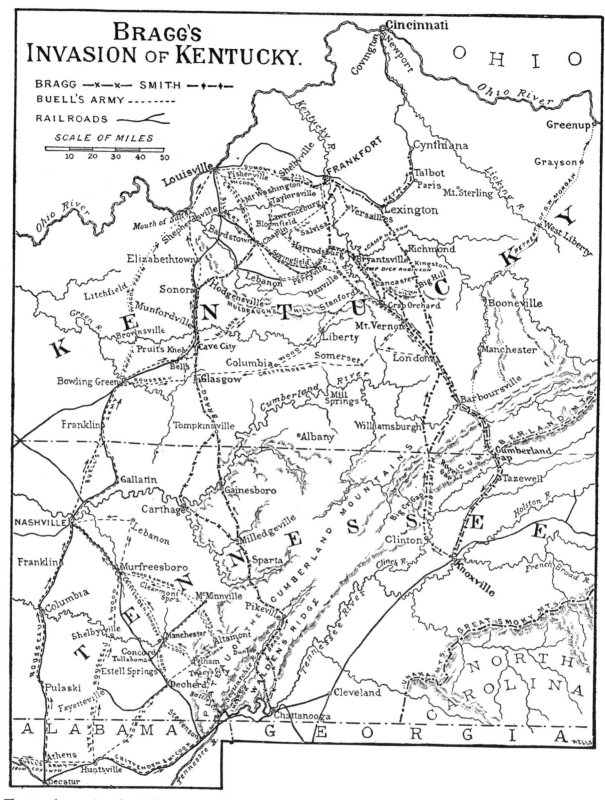

Theater of operations for Kirby Smith's and Braxton Bragg's invasion of the Bluegrass State.

General Heth was far to the rear, General Smith determined upon an immediate attack. He was in the heart of Kentucky, and the Confederate commander rightly judged that boldness was the surest road to victory.

Early on the 30th, General Cleburne, being in advance with his two brigades, found that the Federal force had moved forward and was in line of battle about a mile north of Kingston and probably five miles south of Richmond. The extreme advance-guard of the enemy, about six hundred yards in front of their main line, became engaged with Cleburne's leading brigade, commanded by Colonel Hill, but after a light brush retired upon the mainbody of the Federal army. Hill's brigade was soon formed in line behind the crest of a low ridge which was nearly parallel with and about five hundred yards south of the position occupied by the enemy. Cleburne also brought up Douglas's battery, which he placed in a favorable position near the center of his line. A fire of artillery and infantry commenced, and Captain Martin, with a second battery, having arrived, it was also brought into action, and for two hours both infantry and artillery were engaged from their respective positions. General Mahlon D. Manson, who was in command of the Federal army before General Nelson arrived, and who commenced the battle, now pushed his left forward to turn our right. Cleburne met this with one regiment of Preston Smith's brigade, which had been formed behind a crest in his rear, but the persistence of the enemy in that quarter made it necessary to reënforce the right with all of the reserve brigade under Preston Smith.

In the meantime General Kirby Smith had reached the field with the two brigades (McCray's and McNair's) forming General Churchill's division. He promptly dispatched that officer with one brigade to turn the enemy's right. The Federal commander, apparently disregarding this movment, still boldly advanced his own left to carry out his plan of turning the Confederate flank. This well-conceived manœuvre at first seemed to endanger the Confederate army, but Colonel Preston Smith with his brigade stood firm, and after a severe struggle checked and finally drove back the advancing enemy. General Cleburne, who up to this time had displayed both skill and gallantry, was severely wounded and left the field. General Churchill had now gained the enemy's right, and by a bold and determined charge threw the enemy into disorder

Two miles farther north the Federal force made a stand, and McCray's gallant brigade, by a rapid march, struck their right, while Cleburne's division, now commanded by Colonel Preston Smith, moved to the attack in front. The celerity of McCray's movements brought him into action before the other troops reached the field, and he suffered from the concentration of a galling and destructive fire; but the approach of Preston Smith, with troops cheering as they advanced again, caused a rout of the Federal army, closely followed by our victorious soldiers. When in sight of the town of Richmond the enemy were seen forming for a final struggle upon a commanding ridge, which had been judiciously selected by the Federal commander, Major-General William Nelson, both of the enemy's flanks being protected by skirts of woods. General Smith promptly sent McNair's brigade again to turn the Federal flank, and with the remaining force attacked directly in front. A warm fusillade lasted a few moments, when the Federal army again retreated. Early in the morning Colonel Scott had been sent to gain the rear of the town. His arrival at this moment increased the dis-

may of the enemy, and assisted materially in securing prisoners. The reports of the division and brigade commanders show that General Smith's entire force was about five thousand. The enemy supposed it much greater, their estimate including General Heth, but his division did not join General Smith until the day after the battle. Kirby Smith's loss was 78 killed, 372 wounded, and 1 missing.

Nelson in his report speaks of his own command on the Kentucky river as 16,000 strong, and the official report of casualties is given as 206 killed, 844 wounded, and 4303 captured. The Federal official reports admit that nine pieces of artillery and all their wagon trains were captured by the Confederates. General Manson contends that the Federals engaged did not exceed 6500.

Elated with success, and reënforced by about four thousand troops just arrived under Heth, the victorious army moved forward to Lexington, and was designated by its commander as "The Army of Kentucky." During the month of September the greater portion of the army remained in that vicinity.

On September 4th Colonel Scott, with a brigade of cavalry, was ordered to push on as near as practicable to Louisville, and to destroy the Louisville and Nashville Railroad. Heth, with a division of infantry and a brigade of cavalry, marched north; some of his troops, on September 6th, reached the suburbs of Covington, but his instructions were not to make an attack upon the city. Smith used vigorous efforts to gather and concentrate supplies, arouse the people, and raise and organize troops for the Confederacy.

General George W. Morgan (Federal), who was left at Cumberland Gap with 8682 men, seeing these active movements in his rear, evacuated that position on September 17th and made his way through eastern Kentucky to the Ohio River at Greenupsburg, arriving there October 3d.

While these events were happening, Bragg had organized his army at Chattanooga into two wings. The right, commanded by General Polk, consisted of Cheatham's and Withers's divisions of infantry and Colonel Lay's brigade of cavalry. The left wing, commanded by General Hardee, consisted of Buckner's and Anderson's divisions of infantry and Wheeler's brigade of cavalry. This entire force, on August 27th, reported 27,816 officers and men for duty. On the 28th the army was fairly in motion, but up to this time General Bragg had not positively determined upon his plan of campaign, and much depended upon the course pursued by the Federal army.

As early as the 22d General Buell had established his headquarters at Decherd, on the Nashville Railroad, thirty miles north-west of Stevenson, and had all the supplies .at Steveneson transferred to that place. Two parallel mountain ranges, running northeast and south-west, separated him from Chattanooga. A railroad, connecting McMinnville and Tullahoma, ran nearly parallel to the north-west slope of these mountain ranges. Already he had located General Thomas at McMinnville with Wood's and Ammen's divisions, while the divisions of Schoepf,

Pro-Union citizens of the Bluegrass State dig rifle pits, trenches, and fortifications in the Licking Valley near Covington in an attempt to prepare themselves for the possibility of a Confederate attack.

Troops of the 100th Ohio occupy Fort Mitchell along the Lexington Turnpike in Covington, Kentucky, during Braxton Bragg's invasion of the Bluegrass State.

McCook, and Thomas L. Crittenden were near the Nashville and Stevenson Railroad within easy call of headquarters of Decherd. Buell seemed impressed with the belief that Bragg's objective point was Nashville, and that he would take the short route over the mountain by way of Altamont, which movement, if made, would have placed Bragg between the force under Thomas and the rest of Buell's army. To prevent this Beull, on the 23d, ordered these five divisions to concentrate at Altamont. General Thomas reached his destination on the 25th, but, finding no enemy to confront him and learning that there was no enemy on the mountains, the nearest Confederates being at Dunlap's in the Sequatchie Valley, he reported these facts to Buell and returned to McMinnville. Crittenden's division halted near Pelham, and Schoepf at Hillsboro'. McCook pressed on and reached Altamont on the 29th, where, on the 30th, Wheeler attacked his outposts, and McCook retired down the mountain. The same day General Buell ordered his entire army to concentrate at Murfreesboro'.

By September 5th, the five divisions just mentioned had reached that place, together with all detachments from along the lines of railroad except Roussseau's division, which, being on the Nashville and Decatur Railroad, marched directly to Nashville. The strength of Buell's forces during the months of July, August, and September was estimated by witnesses before the Buell Commission, in 1863, at from 45,000 to 59,309. His own returns for June, deducting the force at Cumberland Gap, showed 56,706 present for duty, and his October returns, with the same deduction, 66,595. General Buell presented a paper to the Commission which does not question any of these statements regarding strength, but states that he could not have concentrated more than 31,000 men at McMinnville to strike the Confederate forces as they debouched from the mountains; and the same paper estimated Bragg's army at 60,000, while his returns of August 27th showed but 27,816 officers and men for duty. These facts prove the large preponderance of the Federals.

At Murfreesboro' Buell heard of Nelson's defeat at Richmond, and without halting he marched to Nashville. On September 7th he intrusted General Thomas with the defense of that city with the divisions of Palmer, Negley, and Schoepf, while with the infantry divisions of McCook, Crittenden, Ammen, Wood, Rousseau, and R. B. Mitchell, and a cavalry division under Kennett, General Buell determined to race with Bragg for Louisville.

It was a fair race, as on that day most of Bragg's army was south of the Cumberland River, at Carthage and Greensboro'. Bragg was nearest to Louisville by some twenty-five miles, but Buell had the advantage of a bridge at Nashville and the assistance of the railroad to aid in his march. With seven hundred cavalry, I hastened to strike and break the railroad at points between Bowling Green and Nashville, and otherwise sought to retard the northern march of the Federal army. By the 12th it was evident to Buell that no attack would be made on Nashville, and he ordered

General Thomas to join him with his own division, which had been commanded by General Schoepf. Beull reached Bowling Green with his cavalry and two divisions of infantry on the 14th, and turned his column in the direction of Munfordville. I interposed my cavalry on the Munfordville road, and also on the roads leading to Glasgow, and reported Buell's movements to Bragg. General Chalmers, with Bragg's advance, reached Munfordville at daylight on the 14th and learned that Colonel Scott, with a cavalry brigade, had demanded the surrender on the night previous. Chalmers was misinformed regarding the strength of the garrison and the character of the defensive works. He attacked with vigor, but was repulsed. He reported his force at 1913 men, and his loss at 35 killed and 253 wounded. On the 14th all of Buell's six divisions had reached Bowling Green, and on the 16th he advanced vigorously to succor the

Citizens of Louisville flee the city as the army of Braxton Bragg runs on a rampage across the state. While Bragg was able to cause a good deal of panic among the pro-Union element in Kentucky, the groundswell of support he expected for the Confederacy during his invasion did not materialize.

Refugees from the war in Kentucky attempt to warm themselves near fires by the banks of the Ohio River outside of Louisville, Kentucky.

garrison at Munfordville, the head of his column being opposed by cavalry. Bragg, hearing of Chalmers's attack and of Buell's movements, ordered his entire army, which had rested two days at Glasgow, to start early on the 15th *en route* for Munfordville. On the next day he reached that place, boldly displayed his army, and on the 17th at 2 P.M. the fort and garrison surrendered. The Federals reported their loss at 15 killed, 57 wounded, and 4076 prisoners. We also captured their armament, 10 pieces of artillery, and 5000 stand of small-arms. As might be expected, the Confederate army was much elated, and were eager to grapple with the dispirited army under General Buell.

Bragg placed his troops in a strong position south of the river, using the fort as a part of his line of defense. My command was thrown forward to meet and skirmish with the enemy, who, on the 19th, commenced preparations for an attack. On the 20th General Thomas joined the Federal army with his division. General Bragg, in referring to the situation of September 20th, wrote:

> With my effective force present reduced by sickness, exhaustion, and the recent affair before the intrenchments at Munfordville to half that of the enemy, I could not prudently afford to attack him there in his selected position.

If Kirby Smith's command had been ordered from Lexington to Munfordville even as late as the 12th, a battle with Buell could not have been other than a decided Confederate victory. Bragg at first had determined to fight with his four divisions, and no doubt would have done so had Buell advanced on the 17th, or 18th, or 19th. Early on the morning of the 18th, General Bragg sent for me and explained his plans. I never saw him more determined or more confident. The entire army was in the best of spirits. I met and talked with Generals Hardee, Polk, Cheatham, and Buckner; all were enthusiastic over our success, and our good luck in getting Buell where he would be compelled to fight us to such a disadvantage. It is true our back was to a river, but it was fordable at several places, and we felt that the objection to having it in our rear was fully compensated by the topographical features, which, with the aid of the fort, made our position a strong one for defense. So anxious was Bragg for a fight that he sent Buckner's division to the front in the hope that an engagement could thus be provoked; but after the arrival of General Thomas, Bragg did not deem it advisable to risk a battle with the force then under his command, believing that another opportunity would offer after being joined by Kirby Smith. He therefore withdrew to Bardstown, sending to me, who still confronted Buell, the followng order, dated September 20th, through General Hardee:

General Bragg directs that, if possible, the

The Army of the Ohio under Major General Don Carlos Buell enters the relieved town of Louisville during that general's pursuit of Bragg and Smith.

enemy be prevented from crossing Green River tomorrow, and General Hardee instructs me to say that he expects you will contest the passage of that river at Munfordville to that end.

Buell heard of Bragg's movements and pressed forward with determination. My small brigade of cavalry contested his advance on the 20th and 21st, in efforts to comply with the instructions from General Bragg. On the afternoon of the 21st, Buell's right approached the river above the town, and at the same time he pressed forward his line of battle so rapidly as almost to command the only ford by which I could cross Green River with both artillery and cavalry. Allen's 1st Alabama Regiment, being directly in front, was thrown into column and, charging gallantly, defeated the opposing cavalry and broke through their infantry. Among our killed was the noble Lieutenant-Colonel T. B. Brown, but the charge sufficiently checked the advance to enable the command to cross the ford in good order.

On the 22d, with a clear road to Louisville, Buell moved with celerity in that direction. My cavalry contested his advance, but the country was too open to allow of effective opposition with so small a force. On the 25th the leading Federal column reached the city, and the seven divisions were all up on the 27th. Bragg, Polk, and Hardee had been kept thoroughly informed of Buell's march and of the exposure of his flank, which presented an inviting opportunity for attack, but so worn and wearied was the condition of our army that these officers did not feel justified in

attempting an aggressive movement. On the 8th Bragg left Bardstown with his staff to confer with Kirby Smith at Lexington, and then proceeded to Frankfort, where, on the 4th of October, a day was occupied in the installation of the Hon. Richard Hawes as Confederate Provisional Governor of the Commonwealth.

While these events were happening Buell was making active preparations for an aggressive campaign. On the 26th Major-General Wright, commanding the Department of the Ohio, went from Cincinnati to Louisville to confer with him, and on the 27th General Halleck issued an order placing Buell in command of the troops of both departments, then in Louisville. . . .

The above [48,776] was the reported strength of the Confederate troops when the campaign began, but to make sure and to compensate for any omitted cavalry let us add 1000, making the entire force, 49,776. The losses at Richmond and Munfordville were very slight, compared to the daily depletion caused by dropping out along the route. Some were allowed to organize in squads and make their way back to east Tennessee; some sought shelter among the kind and hospitable people; some struggled along with the ambulance trains, and some were left at temporarily established hospitals, one of which, containing two hundred inmates, was captured by the enemy at Glasgow.

This character of loss always attends a rapidly moving army, and its extent can be realized when we see that Hardee's wing left Chattanooga 12,825 strong, was reënforced by Cleburne's brigade early in October; yet, even with Cleburne included, Hardee, in stating officially the force with which he fought at Perryville, says: "Thinned by battle and long and arduous service, my effective force did not exceed 10,000 men." It will be seen, therefore, that these causes reduced the Confederate ranks in much greater proportion than they were increased by enlistments and other accretions, and General Bragg in his official report of the campaign asserts that we were able "at no time to put more than forty thousand men of all arms and at all places in battle." This included Bragg's, Smith's, and Marshall's columns, and although it is probably true that their aggregate strength in August was 48,776, it would have been as difficult for Bragg and Smith to have concentrated that number as it would have been for Buell and Wright to have concentrated the 163,633 which they commanded. Even with such a force available to drive 40,000 men out of Kentucky, General Wright on the 16th appealed to the governors of Indiana, Illinois, Wisconsin, and Michigan for additional troops. What troops came in answer to these calls I could not venture to say; but leaving these and the troops in West Virginia under General Wright out of the calculation, our strength, even after Stevenson joined us, was less than half, and but little more than one-third that of the enemy, and that powerful enemy was directly on its base of supplies, with unlimited commissary and ordnance stores, while the Confederate army had no base, was living off the country, and had no possiblity

of replenishing ammunition. Bragg felt very keenly the misfortune caused by his inability to concentrate and gain a victory over Buell before he should reach the reënforcements which awaited him at Louisville.

In writing to the Government, September 25th, Bragg says:

> I regret to say we are sadly disappointed in the want of action by our friends in Kentucky. We have so far received no accession to this army. General Smith has secured about a brigade—not half our losses by causalties of different kinds. Unless a change occurs soon we must abandon the garden spot of Kentucky. . . .

On September 18th, Kirby Smith writes to General Bragg:

> The Kentuckians are slow and backward in rallying to our standard. Their hearts are evidently with us, but their blue-grass and fat-grass are against us. Several regiments are in process of organization, and if we remain long enough recruits will be found for all the disposable arms in our possession.

These letters illustrated why a victory over Buell was necessary.

Although Kentucky maintained her neutrality as long as it was possible, the chivalric spirit of her gallant sons was fully manifested at the earliest opportunity—each obeying only the dictates of his own convictions of duty. While thousands united their fortunes with the South, other and more thousands flocked to the standard of the North.

The proud old families—descendants of the pioneers of the Commonwealth—each sent sons to do battle in the opposing armies. Friends, neighbors, kinsmen, and even brothers bade each other adieu—one to the Northern army, the other to the Confederate. Wherever daring courage, rare intelligence, extraordinary fertility of resource, or fortitude under privation and suffering were displayed, Kentuckians were conspicuous and when the fight was over and the battle-rent banner of the vanquished Confederacy furled about its shattered staff was buried in that grave from which a resurrection is no less unwished for than impossible, the survivors of the contest from that State returned to their homes with no feelings of animosity, no brooding hopes of vengeance to be wreaked upon their late opponents.

On October 1st Buell commenced his march from Louisville upon Bragg at Bardstown. On September 29th General Thomas had been assigned by President Lincoln to the command of the army, but at Thomas's request the order was revoked, and he was announced in orders as second in command.

Buell organized his infantry into three army coprs, of three divisions each. The First Corps on the left, under Major-General McCook, marched through Taylorsville. The Second Corps, under Major-General Crittenden, marched through Mount Washington, and the Third Corps, under Major-General Gilbert, which formed the Federal right took the route by way of Shepherdsville. General Sill, of McCook's corps, reënforced by Dumont's independent division, marched direct to Frankfort to threaten Kirby Smith.

Skirmishing with the enemy's cavalry and artillery marked the movement of each column from within a few miles of Louisville. It was more stubborn and formidable near Bardstown, but the rear of the enemy's infantry retired from that place eight hours before our arrival, when his rear-guard of cavalry and artillery retreated after a sharp engagement with my cavalry. The pursuit and skirmishing with the enemy's rear-guard continued toward Springfield.

General Smith prepared to meet Sill and Dumont, and on October 2d Bragg ordered General Polk to move the entire army from Bardstown via Bloomfield toward Frankfort, and to strike Sill's column in flank while Smith met it in front. For reasons which were afterward explained that order was not complied with, but, on the approach of Buell, Polk marched via Perryville toward Harrodsburg, where he expected the entire army would be concentrated. General Smith, confronted by Sill and Dumont near Frankfort, had several times on the 6th and 7th called upon Bragg for reënforcements, and Withers's division of Polk's corps was ordered to him. Reports reached Bragg exaggerating the strength of the movement upon Frankfort. He was thus led to believe that the force behind Polk was not so heavy as represented, and on the evening of October 7th he directed him to form the cavalry and the divisions of Cheatham, Buckner, and Patton Anderson at Perryville, and vigorously attack the pursuing column. Since October 1st our cavalry had persistently engaged the two most advanced of Buell's columns.

The reader should now observe, by the map that McCook's corps approached Perryville by the road through Bloomfield, Chaplin, and Mackville, its general direction being nearly south-east. General Gilbert's corps approached by the road from Springfield, its general direction being east, but bearing north-east as it approached the town. Crittenden's corps, accompanied by General Thomas and preceded by cavalry, having crossed Gilbert's line of march, was on a road which runs due east from Lebanon to Danville. At a point about five miles south-west of Perryville this road has a branch which turns north-east to that place. Now remember that our stores and supplies were at Bryantsville and Camp Dick Robinson about eighteen miles east of Perryville, and that Kirby Smith was at McCown's Ferry, on the Kentucky River, *en route* for Versailles, menaced by two divisions under General Sill. Also observe the important feature that McCook was at Mackville during the night of the 7th, at which place a road forks, running east to Harrodsburg and thence to our depot at Bryantsville; and also consider that Mackville was as near Bryantsville as were our troops in front of Perryville.

On the 7th our cavalry fought with considerable tenacity, particularly in the evening, when the enemy sought to get possession of the only accessible supply of water. General Buell, in his report, says:

The advanced guard, consisting of cavalry and artillery, supported toward evening by two regiments of infantry, pressed successfully upon the enemy's rear-guard to within two miles of the town, against a somewhat stubborn opposition.

After dark, at General Hardee's request, I went to his bivouac and discussed the plans for the following day. I explained to him the topography of the country and the location of Buell's columns. I understood from him that the attack would be made very early the next morning, and I endeavored to impress upon him the great advantage which must follow an early commencement of the action. An early attack on the 8th would have met only the advance of Gilbert's corps on the Springfield road, which was four or five miles nearer to Perryville than any other Federal troops, and their overthrow could have been accomplished with little loss, while every hour of delay was bringing the rear divisions of the enemy nearer to the front, besides bringing the corps of McCook and Crittenden upon the field. I explained, also, that Thomas and Crittenden on the Lebanon and Danville road could easily gain our rear, while all our forces were engaged ith McCook and Gilbert. For instance, if Crittenden turned toward Perryville at the fork five miles from that place, he would march directly in the rear of our troops engaged with Gilbert's corps. If he kept on toward Danville and Camp Dick Robinson, our position would be turned, and a rapid retreat to our depot

Major General George H. Thomas' division in pursuit of Bragg's Confederates in Kentucky.

of supplies, closely followed by McCook and Gilbert, would be the inevitable result. With equal ease, Mc-Cook, by marching from Mackville to Harrodsburg, could reach our depot, thus turning our right flank.

The reader will plainly see that Perryville was not a proper place for sixteen thousand men to form and await the choice of time and manner of attack by Buell, with his tremendous army, and that every moment's delay after daylight was lessening the probabilities of advantage to the Confederates. The cavalry under my command was pressed forward at dawn on the 8th, and skirmished with the outposts of the enemy, until, on the approach of a Federal brigade of cavalry supported by a line of infantry, we charged, dispersing the cavalry, and, breaking through both infantry and artillery, drove the enemy from their guns and took 140 prisoners.

The Federal army was now being placed in line: McCook's corps on the left, Gilbert's in the center, and Crittenden's corps, which reached the field at 11 o'clock on the right, its flank being covered by Edward M. McCook's brigade of cavalry. The management of the Federal right wing was under the supervision of General Thomas.

General Bragg reached Perryville about 10 o'clock. General Liddell's brigade, of Buckner's division, had been advanced with his left near the Springfield road, and his skirmish line became engaged. The cavalry on the Confederate left apparently being able to hold their own against the enemy upon that part of the field, Cheatham's division, composed of Donelson's, Stewart's, and Maney's brigades, was ordered to the right, where, between 1 and 2 o'clock, with its right supported by cavalry, it moved forward to the attack.

Generals Hardee and Buckner, seeing Cheatham fairly in action, ordered General Bushrod Johnson's and Cleburne's brigades forward. There being considerable space between Cheatham's left and Buckner's right, General John C. Brown's and Colonel Jones's brigades, of Anderson's division, and General S. A. M. Wood's, of Buckner's division, had been placed in position to fill the vacancy. Adams's and Powell's brigades, of Anderson's division, were to the left of Buckner, and the line thus arranged with cavalry on both flanks gallantly advanced upon the enemy. Cheatham was first in action and was almost immediately exposed to a murderous fire of infantry and artillery, which soon spread to the left of our line.

Our artillery, handled with great skill, told fearfully on the enemy, who sought, when practicable, to take shelter behind stone walls and fences. Fortunately we were enabled to enfilade many of their temporary shelters with a well-directed fire from our batteries, and this, added to our musketry, was so effective that first one regiment, then another, and finally the entire Federal line, gave way before the determined onset of our troops.

At one time Cleburne and Johnson seemed checked for a moment, as they assailed a very strong position, the fire from which cut down our men and severely wounded General Cleburne. But encouraged by the steady advance on both right and left, these troops recovered from the shock, and with increased speed the entire line overran the enemy, capturing three batteries and a number of prisoners. Among the dead and wounded Federals lay one who, the prisoners told us, was General James S. Jackson, the commander of one of McCook's divisions. General Liddell, who had been placed in reserve followed the movement, and when the contest became warmest was sent to reënforce Cheatham, where he did valiant service.

During this sanguinary struggle, our line had advanced nearly a mile. Prisoners, guns, colors, and the field of battle were ours; not a step which had been gained was yielded. The enemy, though strongly reënforced, was still broken and disordered. He held his ground mainly because our troops were too exhausted for further effort. At one point just at dusk we captured a disorganized body, including a number of brigade and division staff-officers. Soon darkness came on and we rested on the field thus bravely won.

Our entire force engaged, infantry, cavalry and artillery, was but 16,000 men. Our loss was 510 killed, 2635 wounded, and 251 missing. Generals S. A. M. Wood and Cleburne were disabled, and a large proportion of higher officers were killed or wounded. Three of General Wood's staff were among the killed.

General Buell lost 916 killed, 2943 wounded, and 489 captured by the Confederates. General Jackson, commanding a division, and General Terrill and Colonel Webster, commanding brigades, were among the Federals killed, and Colonel Lytle was among the wounded.

At every point of battle the Confederates had been victorious. We had engaged three corps of the Federal army; one of these McCook's, to use Buell's language,

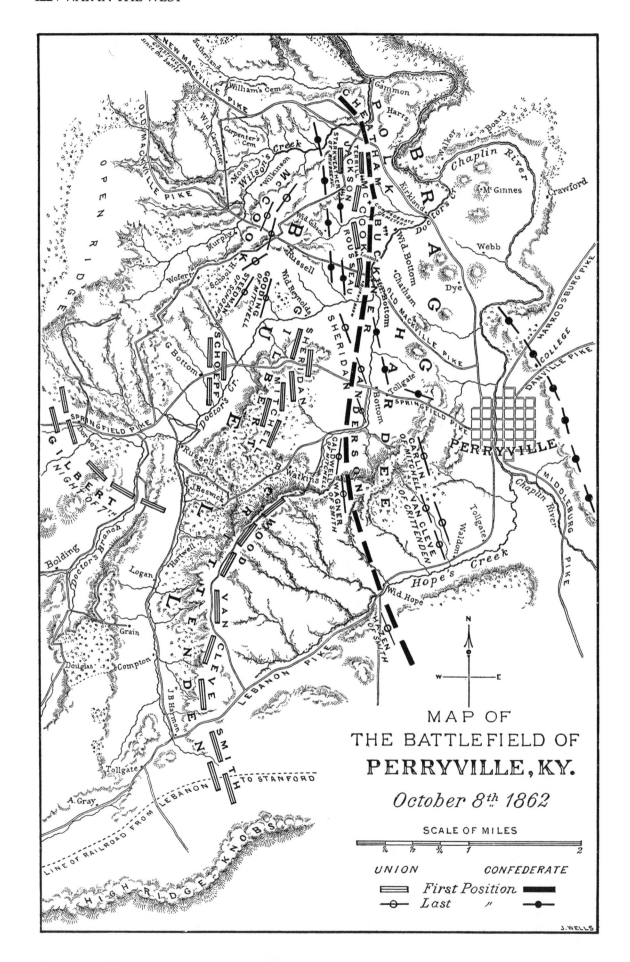

MAP OF
THE BATTLEFIELD OF
PERRYVILLE, KY.

October 8th 1862

SCALE OF MILES

UNION   CONFEDERATE

First Position

Last   *"*

J. WELLS

Bragg's associate during the Perryville Campaign, Major General Edmund Kirby Smith.

Commander of Bragg's cavalry, Colonel Joseph Wheeler.

was "very much crippled," one division, again to use his language, "having in fact almost entirely disappeared as a body."

After darkness had closed a battle, it was a custom to send messengers or notes to the nearest generals, detailing results, telling of this or that one who had fallen, and asking information from other portions of the field. Resting quietly on the ground, the army expected, and would gladly have welcomed, a renewal of the fight on the next day, but the accumulation of Buell's forces was such as not to justify further conflict in that locality. Kirby Smith was near Lawrenceburg with his own troops and Withers's division, and after full consultation it was determined to march to Harrodsburg, where it was hoped the entire Confederate force in Kentucky might be concentrated. I was directed with the cavalry to prevent an advance on the road leading to Danville. At night the troops withdrew to Perryville, and at sunrise continued the march. It was long after this when the Federal pickets began to reconnoiter, and it was fully 10 o'clock when, standing on the edge of the town, I saw the advance of the skirmish line of Buell's army. Bragg prepared for battle on the Harrodsburg road, only eight miles from Perryville, and awaited Buell's advance.

Two days elapsed, and the Federal army evinced no disposition to attack. A division of infantry and a brigade of cavalry fought me back to near Danville,

and at the same time Buell formed with his right within four miles of that place, making a feint in Bragg's immediate front on the road leading from Perryville to Harrodsburg. Buell, no doubt, hoped to cut him off from the crossing of the Dick River near Camp Dick Robinson.

I sent General Bragg information of Buell's dispositions, whereupon he issued orders to his army and wrote me as follows:

HARRODSBURG, KY., October 10th, 1862.
COLONEL WHEELER. DEAR COLONEL: I opened your ispatch to General Polk regarding the enemy's movements. The information you furnish is very important. It is just what I needed and I thank you for it. This information leaves no doubt as to the proper course for me to pursue. Hold the enemy firmly till to-morrow. Yours, etc., BRAXTON BRAGG

Bragg had now determined to retreat to Knoxville by the way of Cumberland Gap. It was evident that Buell's large army would enable him to select his own time and position for battle unless Bragg chose to attack. Bragg already had 1500 sick and over 3000 wounded. A severe battle would certainly have increased the wounded to 4000 or 5000 more. The care of such a number of wounded would have embarrassed, possibly controlled, our movements.

Hardee states that he had but 10,000 men before the battle of Perryville, and Bragg said that the three divisions which fought that battle had but 14,500. If

Left:

Battlefield map of the bloody confrontation of Perryville.

that was correct they had now but 11,000.

It was too hazardous to guard our depot of supplies and contend with the Federal forces within easy march. Our wagon trains were immense, and our artillery large in proportion to other arms.

The enemy pushed up close to Danville on the night of the 10th, but we easily held him in check until all our army had crossed Dick River. On the 11th we contended against a force of infantry, which finally pressed us so warmly that we were compelled to retire east of Danville. Here the enemy was again driven back, and we held our position near the town.

Before day on the 13th I received the following appointment and instructions in a special order from General Bragg, dated Bryantsville:

> Colonel Wheeler is hereby appointed chief of cavalry, and is authorized to give orders in the name of the commanding general. He is charged under Major-General Smith with covering the rear of the army and holding the enemy in check. All cavalry will report to him and receive his orders.

Compliance with the above of course involved considerable fighting, but by using the cavalry to the best advantage, and adopting available expedients, the movement of our infantry and trains in retreat was unmolested. These engagements were constant, and were often warmly and bitterly contested.

The large trains of captured stores made the progress of our infantry very slow, and the corps commanders sent frequent admonitions to me urging the importance of persistent reistance to Beull's advance.

Yankee skirmishers advance beyond the safety of their own line to feel the enemy's position.

In crossing Big Hill, and at other points, the trains hardly averaged five miles a day, and General Kirby Smith at one time regarded it as impossible for the cavalry to save them. In his letter to Bragg, on the 14th, he says: "I have no hope of saving the whole of my train"; and in his letter on the 15th he says: "I have little hope of saving any of the trains, and fear much of the artillery will be lost." But fortunately nothing was lost. Our cavalry at times dismounted and fought behind stone fences and hastily erected rail breastworks, and when opportunity offered charged the advancing enemy. Each expedient was adopted several times each day, and when practicable the road was obstructed by felling timber. These devices were continually resorted to until the 22d, when the enemy ceased the pursuit, and early in November the cavalry force, which covered the retreat from Kentucky, reached middle Tennessee and was close to the enemy, less than ten miles south of Nashville.

The campaign was over. Buell was deprived of his command for not having defeated Bragg, who, in turn, was censured by the Southern people for his failure to destroy the Federal army commanded by Buell.

This campaign was made at a time when the opposing Governments hoped for more from their generals and armies than could reasonably be accomplished. The people of the South were misinformed regarding the resources at the disposal of Generals Bragg and Kirby Smith, and our first successes aroused expectations and hopes that the Kentucky movement would result in the defeat, or at least the discomfiture, of Buell's army, the possible invasion of the North, and certainly the recovery of Confederate power in the central and eastern portions of Kentucky and Tennessee. They were sorely disappointed when

they heard of General Brag's withdrawal through Cumberland Gap, and could not easily be convinced of the necessity of such a movement immediately following the battle of Perryville, which they regarded as a decisive victory. The censure which fell upon Bragg was therefore severe and almost universal. It somewhat abated after the prompt advance of the army to Murfreesboro'; but to this day there are many who contend that Bragg should have defeated Buell and maintained himself in the rich and productive plans of Kentucky. On the other hand the Federal Government was, if possible, more severe in denunciation of General Buell, and held that, far from allowing Gneral Bragg to cross the Tennessee River and the mountains into middle Tennessee, Buell should have anticipated these movements, occupied Chattanooga, and, as some even contended, marched his army toward Atlanta. The Government was convinced that he could easily have met and halted Bragg as he debouched from the mountains before entering middle Tennessee. It was emphatic in its assertion that ordinary celerity on the part of General Buell would have saved Munfordville and its garrison of 4200 men; that proper concentration would have destroyed the Confederate forces at Perryville, and that the plainest principles of strategy represented the opportunity of throwing forward a column to cut off Bragg's retreat via Camp Dick Robinson, or that at least after the commencement of the conflict at Perryville he should have pressed close to his antagonist and forced Bragg to continuous battle, contending, as they did, that superior numbers and proximity to his base gave the Federal commander advantages that, if properly improved, would have resulted in the destruction of the Confederate army.

Buell's strategy and tactics were the subject of Congressional investigation and inquiry by a military commission. With regard to the adverse criticisms on Bragg's campaign it must be admitted that there were opportunities, had they been improved, to cripple, if not to defeat, the Federal army.

The failure to "concentrate and attack" tells the story of the campaign. The first opportunity was on September 18th, when we caught Buell south of Munfordville. Bragg could not have attacked at Altamont, because it will be remembered that on August 30th, at the first appearance of our cavalry, the Federal force retreated from that place down the mountain. Neither could he have overtaken Buell's troops at McMinnville, because, fully three days before Bragg could have reached that place, Buell had ordered all his army to Murfreesboro'.

Those who contend that Bragg should have followed Buell to Nashville do not consider that he would have found him in a good position, strengthened by fortifications, and defended by 9 divisions of infantry and 1 of cavalry; his available force for duty then being 66,595.

After the surrender of the Federal fort at Munfordville, it became painfully apparent that a single mind should control the Confederate troops in Kentucky, and concentrate our entire force and attack the divided enemy; but a condition existed which has been repeated in military operations for four thousand years, and always with disastrous results. The troops in Kentucky had two commanders. The troops of two different departments were expected to coöperate.

Both Kirby Smith and Bragg were brave and skillful generals. The devotion of each to the cause in which they were enlisted was absolute, and their only ambition was to contribute to its success. In their characters the pettiness of personal rivalry could find no place, and either would willingly have relinquished to the other the honor of being the victor, if victory could only have been won.

It will be remembered how promptly, in the preceding June, General Bragg had weakened his own army and strengthened Smith's by sending McCown's division from Tupelo to Chattanooga, and again in August by sending the brigades of Cleburne and Preston Smith from Chattanooga to Knoxville; and again, when Smith was pressed at Frankfort, that Bragg reënforced him promptly with one of his best divisions. That Kirby Smith would, at any time, have been as ready and prompt to give Bragg any part or all of his army there can be no doubt, but when the decisive moment came, the two independent armies were more than one hundred miles apart, and neither commander could be informed of the other's necessities. Bragg and Smith conferred together, but neither commanded the other. If all the troops had belonged to one army, Bragg would have ordered, and not conferred or requested.

To aggravate the difficulties inherent in the system of independent commands and divided responsibility, Brigadier-General Marshall, who had commanded in West Virginia, appeared upon the field of active operations with 2150 men. He was an able and distinguished man and determined in his devotion to the Confederacy. He wished to do his full duty, but he appeared to feel that he could render more efficient service with a separate command than if trammeled by subordination to a superior commander; and his aversion to having any intervening power between himself and the President was apparent.

While General Smith was anxious to coöperate, he nevertheless, in reply to Bragg's request for coöperation, wrote indicating very forcibly that he thought other plans were more important; and, in fact, the only coöperative action during the campaign was Bragg's compliance with Smith's request to transfer to him two brigades on August 5th, and to transfer Withers's division to him on October 7th.

In reply to the question as to what one supreme commander could have done, I confidently assert he could have concentrated and attacked and beaten Buell on September 18th south of Munfordville. He could then have turned and marched to Louisville and taken that city. If it should be argued that this plan involved unnecessary marching on the part of Kirby Smith, who was then at Lexington, a supreme commander could have adopted the one which was contemplated by Bragg early in the campaign.

After the surrender of Munfordville he could by

September 21st have reached Louisville with all the force in Kentucky, taken the city, and then risked its being held by a small garrison while making another concentration and attack upon Buell.

As an evidence of how easily we could have taken Louisville, it must be observed that on September 22d Buell sent Major-General Nelson orders containing these words:

If you have only the force you speak of it would not, I should say, be advisable for you to attempt a defense of Louisville unless you are strongly intrenched; under no circumstances should you

The Squirrel Rifles on parade in Cincinnati. During the Perryville Campaign, there were fears among the Federals that Bragg would take the war across the Ohio River. In response to this threat, hundreds of Ohio backwoodsmen, called the Squirrel Rifles, answered the call to come to the defense of their state.

make a fight with his whole or mainforce. The alternative would be to cross the river or march on this side to the mouth of Salt River and bridge it so as to form a junction with me. . . .

Nelson seemed to concur with Buell, and it was not until that officer was but a day's march from Louisville that Nelson telegraphed the fact to General Wright, saying, "Louisville is now safe; 'God and Liberty.'"

In further corroboration of this, "Harper's History," p. 311, says:

Just before the Federal army entered Louisville, on the 25th of September, the panic there had reached its height. In twenty-four hours more Nelson would have abandoned the city."

But suppose neither plan had been adopted, the next chance for a supreme commander of the Kentucky forces was to "concentrate and attack" Buell's flank while his army was strung out *en route* to Louisville. Elizabethtown would have been a good

place, and had it been done with vigor about September 23d it certainly would have resulted in victory. But at this time General Smith's forces were all moving to Mount Sterling, 130 miles to the east of that place (Elizabethtown), and General Smith was asking, not ordering, General Marshall to coöperate with him. The next field upon which a supreme commander had an opportunity to concentrate and attack was at Perryville. Three hundred cavalry could have played with Generals Sill and Dumont around Frankfort, and every other soldier, except a few scouts, could then have struck Gilbert's corps as day dawned on the 8th of October.

Since, in the final result, we neither defeated Buell nor took Louisville, it is now evident that it was unfortunate Bragg did not foresee the end immediately after his victory at Munfordville. He could certainly have crippled Buell to some extent as he attempted his hazardous flank movement *en route* to Louisville, and then, by a rapid march, he could have reached and captured Nashville and returned and es-

tablished himself at Bowling Green.

I have pointed out these lost opportunities as an additional proof of the adage, as old as war itself, "that one bad general is better than two good ones." The very fact that both the generals are good intensifies the evil; each, full of confidence in himself and determined to attain what he has in view, is unwilling to yield to any one; but if both are weak the natural indisposition of such men to exertion, their anxiety to avoid responsibility, and their desire in a great crisis to lean on some one, will frequently bring about the junction of two independent armies without any deliberately planned concert of action between the commanders. Both Bragg and Kirby Smith were men who had, to an eminent degree, those qualities that make good generals, and, once together with their armies upon the same field, victory would have been certain. Both fully appreciated the fact that, when an adversary is not intrenched, a determined attack is the beginning of victory. By this means Smith had been victorious at Manassas and at Richmond, Ky., and by vigorous attack Albert Sidney Johnston and Bragg had won at every point of battle at Shiloh, on the 6th of April. Later, the Confederate points of attack were Bragg's scene of victory the first day at Murfreesboro', and the boldness of his onset gave Bragg his great triumph at Chickamauga. Nothing was therefore wanting in Kentucky but absolute authority in one responsible commander. Coöperation should be stricken from military phraseology.

In writing to the Government on August 1st, after he had met General Smith, General Bragg says: "We have arranged measures for mutual support and effective coöperation." On August 8th Bragg writes to Smith: "I find myself in your department; without explanation this might seem an unjustifiable intrusion." While it is no doubt true that General Smith was at all times willing to yield to the authority of General Bragg, yet the fact that Smith was the commander of an independent department, receiving orders from and reporting directly to the President, made him primarily responsible to the Executive, and this limited the authority of General Bragg. Nevertheless the Kentucky campaign was attended with great results to the Confederacy. Two months of marches and battle by the armies of Bragg and Smith had cost the Federals a loss in killed, wounded, and prisoners of 26,530. We had captured 35 cannon, 16,000 stand of arms, millions of rounds of ammunition, 1700 mules, 300 wagons loaded with military stores, and 2000 horses. We had recovered Cumberland Gap and redeemed middle Tennessee and north Alabama. Yet expectations had been excited that were not realized, and hopes had been cherished that were disappointed; and therefore this campaign of repeated triumphs, without a single reverse, has never received—save from the thoughtful, intelligent, and impartial minority—any proper recognition.

★★★

B. P. STEELE

Charge of the First Tennessee at Perryville

With no stunning result save forcing the Confederates to abandon Kentucky once more, Perryville was a terribly bloody battle with the Confederates losing over 3000 men and the Federals suffering some 4000 casualties. Distinguishing itself on that "ensanguined" Kentucky battlefield was the First Tennessee, called the Kid Glove Regiment, as the unit primarily consisted of youths from Nashville and central Tennessee.

Far and wide on Perryville's ensanguined plain,
    The thunder and carnage of battle resounded;
And there, over thousands of wounded and slain,
    Riderless steeds from battle's shock rebounded.
Cheatham's division was fiercely attacking,
    And proudly from his men rose cheer after cheer,
As before them McCook was sullenly backing,
    Gallantly fighting as he moved to the rear.
On Cheatham's left, Stewart's guns roared and rattled,
    And in the center, Donelson onward bore;
On the right, Maney's brigade charged and battled,
    Valiantly driving the stubborn foe before.
'Twas there, held in reserve, impatiently lay,
    The First Tennessee, the "Knights of the Kid Glove,"
Eager and chafing to join the bloody fray—
    Help their brave comrades, and their own powers prove.
Soon was their impatient valor to be tried,
    Soon were they to charge to the cannon's grim mouth—
Soon upon the battle's crimsoned wave to ride—
    Soon to prove themselves worthy "Sons of the South."
For soon, at headlong speed, there came dashing down—
    His steed flecked with sweat and foaming at the mouth—
The warrior-bishop—he of the "Sword and Gown"—
    Who with like devotion served God and the South.
Every eye and ear of that gallant band,
    Was eager turned to catch the old hero's words;
On the guns more firmly clenched was every hand,

And from their scabbards quick leaped two score of swords;
For all knew by the flash of the old chief's eye,
    That he had hot work for every trusty gun;
And ready was each man to fight and to die,
    In the bloody work then and there to be done.
A moment along their solid ranks he glanced,
    And with just pride his eagle-eye beamed o'er them—
Assured by their firm main, that when they advanced,
    No equal numbered foe could stand before them.
He noted the firm set lip and flashing eye,
    And on their sun-burnt cheeks the brave man's pallor;
And knew they had the spirit to "do or die,"
    For Southern honor and with Southern valor.
Then pointing towards the cannon-crested height,
    Where Loomis' guns volleyed in death-dealing wrath,
He seemed as a war-god gathering his might,
    To hurl missiles of destruction on his path,
And with a look that plainly said, "You must win,
    For the sake of the Sunny Land that bore you,"
He shouted above the battle's fierce din,
    "Forward! and carry everything before you!"
Forth they sprang, four hundred, less fifty, all told;
    And as their ranks were thinned by iron and lead,
With true discipline, fearless courage, and bold,
    They closed their files and rushed on over the dead.
Towards the height, bristling in hostile array,
    With unwavering line the heroes rushed on—
Oh! truly was it a glorious display
    Of courage—worthy the fame the "Old Guard" won.

All *dressed by the right* with veteran skill,
  They moved on their way with step steady
    and true,
And guns at shoulder, to the foot of the hill,
  As if on parade, for the "soldiers in blue."
But then their muskets spoke, their wild shouts
    leaped,
  As before them, in rout, a regiment fled;
Many of which their bullets halted and heaped
  In bloody confusion, the wounded and dead.
Now more dreadful the carnage volleyed and
    roared,
  A volcanic crater the hill's frowning crest,
Down whose bloody sides, death's fiery lava
    poured,
    Sweeping the young and the brave upon its
      breast.
    Like sear leaves before the autumn blast"
      they sank,
    But their undaunted comrades pressed on
      o'er them—
Pressed on, with quick, steady step and closed
    up rank,
  Hurling death into the blue links before
    them.
Brave Loomis' support were veterans long tried,
  And nobly did they second his fatal blows;
But their numbers and valor were all defied,
  By the impetuous ranks of their Southern
    foes.
Loomis' gunners and horses went to the dust,
  And his terrible war-dogs were hushed and
    still;
A few more quick bounds and a bayonet thrust,
  And the "kid glove soldiers" had captured the
    hill.
But then came stern Rousseau, a Federal
    "brave,"
  Rapidly sweeping down with his fine com-
    mand,
And threw it like a torrent, wave upon wave,
  Against the brave First's shattered and bleed-
    ing band.

But they met it as meets the breakers firm rock,
  The wild, towering waves of the storm-
    lashed sea—
Met it to hurl it back with a fearful shock—
  Back, like the foiled, rock-broken waves of
    the sea.
But just then the cry was passed along the line,
  "They are flanking by the left! fall back! fall
    back!"
Ah! 'twas then more brilliant did their valor
    shine,
  As with face to the foe, they retraced their
    track.
Proudly, their reluctant, backward way they
    bent,
  With sullen, defiant mien, firm step and
    slow,
Sending back defiance and death as they went,
  And moved more to the left in the plain be-
    low.
And then "forward!" was again the cheering cry,
  And quickly did those noble Southerners re-
    spond;
They again sprang forward, and their shouts
    rose high,
  As they swept the hill and the wide plain
    beyond.
And then, when the fierce, bloody conflict was
    o'er,
  The heroes sank down with fighting sore
    wearied;
And wept that of their brave comrades, full ten
    score,
  Were wounded or dead; *but the height had
  been carried.*

**The 4th Indiana and 1st Kentucky Batteries are sup-
ported by Colonel John C. Starkweather's brigade as
they fight off a threat posed by the Confederate right
wing at the battle of Perryville.**

WILLIAM L. B. JENNY

"On to Vicksburg . . ."

In attempting to assail Vicksburg, Union commanders were faced with numerous difficulties; the swampy terrain made any assault down from the North an almost complete impossibility and the Confederates blocked most of the landings on the eastern bank of the Mississippi River. The quandary of how to get around Vicksburg in order to take the town occupied Federal planners for months. An eyewitness to these and subsequent events, William Jenny wrote an account of the attempts to take the Confederate stronghold entitled Personal Recollections of Vicksburg.

It is not my intention to write a history of the Vicksburg campaign. The story of that historic event has been told by Colonel Green and others who have had access to the archives both of the Union and Confederates armies, and I shall therefore confine myself to personal recollections of the military movements and events which resulted in the surrender of General Pemberton at Vicksburg on July 4, 1863, re-

ferring only to standard authorities for dates.

Those bloody contests occurring in the autumn of 1862 at Antietam, Perryville, and Corinth had checked the advance of the Confederate forces and compelled them to assume the defensive along the entire line from the Atlantic Ocean to the Mississippi River. General Halleck was then commander-in-chief at Washington; Rosecrans had succeeded to the com-expedition with his division at Helena on the 21st of December. In all, the command numbered about 32,000 men and sixty guns, and reached Milliken's Bend about twenty miles above Vicksburg on Christmas Day. Among the earliest visitors at General Sherman's headquarters at Milliken's Bend was an old planter, in fact about the only caller from the scattered resident population in that vicinity. The vocabulary of this old planter was by no means fertile. He

Grant just before he engaged in his epic Vicksburg Campaign; his diligent facial expression and forceful pose reflect his determination to accomplish his mission and take the Confederate citadel on the Mississippi River.

Below:
Object of many months of campaigning fraught with adversity and bloodshed, the city of Vicksburg.

designated all manner of men and all sorts of things as "improvements," and told General Sherman that he "had never seen so many improvements in them parts before." He seemed very anxious to learn what was to be done with them, and was probably a spy. But we allowed him to sample our stock of commissary supplies freely, the quality of which he gratefully and cheerfully approved, and left headquarters for his home stepping quite high and appearing to be very jolly.

The division under A. J. Smith proceeded to destroy the railroad running from the west to Vicksburg, over which the Confederates under General Pemberton were receiving supplies. On December 26 the other three divisions, under command of General Sherman, ascended the Yazoo about thirteen miles, and were landed on the low bottom-lands between the Yazoo and the Walnut Hills. The troops moved forward with little opposition along Chickasaw Bayou until it turned and ran parallel with the bluffs, on which the enemy were posted in great numbers and in strong position. An assault which was immediately made demonstrated that the ground was too difficult and the enemy too well fortified to be dislodged. The only passage across this bayou was in front of General

Morgan's division, and this passage was much in the nature of a breach, admitting only a few men at a time, and was swept by numerous guns of the enemy. The way was then across a broad and gently sloping bottom without cover to the foot of the hills, which had to be scaled under the fire of an enemy so securely posted that almost every man amounted to an army on his own account. It was then determined to try a night attack higher up the river at Haines's Bluff, which was also protected by a bayou at its foot known as "Skillet Goliah," and beyond which the troops must be landed in order to reach the high land. The landing and assault were intended to be made under cover of an attack by the gunboats. For this purpose 10,000 men were embarked on the transports, but the night was so intensely foggy that the boats could not move and the moon rendered no service whatever to such a movement. On learning the next morning that

Brigadier Stephen G. Burbridge plants the Union colors at Fort Hindman. While McClernand managed to capture the fort's garrison of 4800 men, his short campaign was only a slight diversion in Grant's main attempt to move on Vicksburg.

secrecy was no longer possible, the contemplated attack was abandoned as too hazardous and Sherman reembarked his troops, without opposition from the enemy, on the night of January 2, 1863. At daylight the next morning Sherman, learning that General John A. McClernand was at the mouth of the Yazoo with orders from the President to assume command of the river expedition, left his troops all on board of the transports and promptly steamed down the river to report to the new commander. We waited with the boats lying against the river bank for about three hours, expecting every moment to see the enemy coming through the woods, but in this we were happily disappointed, and finally orders were received to proceed to Milliken's Bend, the enemy only showing himself as the last boat left the bank.

On January 5, 1863, the entire force then under command of McClernand left Milliken's Bend for Arkansas Post, which was surrendered after a combined attack by the gunboats and the army. The capture of Arkansas Post was an important event, resulting in the surrender of more than 5,000 men and a large number of guns and a quantity of munitions of war. The event was heralded by General McClernand as a great victory, although he really had but little to do with the details of it. After the gunboats had opened fire the attitude of McClernand became quite theatrical; but the reduction of that rebel stronghold

Workers dig a canal for gunboats to bypass the powerful batteries of Vicksburg.

To get gunboats and transports near Vicksburg via the Coldwater, Tallahatchie and Yazoo Rivers, Grant's troops attempted to create a break in a Mississippi levee built to prevent flooding.

was largely due to the skill and efficiency of the gunboats under Porter.

McClernand next proposed to push on to Little Rock, but peremptory orders were received from General Grant directing the return of the army under McClernand at once to the Mississippi River where Grant met the toops in person at Napoleon. After a conference with his subordinates, Grant returned to Memphis and ordered McClernand to proceed to Young's Point immediately opposite Vicksburg and there complete the canal that had been commenced long before and was known to Sherman's army as "Butler's Ditch." This canal had long been discussed and its completion seems to have been a pet idea of Mr. Lincoln.

As soon as a landing was made in the vicinity of Young's Point, Sherman and his staff rode over to inspect the canal, the completion of which, it was then expected, would give us possession of Vicksburg, and would, as often remarked at that time, "leave that city an inland town"; but all our hopes were doomed to utter disappointment. The line of the canal was soon reached, and as Sherman checked his horse on the bank he remarked, "It is no bigger than a plantation ditch." But this was not all. Both ends of the proposed canal were in slack water and its entire length was within the enfilading fire of the enemy's batteries at Vicksburg, which stretched along the bluff to Warrenton, a point quite as capable of being strongly fortified as any other in the vicinity of Vicksburg. It was soon learned that the proposed canal, if completed, could be of but little practical use. While we are discussing how it could happen that so trifling an affair could have been considered of such great importance that an army of 30,000 men should be collected to complete it, an orderly arrived with a peremptory order from McClernand to General Sherman, which read: "You will proceed immediately to blow up the bottom of the canal. It is important that this be done to-night, as to-morrow it may be too late." General Sherman handed me the order with instructions to go and do it. I read the order, and looked at General Sherman. There was a roguish twinkle in the General's eye, indicating that he knew as little what the order meant as I did. A few minutes later I met General McClernand, and with all the politeness and diplomacy at my command endeavored to obtain some definite instructions. My endeavor, however, to obtain information as to what the order really meant was futile. General McClernand, pursuant to his customary manner in those days, flew into a passion, exclaiming, "You can dig a hole, can't you? You can put powder into it, can't you? You can touch it off, can't you? Well, then, won't it blow up?"

Right:

A Federal steamboat attempts to negotiate the treacherous route created by the levee. The path of the ships was strewn with trees and trunks which had to be pulled out of the way by sailors while under fire from Confederate pickets.

Confederates capture the helpless **Queen of the West,** *run aground while traveling on the Mississippi River. Manned by Southern sailors, the vessel proved instrumental in the capture of the* **Indianola.**

With these interrogatories ringing in my ears I rode away, and a suppressed "Damn" was all the "blowing up" it received that night.

We subsequently learned that a steamboat captain, one of that ignorant class from whom so many absurdities in military affairs were derived, had told General McClernand that the bottom of the canal was a thin stratum of hard clay with sand below, and that by exploding some powder in the sand the clay bottom would be shattered and washed out with untold quantities of sand by the rapidly rising river. No condition of the kind existed save in the turbid fancy and grotesque superstition of an over-officious Misisssippi River steamboat captain. It was one of thsi class of captains who went to General Grant when the army was on the bluffs behind Vicksburg, and in all seriousness proposed to Grant that he should send north for all the steam fire-engines that could be obtained, back them up against the enemy's parapets, and wash Vicksburg into the river. This watery method of reducing the stronghold of Vicksburg was never tried. But inasmuch as we had been directed to

complete the canal at Young's Point the work was commenced and pushed as rapidly as possible. It was nearly completed, when one night during a heavy rain the levee gave way at the upper end of the canal and inundated the whole of the lower peninsula, driving the troops to the levee, where the tents were huddled together as closely as they could be pitched. Dredging machines were then tried, but our men were driven off by the enemy's guns; for although the attempt was made to carry on the work at night, the light of their fires exposed their positions as soon as they opened the boiler furnace doors.

It was at this time that the governor of one of the northwestern states made us a visit. He became the guest of General Sherman, and was entertained as became his high political station. He expressed to the General his great desire to hear the sound of a shell, and, in order to gratify his ambition, Sherman sent him under escort of Colonel Dayton to the dredge, where his curiosity to hear the whiz of a hostile shell was soon adequately satisfied, and this war governor thereupon fully and cheerfully expressed himself as quite ready to go home.

The army remained for nearly four months at Young's Point with the weather very disagreeable, and the troops, huddled together on the levee, by no means comfortable or very cheerful, although complaints were rarely ever uttered either by officers or men. There seemed to be a feeling pervading the rank

The Yankee gunboat Indianola *briskly runs the batteries of Vicksburg in mid-February of 1863. The* Indianola *was sent downstream to join the ram* Queen of the West *in order to disturb Confederate water traffic on the Mississippi and Red Rivers.*

and file that they were the vanguard in a campaign which would be successful, and for that reason whatever of hardship was necessary to the supreme purpose of the campaign was borne with a silent heroism which was at least grateful to General Sherman.

Some amusing incidents, however, relieved the monotony of our stay at Young's Point. It was during this time that Admiral Porter constructed a dummy gunboat from a large coal barge. This dummy was rigged up with smokestacks and sloping sides, and all were covered black with a coat of coal tar so that in the obscurity of darkness, or even of moonlight, she looked very much like an ironclad. One dark night some smoke-making combustibles were lighted below the smokestack, the dummy was pushed down the river as near the Vicksburg batteries as it was prudent to go, and was then set adrift in the middle of the steam, and floated silently and majestically down the current of the Father of Waters. As soon as this dummy was discovered the Confederate batteries one

A dummy gunboat sent down river to scare the Confederates. The maneuver was entirely successful to the point that the captured **Indianola** *was scuttled rather than risk confrontation with the harmless vessel.*

after another opened fire as she came in range, but the dummy behaved admirably and kept steadily on her course without returning a shot. When General Pemberton saw that what he supposed was a real ironclad was likely to run his batteries, he sent a swift messenger down the river to where the ironclad *Indianola*, which had been captured by the Confederates, was being repaired, with orders to blow her up; but when, later, the trick perpetrated by Porter with his dummy was discovered, Pemberton sent another messenger to countermand the order to destroy the *Indianola*. This messenger, however, was too late, for we heard the explosion which destroyed the *Indianola*. Not long after this event Admiral Farragut came up the river and anchored his fleet below Warrenton. Farragut was short of coal and provisions, and in order to supply him Admiral Porter loaded some barges with coal and provisions and sent them down the river as he had sent the dummy. These barges passed the Vicksburg batteries without notice and their contents were appropriated by Admiral Farragut. The next day a flag of truce was received from Vicksburg with General Cheatham in charge. After the business connected with this flag of truce had been concluded, General Cheatham remarked, "You Yanks make very good dummy gunboats and we wasted lots of powder and shot on one of them, but

you must think us green if you expected to fool us a second time by the same trick. We saw your dummies last night, but we do n't waste any more powder on such trash." We smiled pleasantly and bade them an affectionate good-bye, permitting them to go away in ignorance of the fact that the second lot of dummies were really engines of destruction, because they carried the sinews of war to the fleet below.

The numerous projects which were tried one after another for the purpose of reaching high ground in the rear of Vicksburg are known to everyone. One of these expeditions consisted of an endeavor to force the gunboats through the bayous up the Yazoo above Haines's Bluff, but when an effort was made to put this plan in execution it was discovered that the enemy had cut down trees across the bayou above and were doing the same below the gunboats, and that the Confederate sharpshooters from behind the trees killed or wounded almost every man that showed himself. In this situation Admiral Porter sent a colored man with a note to Sherman begging him to come to his relief. Sherman received this note about nine o'clock in the evening, and by midnight had embarked his troops and left the Mississippi. The enemy were soon driven away and some three hundred axes were captured, which were used to help clear the bayou behind the boats, which were backed out into the river. Sherman returned in the night, and the next morning Major Chase, commanding the battalion of the Thirteenth regulars, came to my room, carefully closed the door, looked around to see that we were alone, and in a manner that indicated that he had a great secret to impart, whispered to me, "I command a battalion of

The **Indianola** *is run aground and blown up in the face of the "quaker" vessel which was thought to be a powerful ironclad.*

regulars,—I have been on an expedition,—I must write a report,—I want you to tell me where I have been, how I went there, what I did, and if I came back the same way I went, or if not, how I did get back." Major Chase was an old soldier who had won his shoulder-straps on a battlefield in Mexico, and this incident serves to illustrate how little even battalion commanders knew of what was being done at this time. Many of these moves on the Vicksburg chessboard were very bold in their conception, made with secrecy, energy, and rapidity, and all failed from a combination of natural causes, very materially assisted by an active and watchful enemy.

General Grant finally decided to make a landing below the Vicksburg batteries, and a new canal was started farther up the river where a short cut would open into a system of bayous that would take small steamboats from a point below Warrenton. These bayous were filled with trees of young growth averaging about six inches in diameter.

I was sent with the One Hundred and Seventeenth Illinois, under command of Colonel Eldredge, to clear out these trees. For that purpose we made saw-frames in the shape of the letter A with a crosscut saw across the bottom, and hung them to the trees to be cut, by a pin at the apex. The saws were put in motion by ropes worked by men on rafts. We soon found, however, that our work was rendered especially dangerous by an enemy that did not carry rebel guns. Poisonous snakes were very numerous at that season of the year in that region, and frequently hung from the trees which stretched their branches across the water. A slight tap on the branch and the snake would fall, so that, in order to keep them out of our boats and rafts, we were obliged whenever we moved to station men forward with long poles to clear the track from snakes. With our force we cut off at a point six feet

*The Federal rams **Switzerland** and **Lancaster** run the formidable batteries at Vicksburg.*

under the water about seven hundred trees per day, but the trees were in great numbers and our progress was slow. One stern-wheeler forced her way through the bayou; but the next day the river began to fall and the passage of the bayous became impracticable.

Next came the running of the Vicksburg batteries, and a fleet was soon collected below Warrenton sufficient to transport the troops designed for the expedition in the rear of Vicksburg. The gunboats attacked the batteries at Grand Gulf, silencing the guns, but failing either to force the evacuation or the surrender of the works at that point. That night the attack was renewed, and under its cover the transports passed below, and the next morning picked up a part of McClernand's corps, the Thirteenth, and ran up and down the river so that the enemy could form but little idea where the landing was to be attempted. After some maneuvering the troops were landed at Bruinsburg, and the balance of McClernand's corps was ferried over. By noon of May 1, 1863, 18,000 men were on the east bank of the Mississippi, with no enemy in sight. Grant's movements were so well

Left·
The greatest obstacle to Grant's Vicksburg Campaign, the depths of the Mississippi Delta country.

planned, and conducted with so much celerity and skill, as to have caused the utmost confusion to the enemy's camp.

General Grierson was at this same time making his raid from La Grange to Baton Rouge, and this daring attempt had caused Pemberton to send various detachments from the Confederate army at Vicksburg in several different directions in an effort to intercept and capture Grierson. This added to the confusion of Pemberton and the army under him. In order to further increase the confusion in the mind of Pemberton, Grant, before he attempted to cross the river with his troops, wrote to Sherman at Milliken's Bend, saying: "If you will make a demonstration against Haines's Bluff it will help to confuse the enemy as to my intentions. I do not give this as an order, for the papers will call it another failure of Sherman to capture Haines's Bluff." When this letter was received by General Sherman he remarked, "Does General Grant think I care what the newspapers say?" and jumped into a boat at once and rowed to Porter's flagship, where Sherman and Porter then arranged a jolly lark.

Some of the newspaper correspondents had written that Sherman protested against the running of the batteries and the crossing of the river below Vicksburg, but Sherman made no protest, and later said to me, "The campaign was entirely Grant's conception, and when Grant told me he had decided to execute it I offered him my hearty support." It was at this time that Grand adopted the motto, "Waste no time in trying to shift the responsibility of failure from one to the other, but take things as you find them and make the best of them." In all his vocabulary Grant found no such word as "can't."

But to return to the lark on the Yazoo. Sherman spread his command over the decks of the transports, with orders that every man should be in sight and look as numerous as possible. Porter ordered every boat to get up steam, and even took a blacksmith shop in tow, which he left behind a point near to and concealed from Haines's Bluff, with orders to fire up every forge and make all the smoke possible. The gunboats and transports whistled and puffed, and made all the noise they could. They showed themselves to the garrison at Haines's Bluff and then drifted back and landed the men, who were marched through the woods toward Haines's Bluff until they were seen by the enemy, marched a mile or so down the river, and taken again on board the transports, to go through the same farce again. The boats were kept in movement up and down the Yazoo all night, as if they were bringing up more and more troops. As soon as Grant had effected his landing he sent word to Sherman, "All right; join me below Vicksburg."

Later we learned the good effect of the demonstration of Sherman and Porter. The commander at Haines's Bluff telegraphed to Pemberton: "The dem-onstration at Grand Gulf must be only a feint. Here is the real attack. The enemy are in front of me in force such as we have never seen before at Vicksburg. Send me reinforcements." Pemberton recalled troops marching against Grant, who had already reached the Big Black, and sent them by forced marches to Haines's Bluff. The citizens turned out with wagons and carriages to help along the stragglers. The Confederates had no sooner reached Haines's Bluff than the nature of Sherman's maneuvers was discovered, and they were marched back again, to arrive finally in front of Grant, tired out and half demoralized.

Pemberton had a force exceeding that of Grant's in number, but it was badly scattered and handled with little ability. Grant kept his forces well in hand, so that at Champion Hills he completely routed the enemy and drove the greater part across the Big Black into Vicksburg, cutting off Loring's division, which joined General Johnson at Jackson, without transportation or artillery.

You all know the details of that brilliant campaign, which had for its object to place the Union army in a position to invest Vicksburg, and at the same time have a base of supplies on the Yazoo River. In speaking of this afterwards, Sherman said: "Any good general will fight a battle when the chances are three to one of success. Grant will fight if the chances are two to three in his favor, but in this campaign he took all the chances of war against himself, and *won*."

The morning after the battle I rode across the field of Champion Hills. At a place where the fight had raged the fiercest there remained a solitary house, with all its surroundings swept away as clean as if a cyclone had passed that way. On the front veranda stood a woman weeping. I was so near her, as I turned the corner of the house, that I could not avoid speaking. I expressed the hope that she had not been unnecessarily annoyed. "Annoyed!" said the good lady, "a big battle passed by here yesterday." "Where were you?" I asked. "I was trembling with fright down cellar," she replied. *Annoyed* was in her opinion too mild a word for the occasion.

On the 18th of May, 1863, Grant's army appeared in sight of the fortifications of Vicksburg, and on the 19th, when Sherman's corps was in position, a general assault was ordered at 2 P.M. which did not result with any success.

That night I was ordered to lay a pontoon across Chickasaw Bayou at the point crossed by Morgan's command some five months before, in the first move in Grant's campaign against Vicksburg. The supplies we had already received had come by way of Haines's Bluff, which had been abandoned with all its artillery the morning after the battle of Champion Hills. I

Federal gunboats passing Vicksburg on the night of 16 April 1863 under a heavy bombardment from Rebel guns. In the distance, fires have been lit to allow gunners to sight their targets. The Yankee vessels successfully passed the batteries without much damage.

U.S. "Sam" Grant finally on the move against Vicksburg.

Federal transport passes by Vicksburg with a barge full of cotton tied to its hull to protect the vessel from enemy guns.

Federal troops storm the almost impregnable entrenchments around Vicksburg. After a few bloody and unsuccessful ventures to break through the for- *tifications before the town, it became evident that only a long siege would force Vicksburg to capitulate.*

A perpetual thorn in Grant's side throughout the Vicksburg Campaign was Major General John Alexander McClernand, the skipper of the XIII Corps.

The powerful fortifications around the city of Vicksburg. Here 21,000 men under Lieutenant General John C. Pemberton held out for less than two months against a Federal force as large as 75,000 men.

started at 9 P.M. with a regiment that had been detailed to do the work. The troops were worn out and hungry, and when we had made half the distance the colonel commanding ordered his men to bivouac. At daylight next morning there was a grand hunt. A flock of sheep had been discovered and soldiers were chasing sheep in every direction. Soon mutton chops were broiling at a hundred fires made from fence rails. I protested against the long delay, but the colonel insisted, stating that his men had not had a square meal since they crossed the Mississippi. At length the last bone was picked, and the march was resumed. On reaching the bayou, we found Lieutenant Freeman of General McClernand's staff, who, not having had a flock of sheep to consume, and looking for his breakfast to come from the Yazoo across that pontoon, had the bridge half completed. With the additional force I had brought the bridge was quickly finished, the wagon trains from the Yazoo commenced to cross, and the campaign of investment was complete.

A little incident occurred here. Lieutenant-Colonel McFeeley, then chief commissary and now commissary-general, came to the bank from the hills at a moment when the bridge was filled with wagons coming from the Yazoo. He was about to cross, when the guard said to him, "The orders are to pass but one way at a time"; but McFeeley, knowing that it was important that he should reach the transports at once, and being impatient of delay, attempted to force his horse beside the wagons, when, in the middle of the bridge, the animal took fright and leaped with his rider into the middle of the muddy bayou. They both went out of sight, but were quickly pulled out on the opposite bank.

Another attack was made on the Vicksburg fortifications on the 22d. By noon, when it was evident to General Grant that the place could not be carried

by assault, he received a note from General McClernand stating that he had taken three of the enemy's works, "that the flag of our beloved country floated over the stronghold of Vicksburg"; he asked for reinforcements and begged that the enemy be pushed at every point, so that he might not be overwhelmed. Grant read the note and handed it to Sherman, with the remark, "If I could only believe it." Sherman, however, favored a renewal of the assault, saying, "A corps commander would not write a misstatement over his own signature at such a time." Grant replied, "I do not know," but finally decided to renew the assault, with no other results than a heavy loss.

That night there were stirring times at Grant's headquarters, where most of the corps and division commanders were assembled. McClernand was spoken of in no complimentary terms. Rawlins ordered Major Bower to open the record book and charge a thousand lives to that —— McClernand. Rawlins used strong language when the occasion required, and this was one of them.

The only works McClernand had captured were some advanced picket posts abandoned by the enemy before our line came in sight.

In due time the St. Louis *Democrat* arrived in

With the fall of Vicksburg, the Mississippi River was soon completely open to Federal military and commercial vessels. The Federal gunboat **Choctaw** *rests before the city under Union control.*

camp containing a vain-glorious congratulatory order from McClernand to his corps, telling them in the most laudatory language what "bully boys" they were, and what they had done. It also asserted that "at Champion Hills, where they were truly the Champions, and at Vicksburg, where, had the other corps but done their duty, the stronghold would now be ours." The publication of this untimely and indiscreet order created much excitement and indignation among the other corps. General Frank Blair wrote a letter to General Sherman and told him that if he and McPherson did not take it up, he, who had already made a campaign against another general officer, Fremont, would commence another against McClernand. Thereupon General Sherman and General McPherson each wrote a letter to General Grant, enclosing letters from their subordinates. Grant wrote to McClernand asking him if the order published in the St. Louis *Democrat* was substantially correct, and stating that he had not received a copy of the order as regulations required. McClernand replied that the order as published was correct, and that he was ready to maintain its statement; that he supposed a copy had been duly forwarded to headquarters, and charged his adjutant-general with the neglect.

Grant immediately relieved McClernand, and appointed General Ord to the command of the Thirteenth corps. The order relieving him was sent to McClernand by Lieutenant-Colonel J. H. Wilson, then of General Grant's staff, and later the General Wilson

commanding the cavalry division that captured Jeff Davis.

There was a particular bit of malice in selecting Wilson to carry this order, for Wilson had been a boy in the town where McClernand had formerly lived, and McClernand had never lost an opportunity to annoy Wilson with reminiscences,—of no account were they not told in an unpleasant way. Wilson handed the order to McClernand, who threw it on his table unopened. Wilson stated that he was instructed to wait and see him read it. McClernand then read the order, and, after a few moments' silence, said to Wilson that he much doubted the authority of General Grant to relieve a general officer appointed by the President, but that he would not make a point of it,— a very wise conclusion on McClernand's part, since Grant had all the bayonets.

The departure of McClernand was a relief to the whole army, and the appointment of General Ord materially increased the efficiency of the Thirteenth corps.

Grant enclosed McClernand's published order, the letters of Sherman, McPherson, and Blair, and his own order relieving McClernand and ordering him to return to Illinois and report to the adjutant-general, by letter, and ordered C. C. Chaffee, lieutenant of ordnance on his staff, to take them to Washington.

Chaffee was tenting with me at General Sherman's headquarters at the time, and, as he could not leave until the next morning, we spent the night together. Chaffee remarked that as General Grant had given him the papers unsealed, with the envelope gaping open, he evidently intended that he should read them; so, lying on his cot, by the light of a candle he read them aloud. Sherman's letter was very bitter; he said that it was "the first instance on record of a commanding general congratulating his troops on their defeat"; it was not, however, for the troops at all, but to make political capital to be used thereafter in Illinois. McPherson was more mild, but very sarcastic, and in his letter said, "Although born a warrior as he himself has said, he forgets one of the traits of a true soldier,—generosity and justness to his companions in arms." McPherson alluded to a story often told at that time, that in a public speech in Illinois McClernand was said to have told his audience that "Some men were born to one walk in life, and some to another. Thank God, I [McClernand] was born a warrior insensible to fear."

The siege went on. There were so few engineering officers that Chief Engineer Captain Prime did not attempt to control the approaches, but let each brigade dig as they chose toward the enemy, remarking that they were ready enough to dig in that direction. The engineers were mostly employed in preparing

While effectively cutting off his own supply lines, Grant campaigned south of Vicksburg in late spring of 1863. Since supplies could not be sent from Union sources, Yankees foraged from the Mississippi farms and citizenry.

gabions and sap-rollers; in building batteries and in making parallels connecting the numerous zigzags, and in mining.

During the night pickets were advanced beyond the parallels by both parties. When no officers were within hearing the pickets would indulge in a friendly truce, and it was not unusual to hear, "Johnny!" "Hello, Yank!" "Do n't shoot and I'll come out." "Come on." "Any tobacco, Johnny?" "Yes; have you any coffee, Yank?" Our men used to dry their coffee-grounds and exchange them with the "Rebs" for to-bacco. "It is n't real strong, Johnny," they would say, "but it will give you some *grounds* for calling that rye drink of yours coffee." They would also exchange newspapers, and every morning we had at headquar-ters the Vicksburg paper of the day before. Toward the latter part of the siege these newspapers were printed on the back side of cheap wall-paper.

By the end of June the approaches were within a few feet of the enemy's ditch at several points, and General Grant then ordered preparations to be made for a general assault on the 6th of July. The ditches in the immediate vicinity of the enemy were widened and straightened, and long lines of rifle-pits were built with sand-bag embrasures for riflemen to command the enemy's parapet, so that not a man might show

himself above the rebel breastworks and live.

Pemberton saw all these preparations, and fearing an assault on the 4th which he felt must be suc-cessful, surrendered on the 3d, and the Fourth of July was celebrated by the ceremony of the surrender,— the army marching with colors flying and bands play-ing, while on the river the fleets from above and below, with vessels decorated with flags, sailors in holiday dress, and guns firing, were united once again.

As soon as our men were relieved from duty they made friends with their late enemy, separated into squads, and as usual commenced to boil coffee and fry hard-tack and bacon. At noon I rode inside the for-tifications of Vicksburg.

The place seemed filled with a gigantic picnic; thousands of little parties were seated here and there on the ground, the "Yanks" playing the host. They were talking and laughing and telling the incidents of the siege, and comparing notes. I stopped several times to listen to some of the Confederate tales of what "You-uns" and "We-uns" did. I heard one "Reb" say, "You outgeneraled us, you did. 'T was General Starvation that outflanked us."

The fall of Vicksburg gave us Port Hudson and opened the Mississippi River from Canada to the Gulf.

★★★

ALBERT O. MARSHALL

Champion Hills and Black River

In order to attain his objective of finally taking Vicksburg, Grant boldly cut his lines of supply and communications and went tearing into Mississippi to the south of the town. After defeating the forces under Confederate General Joseph John-ston at the state capital, Jackson, on 14 May, the Federals learned from a Confed-erate courier turned Yankee spy that enemy forces from Vicksburg under John C. Pemberton were attempting to link up with Johnston's army to strike at Grant's rear. Rather than allow this event to pass,

the Federal General struck at Pemberton as he moved to comply, defeating the Southerners decisively at Champion's Hill on 16 May 1863. On the following day, Grant's troops crushed the Confederate force guarding a crossing of the Big Black River. Both battles enabled Grant to lay siege to the beleaguered Confederates in their entrenchments before Vicksburg. Serving with the 33rd Illinois Regiment at the time, Albert O. Marshall wrote of his experiences in the campaign in his work Army Life: From a Soldier's Journal.

At an early hour on Saturday morning, May 16, 1863 our entire army was aroused, a hasty breakfast con-

sisting of some coffee and hard tack eaten, and every thing put in readiness for the coming contest. The

Members of Sherman's corps of Grant's army set Confederate military stores and citizens' property ablaze after the Army of the Tennessee took Jackson, Mississippi, on 14 May.

thick woods in our front covered the Confederate army lying there and waiting for us. The ground was broken and hilly as well as covered with a heavy growth of timber. Many capital positions could be selected by an army that chose to stand on the defensive. This was the course taken by the enemy. Between where we had camped for the night and the wooded hills where the rebels had taken their stand was some open ground.

Our army corps, the thirteenth, was the left of the advancing Union army. At an early hour, between seven and eight o'clock, and before we were fairly under way, we heard the first guns of the day's contest. It was commenced by the advance of our corps and to our extreme left. This first firing being thus to the left of our army suggested the probability that the enemy was attempting to pass from the immediate front of our army and probably looking for a way to escape instead of maintaining his fighting ground.

Our heavy infantry columns immediately went forward. As they did so the slight firing we had heard in front of our left passed along to our center and became somewhat heavier. It now became apparent that the rebels had determined to make a stubborn stand. Of course all the firing yet done had been only that of the advance skirmishers on both sides. The tell-tale stubbornness with which the rebel skirmishers stood their ground, in our front, plainly showed that heavy forces of the enermy were immediately behind them. A soldier, by observation, will learn so as to know when a strong force of the enemy is near at hand as plainly as an experienced sea captain, when upon the water, can tell when a fierce storm is approaching. As we neared the open woods in our front we formed in army line in the open fields and were all ready to march in and attack the waiting rebels.

Now a strange and wonderful day's experience opened before us. Although we were the first of the Union troops upon the ground, and within striking distance of the enemy, we lay still and made no forward move. A ten minutes' march would have brought us upon the main rebel line. The real battle had not yet commenced. We formed in line and waited. During the day all of the varied phases of the fierce battle could be noted by us.

Heavy firing soon told us that the real battle had commenced. Now a fierce artillery duel would be fought and then succeeded by the more desperate and stubborn conflict of small arms. Then a seeming lull in the contest would be again followed by the fierce roar of artillery, and this again followed by an infantry contest. Up and down the line the thunder roar of the battle would go; at one time fierce at one point, then to quiet there and rage with increased fury at another. The heavy cloud of battle smoke, as the dark mass arose above the trees, also told its story of the fierce contest. Now and then we would plainly hear the wild cheers of the Northern boys as some of our troops would charge upon and carry some point held by the enemy. During all this time we lay still. No order for us to go forward was given.

As the hours passed by some of our impatient soldiers would leave the ranks and go forward into the woods and then return with news of the battle. From them and other sources we had almost continual information from the front. This was hardly necessary, however, for we were so near that the smoke of battle, the firing guns and the varied sounds of the fierce struggle plainly told us of advances and retreats made. The progress of the battle was ever before us.

At last, after long waiting and much wondering why we were not permitted to go forward and share in the fierce conflict, the order to "Forward, march," was given. In a brief moment we were on the way. As we started the wild and advancing cheers that rose above the battle roar told us that the Union troops were making a fierce and successful charge upon the rebel lines. As we went in the battle was well-nigh over; we went into the woods and struck the right wing of the rebel army. It vanished before us like snow beneath the summer sun. Had we struck this wing of the rebel army an hour earlier it would have been thrown upon the enemy's center and the confusion that would then have overwhelmed them would have led to the destruction of the entire rebel army. As it was, at the time when we struck them, the Union troops under McPherson had made their last charge and driven in the main rebel line, so that all were now upon a fierce run to escape. Had we been soon enough the confusion in the rebel lines would have been so great that they could not have seen any open way of escape and they would have been obliged to throw down their

Carnage at Champion's Hills; a Confederate battery comes under attack by soldiers of Brigadier General Alvin P. Hovey's division of McClernand's XIII Corps. By the end of the day, Hovey counted almost a third of his command as casualties.

arms and surrender *en masse.*

We drove all before us and then rushed on to the main road where the fiercest contest of the battle had been fought. The hill upon which the enemy had made his most desperate contest was thickly covered with the dead of both sides. Broken guns and ruin covered the field. Rebel artillery with its horses and men were here and there all heaped together in a mountain of death and ruin. Over this gory field we

A Federal artillery battery engaged at the battle of Champion's Hill. With the Confederate loss of this crucial battle, Pemberton and his men were forced to fall back to Vicksburg.

rushed, and on into the woods beyond where we struck all that was left of the rebel army. It was the last shot of the day. The frightened enemy hardly having courage to return our first fire. We cut the remains of the rebel army apart. The largest force was driven toward Vicksburg. The other part ran over the hills and went to the east. The Thirty-third had been given the advance of the reserve force as it went upon the field. The last guns fired in the battle of Champion Hills was by our men and at the force of the enemy we drove to the rear.

Many pieces of rebel artillery fell to our hands. Hosts of rebels surrendered as we advanced. These were left for others to guard, as we pushed on, rapidly following the retreating rebels. Letting those who had gone to the east pursue their way to escape or be captured by other Union forces as their fate might be, we pushed toward the west after the rebels who were retreating toward Vicksburg. Darkness soon ended our pursuit and we stopped for the night at Edwards' Station.

At night, as the full results of the battle became known, it was found that a great victory had been won by our troops.

Having become historical, and its general results being open to all who choose to refer to the pages of written history, it is not necessary to here recount at large the scenes and results of the battle of Champion Hills.

Sunday morning, May 17, 1963, found us ready to move forward as soon as it was light enough to march. We were now given the advance. A rapid march brought us within sight of the rebel works at Black River. The outside picket guards were driven in without difficulty.

The conditions for a stubborn defense were ample. The rebel position was a strong one. At this point Black River is a stream of considerable size. The wagon road to Vicksburg, as well as the railroad, here crosses the river. On the west side of Black River are some high bluffs. We were approaching from the east. Why the Confederates did not select these bluffs on the west side of the river as the place for their fortifications, it is hard to tell; they probably thought the position chosen preferable. It certainly was a mistake. Still, the place selected for their fortifications was by no means a weak one. Had not the west bank of Black River furnished stronger natural positions, that selected by the rebels would have been considered a wise selection. Some little distance from the east side of the main river was a channel of considerable width and depth. This virtually created an island, which lay between the main river and this channel or bayou. The island was the place selected by the enemy for his fortifications. The island was of sufficient size, and the ground being comparatively level and unbroken, it was probably selected by the rebels as a better place for the movement of troops than would have been the uneven hills upon the west side of the river. Again, east of the bayou was a smooth valley varying from half a mile to a mile in width. As the attacking force would have to pass over this level ground, the rebels doubtless thought that they could easily destroy all who attempted to approach, before their works could be reached.

A range of forts well supplied with heavy artillery had been built along the east side of the bayou. These had been connected with a complete chain of breastworks for the enemy's infantry. Thus an attacking force would have to first charge over a wide space of level ground; then pass a deep and wide stream of water, and then climb the rebel fortifications upon the bank of the channel before they could reach the well fortified rebels. What possessed the enemy to waste so much valuable strength in fighting in the open woods upon Champion Hills when Black River, so near at hand, afforded them such superior positions of defense, is, indeed, a marvel.

We were upon the skirmish line and consequently the first troops in sight of the enemy that morning. The position our company held was next to and upon the south side of the road running west toward Vicksburg. This brought us in front of the center and

strongest part of the enemy's works. The valley between the rebel works and the small wood-covered hills was at this point a little over half a mile in width. The valley at this point had been a cultivated corn or cane field. The previous year's furrows ran parallel with the rebel works. The small hills back of this field were covered with a thick growth of underbrush. Had the enemy been thoughtful and industrious enough to have cut and burned all of the small trees and brush upon these hills as far back as heavy artillery could reach, it would have been of untold advantage to him. To our right the valley lessened in width so that the ground covered with trees reached nearer to the rebel works. To our left it continued to widen so that the rebel works upon that part of the line had at least a mile of level ground over which to fire.

Our early morning call had evidently greatly surprised the indolent enemy. As we, upon the skirmish line, came out of the woods and upon the level field in front of their works, we beheld wild confusion in the rebel lines. Evidently they had not yet all got up and finished their breakfast, much less formed into line

Entrenched in a strong defensive position, Pemberton's army comes under heavy attack from Hovey's division and McPherson's XVII Corps at Champion's Hill. After maintaining a firm stand, the Confederates were driven back in a retreat that degenerated into a confused rout.

ready to meet us. All were aroused and called into line. If we had been supported by a solid column, at that moment, we could no doubt have rushed over and taken the works before the enemy was prepared to defend them. But just then the Union troops at hand were only those of a small skirmish line of barely sufficient strength to feel of the enemy.

From the ground we were upon, all of the movements of the enemy could be plainly noted. Officers mounted in hot haste and rushed among the rebel soldiers to arouse and hurry them into position. Every movement of the enemy was plainly seen by us. We could note the strength of each rebel command and see to which part of the line it was sent. Probably no battle was ever before fought which was so completely seen from its commencement to its end as was the battle of Black River by those of us who were upon the advance skirmish line.

To get as near to the rebel works as we did upon such ground was wonderful. For any of us to live through the fight that ensued, holding the position we did, was a miracle. Our ability to advance so close to them was no doubt largely owing to the confusion in the enemy's ranks caused by our early approach. The first firing of the rebels was fearfully wild. They seemed only to put the muzzles of their guns over their breastworks and fire into the air at random. Such firing is more apt to hit those far in the rear as the bullets fall to the ground, than to trouble those who,

Site of the sanguinary battle of Champion's Hill.

like us, are near at hand. Now and then a gun in the hands of a cool-headed rebel would be fired with more judgment at our line. A few were hit. I supposed that I was one of the unfortunate ones. A rifle ball passed near enough to "burn" my face. I then knew by experience how it was with so many others who for a moment supposed they were hit, when they were not. I plainly felt a hole cut through my cheek. That the passing bullet had cut a deep, long gash through the side of my face I did not doubt. I immediately put up my hand to see how much of my cheek was left, and to my glad surprise found that the bullet had simply grazed and not cut me. Those who have experienced both, insist that at the first moment, a bullet that passes near enough to "burn" by the "hot wind" of a swift revolving bullet, produces a much sharper sting than that caused by a direct shot.

Our skirmish line pressed well forward, much farther than prudence would have permitted, and then each selected the best place he could find and lay upon the ground and commenced to load and fire as opportunity offered. Amidst thickly flying bullets it is surprising how small an elevation of ground a soldier can make available as breastwork. The rough plowing of the previous year's crop had left deep furrows and corresponding ridges, the best of which served us well during the hot fight in which we were engaged. The success with which a soldier can, under such circumstances, apparently sink into the ground and out of sight while loading his gun, can not be realized by those who have never seen it done.

Some of our artillery were soon in place on the hills behind us and commenced their work upon the enemy. The artillery was supported by the infantry columns. This heavy force on the higher ground in our rear soon claimed the entire attention of the rebels in our front. They no doubt also believed that all who had advanced on the skirmish line had been killed. These things combined caused us to be neglected by the enemy so that we were at liberty to load

and fire at pleasure and almost unmolested. While it, no doubt, did far more harm in the rebel ranks, still the few guns on the skirmish line attracted no attention when mingled with the fierce firing of the two contending armies. And then our nearness to the rebel line made it difficult for them to look over their works to take effective aim at us. Even when the conditions of the ground are favorable, the experience of war is that most of the firing done carries the balls high above the effective point. Situated as we were it was safe to calculate that the rebel bullets would pass above us. There being so much vacant space in the open air compared with the little space occupied by one individual, is the reason why so few are killed compared with the amount of lead shot in battle. The space occupied by a man is but a mere speck compared with all out doors, and there are a thousand chances to miss, to one to hit him with the ball of a random shot.

Our artillery had a capital position. The hills upon which our cannon were placed were within easy range of the rebel works. Our gunners were much better marksmen than those handling the rebel artillery. The thick underbrush completely covered the movements of our men. An entire battery would be run into position under cover of the thick young trees, careful aim taken and then altogether commence a rapid fire upon the rebel works. As soon as the rebel artillery began to get their guns bearing on the spot our men would run their guns to another point and the first notice of the change the enemy would get was another well-aimed volley. With different batteries doing this and a fine range of favorable ground to stand upon our artillery did most effective work. With our sharp-shooters on the skirmish line so near at hand to annoy every one who attempted to handle a rebel cannon, and our artillerymen so well improving

their opportunities, the result of the artillery duel was favorable to the Union side. All things combined produced the strange result, that superior artillery protected by complete works was worsted by smaller guns in the open field. During the fight many of the protected rebel guns were dismounted, while our artillery out in the open field escaped with but little harm.

Thus the battle raged with our cannon in our rear, and the rebel guns in our front, both firing over us. We were fortunately low enough so that both sides fired their balls and shells above us. The smoke and confusion of the heavy contest also served to withdraw all attention from our skirmish line and left us free to use our trusty rifles to the best advantage. After the engagement had commenced in earnest, the greatest danger we were in was from imperfect shells which would burst on the way, and from faulty charges of powder or misdirected guns which now and then sent iron and lead to plow the ground where we lay.

It would be useless to attempt to describe the terrific scenes of this fierce contest as viewed from the position we held between the two contending forces. The heavy battle smoke rapidly rising continually opened the entire scene to our view. Even in the hottest of the fight every move of the enemy could be noted by us. One rebel officer, mounted upon a powerful white horse, attracted unusual attention. As he first started at the beginning of the fight he appeared to be supported by a numerous staff. His daring was so reckless that he often became the mark our riflemen aimed at. As time passed swiftly on, one by one of his

The 14th Division under Brigadier Eugene A. Carr and Brigadier General Peter Osterhaus's 9th Division break through the parapet defended by Pemberton's rear guard at Big Black River.

assistants were seen to be disabled. He rode until the last of his staff had fallen or left the field, and still the rider upon the white horse, within range of our guns, continued to inspire the rebel soldiers. At last, as it became plain that the day was soon to be ours, a desire seemed to spring up to let the reckless rider live, and he was permitted to ride away at the last unharmed. As the artillery battle reached its height, all incidents and individual matters were absorbed by the fierce grandeur of the terrific storm raging around and above us. For a time the cannon in front of us, the cannon behind us, the cannon around us, thundered and roared and poured forth their fierce storm of fire and shot. Look to the front, look to the rear, look everywhere and the red-mouthed artillery seemed opened upon us. Above us was the black cloud of battle smoke, through which crashed and burst and screamed the murderous shell and ball. But few ever looked upon what we saw during that hour, and lived to tell the tale of the day's conflict. Imagination has often suggested that the grandest place from which to view a battle scene would be from a stationary balloon anchored high above the field of battle, and from thence to look down upon both contending forces. Even this would not prove equal to the position we held, because the rising smoke would then obscure the view, while with us, the dense cloud continually rose so that we could look beneath it and see the entire fury of the fierce conflict.

Although the gigantic grandeur of the conflict was created by the heavy artillery and the solid ranks of infantry in our rear, still the most effective work of the entire battle was done by the line of skirmishers, who, with their trusty rifles, had approached so near the rebel works. We held our ground during the entire battle. In fact it was better to do so than to have attempted to go back while so plainly within range of the rebel guns. I had a little experience in this. Near to me was John Spradling of our company. A piece of bursting shell struck him in the side or top part of his hip inflicting a fearful wound. He supposed that it was fatal and told us that he would soon die. His wound bled badly but his strength remained so well that he soon thought that if he could get medical aid there might still be a chance for him to live. If death is inevitable a soldier will die without a single word of complaint. While there is hope of life he is anxious to improve it. Spradling became wildly anxious to get back where his wound could be attended to before he bled to death. He desired me to help him. It was a dangerous undertaking. The artillery on both sides was still firing rapidly. Standing up incurred more danger from the balls and shells swiftly flying from both front and rear over our heads. The worst, however, was to slowly walk over so much exposed ground, and that in plain sight and range of the solid line of rebel riflemen. The hope was that they would not care to waste any shots at a crippled soldier and his assistant, going to the rear. I got our wounded comrade up and started. With my gun fastened upon one shoulder—a soldier never abandons his gun—I lent my other shoulder and arm to the wounded man.

Yankees and Rebels skirmish before Vicksburg as Grant's army moves to surround the town.

He was so injured that practically he could use only one foot to assist in the walk. Going back in this condition was slow and tedious. The hope of magnanimity on the part of the rebels was misplaced. We had not gone far before the screeching rifle balls aimed at us commenced hissing by our ears. Spradling knew that he would die if he stayed upon the field. Another ball could do no more than kill him. He begged to go on. As a soldier who could yet be useful in front I ought not to have taken the chances. But who could withstand the pleading of a wounded soldier. And then who could tell what the result would be? The chances were even that he would be hit as soon as I. Then my mission toward the rear would be ended. A soldier's life makes all reckless of danger. All places in the midst of a fierce battle are dangerous. What great difference did it make, for us to go or stay? I told Spradling to brace up and we would continue until one or the other of us fell. It is not wild to say that, during our tedious journey, at least a thousand rifle balls aimed at us passed near, and, strange to say, neither of us was touched. There must have been some special Providence that protected us. With much difficulty I managed to get back over the open ground, reached the woods, dragged our wounded comrade up over the hill and then back until we met a squad with their white badges and a stretcher in whose hands I placed the wounded soldier and who carried him back to the field hospital where his wounds would be dressed.

Relieved of our wounded soldier I turned and immediately went forward to rejoin my comrades. It is usual in such cases to remain with the main line and not hazard the attempt to reach the skirmish line in front. Probably it would be more correct to state the fact that it is always usual in all battles for the entire skirmish line to fall back out of the way when the actual engagement commences. It was only owing to the peculiar condition of the ground upon which it was fought that in this battle we upon the skirmish line retained our advanced position and allowed the heavy firing to be done over our heads.

Many indications told us that the battle would soon be ended. Most of the rebel cannon had been silenced. The rebel infantry began to exhibit evidences of uneasiness. I was anxious to be in at the end. To go forward was of course far different from what my retreat had been. Being alone I could skip along lively. There was a chance to select the ground and now and then dodge behind some protection. In short, going back was not by any manner of means a matter of recklessness.

My return had been none too soon. I had hardly reached our skirmish line when the last move in the battle of Black River was made. It was a brisk, sharp and successful charge upon the rebel works. This is how it happened: The woods to our right ran well down toward the rebel works. Colonel Bailey of the Ninety-ninth Illinois—"old rough and ready number two," General Benton had called him after the battle of Magnolia Hills—was with the advance. In their zeal the Union soldiers had pressed to the verge of the woods which brought them near to the rebel works. It became right hot for our boys so near to the enemy's lines. They had no orders to go farther; in fact, had already pushed on farther than orders had been given for them to go. The proper thing to have done was to have fallen back to a less exposed position. Colonel Bailey was one of those awkward officers who could never learn military rules. His only idea of war was to pitch in and whip the enemy whenever and wherever he could be found. By his impetuosity he became the hero of the day's battle. Had his unauthorized movement failed he would probably have been at least dismissed from the army. No, he would not. Had it failed and he come out of it alive, he might have been

tried by a court-martial, but that never would have happened. His rash act was bound to succeed or Colonel Bailey would have been killed in the attempt.

Finding it disagreeable to be so near the rebel works and seeing the effective fire upon his soldiers, Colonel Bailey became fighting mad and yelled out in thundering tones that rang along the line: "Boys, it is getting too d——— hot here. Let us go for the cussed rebels!" Before the last word was out of his mouth, with a drawn sword flashing in the air, he was on a fierce run toward the rebel works. With a wild hurrah his entire command joined him in the wild race. Others to the right and left, without a moment's delay or a single command, joined in the mad career, and thus with wild cheers the entire Union line joined in a charge upon the rebel works.

The disheartened Confederates having already suffered so severely, and vividly remembering the fearful pounding they had received the day before at Champion Hills, at once gave up all hope of further defense and immediately abandoned their works, and were in a hot race to the rear before the Union troops had reached their lines. Crossing the bayou was no easy matter. In front of part of our line the water was only breast deep; through this the soldiers easily waded, holding their guns and cartridge boxes above the water. In some places the stagnant water was covered

Federal gunboats and reinforcements join Grant's force besieging Vicksburg.

Delayed by the destruction of a bridge over the Big Black, the Federals eventually crossed the waterway in pontoon boats.

Bridge over the Big Black River was burned in the wake of the Confederate retreat to impede the Federal advance on Vicksburg. In doing so, Pemberton abandoned 1751 of his men fighting a rear guard action against Grant's legion.

with drift-wood. Here some would jump from one log to another like rabbits. In places where the water was more open a soldier running up would jump on to a floating log and the momentum of the fierce run would carry both him and the log across so that he could jump dry shod upon the other side, before the log he thus used for a boat commenced to turn wrong side up. In front of us the water was deeper and wider, but as good fortune would have it, the rebels had only removed the planks from the bridge, leaving the narrow stringers still running over. Our company immediately jumped upon these stringers and ran across like squirrels. The rest of the skirmish line followed, and thus the Thirty-third was soon all inside of the rebel works, being the first troops inside the main part of the fort. Other troops came in hot haste. The rebels were gone. And the battle of Black River was ended.

A fine lot of rebel cannon was taken with the fort. Our boys had learned a little war experience from the fight of the day before. As we drove the enemy from some of his cannon at Champion Hills, we rushed forward without regard to the guns. When we afterward sent back for them we found that the troops who had followed us had taken possession of the captured cannon, and were thus entitled to the credit of their capture. The rule is, that if a command captures artillery it must retain possession of it, or else the next command coming up will have the right to claim it. Infantry troops can not always carry captured artillery along with them, nor stop in the midst of a fight to retain possession of it. To provide for these and other difficulties that might arise, the established rule has become for the troops who capture a cannon to have one of their men "straddle" it, that is, sit upon it as though on horseback. Then the command can go to any other work at hand, and the one soldier upon the gun will be recognized by the entire army as in full possession of it. Thus one man for each piece of artillery is all the regiment need leave to retain possession of captured cannon. Of course, should any of the enemy return, the "straddling" is ended, and it is again a fight for possession of the guns. We had profited by the Champion Hills lesson, and the result was that the captured rebel forts were full of Thirty-third boys "straddling" the captured cannon. Thus we were credited with the capture of cannon enough to supply a good sized army, and were more than made even for the loss of those we had neglected to "straddle" at Champion Hills. The captured guns came near being a burden to us, there were so many of them that they could not be disposed of at once, so an entire company of our regiment was detailed to take care of the captured guns until they could be properly disposed of.

The rebels retreated across the river and went toward Vicksburg. One of their batteries took position upon the high bluffs on the west side of the river and fired a few rounds at us, but as soon as they saw one of our batteries getting into position to reply to them, they "limbered up" and scampered away. This was the last we saw of the rebels at Black River.

★★★

U. S. GRANT
Capturing Vicksburg

After a few bloody repulses, Grant found he could make little headway against the almost impenetrable earthworks surrounding Vicksburg. Thus, both sides settled down to a long drawn out siege in which the Federals continuously threw shells into the enemy ranks and the town itself. In less than two months, lacking food and supplies, with no hope of relief in sight, Pemberton decided to surrender, with Vicksburg capitulating on 4 July 1863. The fall of the town culminated Grant's most brilliant triumph and continued his spectacular rise to fame. His recollections of the siege are taken from Personal Memories of U.S. Grant.

I now determined upon a regular siege—to "outcamp the enemy," as it were, and to incur no more losses. The experience of the 22d convinced officers and men that this was best, and they went to work on the defences and approaches with a will. With the navy holding the river, the investment of Vicksburg was complete. As long as we could hold our position the enemy was limited in supplies of food, men and munitions of war to what they had on hand. These could not last always.

The crossing of troops at Bruinsburg commenced April 30th. On the 18th of May the army was in rear of Vicksburg. On the 19th, just twenty days after the crossing, the city was completely invested and an assault had been made: five distinct battles (besides continuous skirmishing) had been fought and won by the Union forces; the capital of the State had fallen and its arsenals, military manufactories and everything useful for military purposes had been destroyed; an average of about one hundred and eighty miles had been marched by the troops engaged; but five days' rations had been issued, and no forage; over six thousand prisoners had been captured, and as many more of the enemy had been killed or wounded; twenty-seven heavy cannon and sixty-one field-pieces had fallen into our hands; and four hundred miles of the river, from Vicksburg to Port Hudson, had become ours. The Union force that had crossed the Mississippi River up to this time was less than forty-three thousand men. One division of these, Blair's, only arrived in time to take part in the battle of Champion's Hill, but was not engaged there; and one brigade, Ransom's of McPherson's corps, reached the field after the battle. The enemy had at Vicksburg, Grand Gulf, Jackson, and on the roads between these places, over sixty thousand men. They were in their own country, where no rear guards were necessary. The country is admirable for defence, but difficult for the conduct of an offensive campaign. All their troops had to be met. We were fortunate, to say the least, in meeting them in detail: at Port Gibson seven or eight thousand; at Raymond, five thousand; at Jackson, from eight to eleven thousand; at Champion's Hill, twenty-five thousand; at the Big Black, four thousand.

A part of those met at Jackson were all that was left of those encountered at Raymond. They were beaten in detail by a force smaller than their own, upon their own ground.

Of the wounded many were but slightly so, and continued on duty. Not half of them were disabled for any length of time.

After the unsuccessful assault of the 22d the work of the regular siege began. Sherman occupied the right starting from the river above Vicksburg, McPherson the centre (McArthur's division now with him) and McClernand the left, holding the road south to Warrenton. Lauman's division arrived at this time and was placed on the extreme left of the line.

In the interval between the assaults of the 19th and 22d, roads had been completed from the Yazoo River and Chickasaw Bayou, around the rear of the army, to enable us to bring up supplies of food and ammunition; ground had been selected and cleared on which the troops were to be encamped, and tents and cooking utensils were brought up. The troops had been without these from the time of crossing the Mississippi up to this time. All was now ready for the pick and spade. Prentiss and Hurlbut were ordered to send forward every man that could be spared. Cavalry especially was wanted to watch the fords along the Big Black, and to observe Johnston. I knew that Johnston was receiving reinforcements from Bragg, who was confronting Rosecrans in Tennessee. Vicksburg was so important to the enemy that I believed he would make the most strenuous efforts to raise the siege, even at the risk of losing ground elsewhere.

My line was more than fifteen miles long, extending from Haines' Bluff to Vicksburg, thence to Warrenton. The line of the enemy was about seven. In addition to this, having an enemy at Canton and Jack-

The powerful naval guns of Battery Sherman at the Federal fortifications at Vicksburg. By the time the town surrendered, Grant had amassed a formidable array of 220 guns to bombard the enemy's works.

While building siege fortifications outside Vicksburg, Grant's Yankees construct gabions, hollow cylindrical baskets made of sticks and wicker and filled with dirt, to protect themselves from Rebel missiles.

son, in our rear, who was being constantly reinforced, we required a second line of defence facing the other way. I had not troops enough under my command to man these. General Halleck appreciated the situation and, without being asked, forwarded reinforcements with all possible dispatch.

The ground about Vicksburg is admirable for defence. On the north it is about two hundred feet above the Mississippi River at the highest point and very much cut up by the washing rains; the ravines were grown up with cane and underbrush, while the sides and tops were covered with a dense forest. Farther south the ground flattens out somewhat, and was in cultivation. But here, too, it was cut up by ravines and small streams. The enemy's line of defence followed the crest of a ridge from the river north of the city eastward, then southerly around to the Jackson road, full three miles back of the city; thence in a south-westerly direction to the river. Deep ravines of the description given lay in front of these defences. As there is a succession of gullies, cut out by rains along the side of the ridge, the line was necessarily very irregular. To follow each of these spurs with intrench-ments, so as to command the slopes on either side, would have lengthened their line very much. Gener-ally therefore, or in many places, their line would run from near the head of one gully nearly straight to the head of another, and an outer work triangular in shape, generally open in the rear, was thrown up on the point; with a few men in this outer work they commanded the approaches to the main line com-pletely.

The work to be done, to make our position as strong against the enemy as his was against us, was very great. The problem was also complicated by our wanting our line as near that of the enemy as possible. We had but four engineer officers with us. Captain Prime, of the Engineer Corps, was the chief, and the work at the beginning was mainly directed by him. His health soon gave out, when he was succeeded by Captain Comstock, also of the Engineer Corps. To provide assistants on such a long line I directed that all officers who had graduated at West Point, where they had necessarily to study military engineering, should in addition to their other duties assist in the work.

The chief quartermaster and the chief commissary were graduates. The chief commissary, now the Com-missary-General of the Army, begged off, however, saying that there was nothing in engineering that he was good for unless he would do for a sap-roller. As soldiers require rations while working in the ditches as well as when marching and fighting, and as we would be sure to lose him if he was used as a sap-roller, I let him off. The general is a large man; weighs two hundred and twenty pounds, and is not tall.

We had no siege guns except six thirty-two pounders, and there were none at the West to draw from. Admiral Porter, however, supplied us with a battery of navy-guns of large calibre, and with these, and the field artillery used in the campaign, the siege began. The first thing to do was to get the artillery in

Eyewitness to the bloody battle of the crater at Vicksburg, Fred B. Schall, illustrator for **Frank Leslie's Illustrated,** *sketches the Federal attack on the Rebel lines after a mine is blown under the enemy's works.*

batteries where they would occupy commanding posi-tions; then establish the camps, under cover from the fire of the enemy but as near up as possible; and then construct rifle-pits and covered ways, to connect the entire command by the shortest route. The enemy did not harass us much while we were constructing our batteries. Probably their artillery ammunition was short; and their infantry was kept down by our sharp-shooters, who were always on the alert and ready to fire at a head whenever it showed itself above the rebel works.

In no place were our lines more than six hundred yards from the enemy. It was necessary, therefore, to cover our men by something more than the ordinary parapet. To give additional protection sand bags, bul-let-proof, were placed along the tops of the parapets far enough apart to make loop-holes for musketry. On top of these, logs were put. By these means the men were enabled to walk about erect when off duty, with-out fear of annoyance from sharpshooters. The enemy used in their defence explosive musket-balls, no doubt thinking that, bursting over our men in the trenches, they would do some execution; but I do not remember a single case where a man was injured by a piece of one of these shells. When they were hit and the ball exploded, the would was terrible. In these cases a solid ball would have hit as well. Their use is barbarous, because they produce increased suffering without any corresponding advantage to those using them.

The enemy could not resort to our method to pro-tect their men, because we had an inexhaustible sup-ply of ammunition to draw upon and used it freely. Splinters from the timber would have made havoc among the men behind.

There were no mortars with the besiegers, except what the navy had in front of the city; but wooden ones were made by taking logs of the toughest wood that could be found, boring them out for six or twelve pound shells and binding them with strong iron bands. These answered as coehorns, and shells were successfully thrown from them into the trenches of the enemy.

The labor of building the batteries and intrenching was largely done by the pioneers, assisted by negroes who came within our lines and who were paid for their work; but details from the troops had often to be made. The work was pushed forward as rapidly as possible, and when an advanced position was secured and covered from the fire of the enemy the batteries were advanced. By the 30th of June there were two hundred and twenty guns in position, mostly light field-pieces, besides a battery of heavy guns belonging to, manned and commanded by the navy. We were now as strong for defence against the garrison of Vicksburg as they were against us; but I knew that Johnston was in our rear, and was receiving constant reinforcements from the east. He had at this time a larger force than I had had at any time prior to the battle of Champion's Hill.

As soon as the news of the arrival of the Union army behind Vicksburg reached the North, floods of visitors began to pour in. Some came to gratify curiosity; some to see sons or brothers who had passed through the terrible ordeal; members of the Christian and Sanitary Associations came to minister to the wants of the sick and the wounded. Often those coming to see a son or brother would bring a dozen or two of poultry. They did not know how little the gift would be appreciated. Many of the soldiers had lived so much on chickens, ducks and turkeys without bread during the march, that the sight of poultry, if they could get bacon, almost took away their appetite. But the intention was good.

Among the earliest arrivals was the Governor of Illinois, with most of the State officers. I naturally wanted to show them what there was of most interest.

In Sherman's front the ground was the most broken and most wooded, and more was to be seen without exposure. I therefore took them to Sherman's headquarters and presented them. Before starting out to look at the lines—possibly while Sherman's horse was being saddled—there were many questions asked about the late campaign, about which the North had been so inperfectly informed. There was a little knot around Sherman and another around me, and I heard Sherman repeating, in the most animated manner, what he had said to me when we first looked down from Walnut Hills upon the land below on the 18th of May, adding: "Grant is entitled to every bit of the credit for the campaign; I opposed it. I wrote him a letter about it." But for this speech it is not likely that Sherman's opposition would have ever been heard of. His untiring energy and great efficiency during the campaign entitle him to a full share of all the credit due for its success. He could not have done more if the plan had been his own.

On the 26th of May I sent Blair's division up the Yazoo to drive out a force of the enemy supposed to be between the Big Black and the Yazoo. The country was rich and full of supplies of both food and forage. Blair was instructed to take all of it. The cattle were to be driven in for the use of our army, and the food and forage to be consumed by our troops or destroyed by fire; all bridges were to be destroyed, and the roads

Bored by the drawn out siege, Yankees pass time by sniping at the enemy, reading or enjoying a pleasant smoke.

rendered as nearly impassable as possible. Blair went forty-five miles and was gone almost a week. His work was effectually done. I requested Porter at this time to send the marine brigade, a floating non-descript force which had been assigned to his command and which proved very useful, up to Haines' Bluff to hold it until reinforcements could be sent.

On the 26th I also received a letter from Banks, asking me to reinforce him with ten thousand men at Port Hudson. Of course I could not comply with his request, nor did I think he needed them. He was in no danger of an attack by the garrison in his front, and there was no army organizing in his rear to raise the siege.

On the 3d of June a brigade from Hurlbut's command arrived, General Kimball commanding. It was sent to Mechanicsburg, some miles north-east of Haines' Bluff and about midway between the Big Black and the Yazoo. A brigade of Blair's division and twelve hundred cavalry had already, on Blair's return from the Yazoo, been sent to the same place with instructions to watch the crossings of the Big Black River, to destroy the roads in his (Blair's) front, and to gather or destroy all supplies.

On the 7th of June our little force of colored and

Joseph Eggleston Johnston. After being put out of action in the battle of Seven Pines, Johnston returned to active command to take charge of the Department of the West during the Vicksburg Campaign.

A typical day during the siege at Vicksburg. Cannons blast away while marksmen snipe at available targets.

white troops across the Mississippi, at Milliken's Bend, were attacked by about 3,000 men from Richard Taylor's trans-Mississippi command. With the aid of the gunboats they were speedily repelled. I sent Mower's brigade over with instructions to drive the enemy beyond the Tensas Bayou; and we had no further trouble in that quarter during the siege. This was the first important engagement of the war in which colored troops were under fire. These men were very raw, having all been enlisted since the beginning of the siege, but they behaved well.

On the 8th of June a full division arrived from Hurlbut's command, under General Sooy Smith. It was sent immediately to Haines' Bluff, and General C. C. Washburn was assigned to the general command at that point.

On the 11th a strong division arrived from the Department of the Missouri under General Herron, which was placed on our left. This cut off the last possible chance of communication between Pemberton and Johnston, as it enabled Lauman to close up on McClernand's left while Herron intrenched from Lauman to the water's edge. At this point the water recedes a few hundred yards from the high land. Through this opening no doubt the Confederate commanders had been able to get messengers under cover of night.

On the 14th General Parke arrived with two divisions of Burnside's corps, and was immediately dispatched to Haines' Bluff. These latter troops—Herron's and Parke's—were the reinforcements already spoken of sent by Halleck in anticipation of their being needed. They arrived none too soon.

I now had about seventy-one thousand men. More than half were disposed across the peninsula, between the Yazoo at Haines' Bluff and the Big Black, with the division of Osterhaus watching the crossings of the latter river farther south and west from the crossing of the Jackson road to Baldwin's ferry and below.

There were eight roads leading into Vicksburg, along which and their immediate sides, our work was specially pushed and batteries advanced; but no commanding point within range of the enemy was neglected.

On the 17th I received a letter from General Sherman and one on the 18th from General McPherson, saying that their respective commands had complained to them of a fulsome, congratulatory order published by General McClernard to the 13th corps, which did great injustice to the other troops engaged in the campaign. This order had been sent North and published, and now papers containing it had reached our camps. The order had not been heard of by me, and certainly not by troops outside of McClernand's command until brought in this way I at once wrote to McClernand, directing him to send me a copy of this order. He did so, and I at once relieved him from the command of the 13th army corps and ordered him back to Springfield, Illinois. The publication of his order in the press was in violation of War Department orders and also of mine.

The capitulation of Vicksburg proved to be another prominent episode in the military career of William Tecumseh Sherman. Originally, he had severe doubts that Grant's campaign would actually succeed.

On the 22d of June positive information was received that Johnston had crossed the Big Black River for the purpose of attacking our rear, to raise the siege and release Pemberton. The corrspondence between Johnston and Pemberton shows that all expectation of holding Vicksburg had by this time passed from Johnston's mind. I immediately ordered Sherman to the command of all the forces from Haines' Bluff to the Big Black River. This amounted now to quite half the troops about Vicksburg. Besides these, Herron and A. J. Smith's divisions were ordered to hold themselves in readiness to reinforce Sherman. Haines' Bluff had been strongly fortified on the land side, and on all commanding points from there to the Big Black at the railroad crossing batteries had been constructed. The work of connecting by rifle-pits where this was not already done, was an easy task for the troops that were to defend them.

We were now looking west, besieging Pemberton, while we were also looking east to defend ourselves against an expected siege by Johnston. But as against the garrison of Vicksburg we were as substantially protected as they were against us. Where we were looking east and north we were strongly fortified, and on the defensive. Johnston evidently took in the situation and wisely, I think, abstained from making an assault on us because it would simply have inflicted loss on both sides without accomplishing any result. We were strong enough to have taken the offensive against him; but I did not feel disposed to take any risk of losing our hold upon Pemberton's army, while I would have rejoiced at the opportunity of defending ourselves against an attack by Johnston.

Federal soldiers dig the tunnel for a mine to be placed under the Confederate works.

At 1500 on 25 June 1863, a mine dug under Confederate lines was exploded and Grant launched an attack into the gap caused by the crater. Men and parts of men were thrown high into the air by the huge explosion.

From the 23d of May the work of fortifying and pushing forward our position nearer to the enemy had been steadily progressing. At three points on the Jackson road, in front of Leggett's brigade, a sap was run up to the enemy's parapet, and by the 25th of June we had it undermined and the mine charged. The enemy had countermined, but did not succeed in reaching our mine. At this particular point the hill on which the rebel work stands rises abruptly. Our sap ran close up to the outside of the enemy's parapet. In fact this parapet was also our protection. The soldiers of the two sides occasionally conversed pleasantly across this barrier; sometimes they exchanged the hard bread of the Union soldiers for the tobacco of the Confederates; at other times the enemy threw over hand-grenades, and often our men, catching them in their hands, returned them.

Our mine had been started some distance back down the hill; consequently when it had extended as far as the parapet it was many feet below it. This caused the failure of the enemy in his search to find and destroy it. On the 25th of June at three o'clock, all being ready, the mine was exploded. A heavy artillery

fire all along the line had been ordered to open with the explosion. The effect was to blow the top of the hill off and make a crater where it stood. The breach was not sufficient to enable us to pass a column of attack through. In fact, the enemy having failed to reach our mine had thrown up a line farther back, where most of the men guarding that point were

After the Vicksburg mine was exploded, the enemy ranks were saturated with a heavy bombardment as the 31st and 45th Illinois moved through a trench to storm the crater. While becoming lodged in the gap caused by the explosion, the Federals failed to make any headway and were eventually forced to withdraw.

placed. There were a few men, however, left at the advance line, and others working in the countermine, which was still being pushed to find ours. All that were there were thrown into the air, some of them coming down on our side, still alive. I remember one colored man, who had been under ground at work when the explosion took place, who was thrown to our side. He was not much hurt, but terribly frightened. Some one asked him how high he had gone up. "Dun no, massa, but t'ink 'bout t'ree mile," was his reply. General Logan commanded at this point and took this colored man to his quarters, where he did service to the end of the siege.

As soon as the explosion took place the crater was

Illinois troops attempt to break through Confederate lines at the crater. With the bloody repulse of the attack, Grant detonated another mine on 1 July, but opted against following the explosion with an attack.

The battle for the crater towards the evening of the 25th. By this time, Grant was coming to the conclusion that Vicksburg could only be taken by siege and not battle.

seized by two regiments of our troops who were near by, under cover, where they had been placed for the express purpose. The enemy made a desperate effort to expel them, but failed, and soon retired behind the new line. From here, however, they threw hand-grenades, which did some execution. The compliment was returned by our men, but not with so much effect. The enemy could lay their grenades on the parapet, which alone divided the contestants, and roll them down upon us; while from our side they had to be thrown over the parapet, which was at considerable elevation. During the night we made efforts to secure our position in the crater against the missiles of the enemy, so as to run trenches along the outer base of their parapet, right and left; but the enemy continued throwing their grenades, and brought boxes of field ammunition (shells), the fuses of which they would light with port-fires, and throw them by hand into our ranks. We found it impossible to continue this work. Another mine was consequently started which was exploded on the 1st of July, destroying an entire rebel redan, killing and wounding a considerable number of its occupants and leaving an immense chasm where it stood. No attempt to charge was made this time, the experience of the 25th admonishing us. Our loss in the first affair was about thirty killed and wounded. The enemy must have lost more in the two explosions than we did in the first. We lost none in the second.

From this time forward the work of mining and pushing our position nearer to the enemy was prosecuted with vigor, and I determined to explode no more mines until we were ready to explode a number at different points and assault immediately after. We were up now at three different points, one in front of each corps, to where only the parapet of the enemy divided us.

At this time an intercepted dispatch from Johnston to Pemberton informed me that Johnston intended to make a determined attack upon us in order to relieve the garrison at Vicksburg. I knew the garrison would make no formidable effort to relieve itself. The picket lines were so close to each other—where there was space enough between the lines to post pickets—that the men could converse. On the 21st of June I was informed, through this means, that Pemberton was preparing to escape, by crossing to the Louisiana side under cover of night; that he had employed workmen in making boats for that purpose; that the men had been canvassed to ascertain if they would make an assault on the "Yankees" to cut their way out; that they had refused, and almost mutinied, because their commander would not surrender and relieve their sufferings, and had only been pacified by the assurance that boats enough would be finished in a week to carry them all over. The rebel pickets also said that houses in the city had been pulled down to get material to build these boats with. Afterwards this story was verified: on entering the city we found a large number of very rudely constructed boats.

All necessary steps were at once taken to render such an attempt abortive. Our pickets were doubled;

While fighting at close quarters in the crater, both sides resorted to the use of short fused shells or grenades. The Confederates were able to use these weapons with some effect as they occupied the higher ground and easily rolled or dropped the devices down on the attacking Federals.

Admiral Porter was notified, so that the river might be more closely watched; material was collected on the west bank of the river to be set on fire and light up the river if the attempt was made; and batteries were established along the levee crossing the peninsula on the Louisiana side. Had the attempt been made the garrison of Vicksburg would have been drowned, or made prisoners on the Louisiana side. General

Richard Taylor was expected on the west bank to co-operate in this movement, I believe, but he did not come, nor could he have done so with a force sufficient to be of service. The Mississippi was now in our possession from its source to its mouth, except in the immediate front of Vicksburg and of Port Hudson. We had nearly exhausted the country, along a line drawn from Lake Providence to opposite Bruinsburg. The roads west were not of a character to draw supplies over for any considerable force.

By the 1st of July our approaches had reached the enemy's ditch at a number of places. At ten points we could move under cover to within from five to one hundred yards of the enemy. Orders were given to make all preparations for assault on the 6th of July. The debouches were ordered widened to afford easy

Snipers in the trenches before Vicksburg pick off unwary and unlucky individuals that expose themselves from cover.

egress, while the approaches were also to be widened to admit the troops to pass through four abreast. Plank, and bags filled with cotton packed in tightly, were ordered prepared, to enable the troops to cross the ditches.

On the night of the 1st of July Johnston was between Brownsville and the Big Black, and wrote Pemberton from there that about the 7th of the month an attempt would be made to create a diversion to enable him to cut his way out. Pemberton was a prisoner before this message reached him.

On July 1st Pemberton, seeing no hope of outside relief, addressed the following letter to each of his four division commanders:

Unless the siege of Vicksburg is raised, or supplies are thrown in, it will become necessary very shortly to evacuate the place. I see no prospect of the former, and there are many great, if not insuperable obstacles in the way of the latter. You are, therefore, requested to inform me with as little delay as possible, as to the condition

ot your troops and their ability to make the
marches and undergo the fatigues necessary to
accomplish a successful evacuation.

Two of his generals suggested surrender, and the
other two practically did the same. They expressed
the opinion that an attempt to evacuate would fail.
Pemberton had previously got a message to Johnston
suggesting that he should try to negotiate with me for
a release of the garrison with their arms. Johnston
replied that it would be a confession of weakness for
him to do so; but he authorized Pemberton to use his
name in making such an arrangement.

On the 3d about ten o'clock A.M. white flags appeared on a portion of the rebel works. Hostilities
along that part of the line ceased at once. Soon two
persons were seen coming towards our lines bearing a
white flag. They proved to be General Bowen, a division commander, and Colonel Montgomery, aide-de-
camp to Pemberton, bearing the following letter to
me:

> I have the honor to propose an armistice for —
> hours, with the view to arranging terms for the
> capitulation of Vicksburg. To this end, if agreeable
> to you, I will appoint three commissioners, to
> meet a like number to be named by yourself, at
> such place and hour to-day as you may find
> convenient. I make this proposition to save the
> further effusion of blood, which must otherwise
> be shed to a frightful extent, feeling myself fully
> able to maintain my position for a yet indefinite
> period. This communication will be handed you
> under a flag of truce, by Major-General John S.
> Bowen.

It was a glorious sight to officers and soldiers on
the line where these white flags were visible, and the
news soon spread to all parts of the command. The
troops felt that their long and weary marches, hard
fighting, ceaseless watching by night and day, in a hot
climate, exposure to all sorts of weather, to diseases

*While some soldiers engage their counterparts in the
opposing trenches, most idle away their time in more
peaceful pursuits. In fact, many Yankees and Rebels
were content to engage in peaceful conversation from
the safety of their trenches.*

and, worst of all, to the gibes of many Northern papers that came to them saying all their suffering was
in vain, that Vicksburg would never be taken, were at
last at an end and the Union sure to be saved.

Bowen was received by General A. J. Smith, and
asked to see me. I had been a neighbor of Bowen's in
Missouri, and knew him well and favorably before the
war; but his request was refused. He then suggested
that I should meet Pemberton. To this I sent a verbal
message saying that, if Pemberton desired it, I would
meet him in front of McPherson's corps at three
o'clock that afternoon. I also sent the following written reply to Pemberton's letter:

> Your note of this date is just received, proposing
> an armistice for several hours, for the purpose of
> arranging terms of capitulation through
> commissioners, to be appointed, etc. The useless
> effusion of blood you propose stopping by this
> course can be ended at any time you may choose,
> by the unconditional surrender of the city and
> garrison. Men who have shown so much
> endurance and courage as those now in Vicksburg,
> will always challenge the respect of an adversary,
> and I can assure you will be treated with all the
> respect due to prisoners of war. I do not favor the
> proposition of appointing commissioners to
> arrange the terms of capitulation, because I have
> no terms other than those indicated above.

At three o'clock Pemberton appeared at the point
suggested in my verbal message, accompanied by the
same officers who had borne his letter of the morning.
Generals Ord, McPherson, Logan and A. J. Smith, and

several of my staff, accompanied me. Our place of meeting was on a hillside within a few hundred feet of the rebel lines. Near by stood a stunted oak-tree, which was made historical by the event. It was but a short time before the last vestige of its body, root and limb had disappeared, the fragments taken as trophies. Since then the same tree has furnished as many cords of wood, in the shape of trophies, as "The True Cross."

Pemberton and I had served in the same division during part of the Mexican War. I knew him very well therefore, and greeted him as an old acquaintance. He soon asked what terms I proposed to give his army if it surrendered. My answer was the same as proposed in my reply to his letter. Pemberton then said, rather snappishly, "The conference might as well end," and turned abruptly as if to leave. I said, "Very well."

General Bowen, I saw, was very anxious that the surrender should be consummated. His manner and remarks while Pemberton and I were talking, showed this. He now proposed that he and one of our generals should have a conference. I had no objection to this, as nothing could be made binding upon me that they might propose. Smith and Bowen accordingly had a conference, during which Pemberton and I, moving a short distance away towards the enemy's lines were in conversation. After a while Bowen suggested that the Confederate army should be allowed to march out with the honors of war, carrying their small arms and field artillery. This was promptly and unceremoniously rejected. The interview here ended, I agreeing, however, to send a letter giving final terms by ten o'clock that night.

CHARLES B. JOHNSON, M.D.

Treating the Wounded at Vicksburg

The post of surgeon in the field armies during the Civil War could hardly be considered an enviable one. Even then, modern warfare was capable of wounding men in most horrible ways while the art of healing had not advanced to pro-vide much supplication for those wounded in combat. A surgeon in the Union ranks at Vicksburg, Charles B. Johnson related tales of horror and humor in his reminiscences entitled Muskets and Medicine.

At 2 P.M., May 19, an assault was made on the Confederate works at Vicksburg. This assault was unsuccessful, so far as capturing the stronghold was concerned, but resulted in giving the Federals an advanced position, which position was made secure by the use of the spade the succeeding night. Believing that the Confederates would not hold out against another determined assault, a second one was ordered at 10 A.M., May 22. This was opened by a terrific cannonade from all the Federal batteries; following this was an incessant rattle of musketry.

It was known at the hospital this charge was to be made, and the constant boom of cannon and continual roll of musketry firing after 10 in the forenoon all knew would soon bring in a frightful harvest of mangled and wounded. The slain would, of course, for the time at least, be left on the field. About 2 P.M.

through the trees was seen a long train of ambulances approaching, all heavily loaded with mangled humanity. Upon reaching the hospital grounds two or three ambulances were backed up at once, and the wounded lifted or assisted out. One of the first that I assisted in taking from the ambulance was a tall, slender man, who had received a terrible wound in the top of his head; a minnie ball had, so to speak, plowed its way through the skull, making a ragged, gaping wound, exposing the brain for three or four inches. He lived but a moment after removal from the ambulance.

The captain of the company in which I enlisted was in another ambulance, mortally wounded, with a bullet in his brain. He lived a day or two in an unconscious stupor—a comatose state—as the doctors say. But the majority of the wounded were boys, young, brave, daring fellows, too often rash, and meeting

Pemberton discusses surrender terms with Grant. Realizing any hope of relief was futile, the Confederate commander of Vicksburg approached Federal lines to seek terms. However, he was not about to accept Grant's demands of unconditional surrender.

Jubilant Federals enter the object of many months of campaigning, the city of Vicksburg, which capitulated on 4 July, a day after the Confederate defeat at Gettysburg.

death, or next to it, oftentimes from needless exposure.

One nice young fellow of eighteen the writer can never forget. He had been wounded in the bowels, and was sitting at the root of a large tree, resting his head against its trunk. His name was Banks, and knowing me well, he recognized me, and calling me by name, said: "Ah, I'm badly wounded." Already his lips were ashy pale, a clammy sweat was upon his face, and from the wound in his abdomen a long knuckle of

intestine was protruding. A few hours more and young Banks was resting in the sleep of death. No danger from enemy's bullets now; the poor, senseless clay, which a little time before had been the dwelling-place of joyous young life, nothing could harm more. By the quiet form sat the father, sad and heart-broken, himself a soldier, but the balance of his term of service would seem lonely and tedious.

Arms and legs of many in the ambulances were hanging useless and lying powerless by the sides of their owners, and soon the surgeons at several tables were kept busy removing mangled and useless limbs. As on all such occasions when there were a great many wounded on hand at one time, but little was done for the mortally injured, save to lay them in a comparatively comfortable position; those having mangled limbs and broken bones were first attended, while those with unextensive, simple flesh wounds were passed by till more serious cases were looked after. Judgment, however, in this direction was not always unerring, and I remember one man, with what seemed a slight wound of the foot, who was rather persistent in asking immediate attention; but the number of dangling limbs and gaping wounds calling for immediate care seemed to justify the surgeons in putting him off for a time. His case was attended to in due course, and later he was sent up the river to a large Memphis hospital, where, some weeks subsequently, he was infected with hospital gangrene, and died from its effects. Of course, the delay in dressing his wound

weeks before had nothing to do with the untoward result, but it did bring sharp criticism upon the surgeons.

All the afternoon and till late at night on May 22 did the surgeons work with the wounded; amputating limbs, removing balls, cleaning and washing wounds, ridding them of broken pieces of bone, bandaging them up and putting them in the best shape possible. A few were bruised from stroke of spent ball or piece of shell, and recovered in a few days. Long lines of wounded now occupied the shaded places, in the yard, and to attend to the wants of these kept all busy. Carbolic acid and other disinfectants were at that time not in use, and all wounds were at first treated with simple water dressings. Old muslin cloth or lint was saturated with cold water and applied to all fresh wounds. As soon as these began to supurate, simple cerate, a mild, soothing ointment, consisting of two parts of fresh lard and one of white wax, was applied. In most bullet wounds, the ball in entering the body carried before it little pieces of the clothing, leather of the belt or cartridge box, tin of the canteens or any such substance first struck by the missile. In nearly all instances these foreign substances were discharged in the form of little dark-colored bits of *débris*.

Every day the wounds were washed and freshly dressed. But, as the weather was warm, many wounds

A Yankee draws a bead on an unfortunate Rebel.

A Federal naval hospital used at the time of the Vicksburg campaign.

became infested with maggots. This looked horrible, but was not deemed specially detrimental. Two or three days' extra work was made by the large number of wounded, resulting from the assault of May 22. After this there was a constant accession of wounded men at the hospital, but only a few at a time.

One man received a wound from some sort of a large missile that made an extensive opening at the place of entrance, the fleshy part of the thigh, in which it buried itself deeply and could not be reached. In a day or two the limb all about the wound began to assume a greenish-yellow hue, and later the man died. Cutting into the wound after death revealed the presence of a copper-tap, more than an inch across, from a shell.

About a week after the siege began a young man from an Ohio regiment died from a wound, resulting from his own imprudence. The first day of the investment, while his regiment was drawn up in line, three or four miles from the enemy's works, there being some delay in the advance, the young man got some loose powder, ran it along in a little trail, covered this with dust and tried to fire it. As it did not ignite he was stooping over with his face close to the ground when the charge took fire. His face was badly burned, and later was attacked with erysipelas, from which death resulted. This seemed an inglorious way of yielding up one's life when the opportunities for dying gloriously for one's country were so plentiful and ready at hand.

As soon as communication by the Yazoo was opened up with the North, supplies in great abundance came in for the sick. In the way of eatables for the hospital were delicacies of various kinds, fruits,

mild home-made wines, etc. Clothing for the sick and wounded was furnished in full quantities. This, for the most part, consisted of cotton garments for underwear, shirts, night-shirts, drawers, gowns, etc., nearly all of bleached muslin. Cotton goods were at the time expensive in the market, from the fact that the supply of the raw material by the South was stopped for the period during which the war continued.

Nearly all these things were donated by individuals and communities. Very many of the garments had the name of the donor stamped upon them with stencil plate. Quite a number of the articles seen by the writer had the name, now forgotten, of a lady with postoffice address at Janesville, Wis.

Yankee soldiers flee for cover as shells fired from Confederate cannons land about them.

The assault of May 22 convinced all, officers and men alike, that Vicksburg was much more securely intrenched than had been supposed, and that the only way to capture it would be by siege. Accordingly all made up their minds to await the result patiently, but of the final fall of the stronghold no one entertained a doubt. Indeed, of ultimate trijmph every man seemed from the start to have full confidence.

As before stated, after settling down to siege operations there were comparatively few wounded. Back of Swett's garden, under some small trees, the dead from the division hospital were buried. It was not possible to provide coffins, and so the dead were wrapped in blankets and covered over with earth—till their shallow graves were filled. As the siege progressed all the wounded and sick, who were able to be moved, were put in ambulances and conveyed to boats on the Yazoo River, from whence they went North.

Cane grew in abundance all about, and by cutting a number of these stocks, tying them together with strings, and putting the two ends on cross-pieces resting upon stakes driven in the ground, quite comfortable and springy cots were improvised for the hospital.

Swett's house had all the time been used as a place for storage of drugs and hospital supplies. Swett was a short, thick-set man with a rotund stomach and about

Federal snipers look out upon the Confederate entrenchments from a crude observation tower as one Yankee takes time out from the conflict to shield himself from the oppressive Mississippi sun.

The bane of the navy, a powerful gun at Vicksburg that guarded the Mississippi from the incursions of Federal naval traffic until the city capitulated on 4 July.

fifty years old. He used to stand around and lean on his cane with much seeming complacency. In his yard were several bunches of fragrant jasmine in full bloom. This is a most beautiful and deliciously fragrant flower, scenting the air with its delightful odor.

In the timber all about were magnificent specimens of magnolia, having upon their branches, in May and June, long beautiful blossoms. Figs ripened in Swett's garden during the siege. These, while not liked by some when gathered fresh from the trees, by others were relished exceedingly. Thus, tree, flower and fruit lent something of their charms to assuage the horrors of war.

As soon as General Joseph E. Johnston discovered that Grant had securely invested Vicksburg, he began organizing a force to relieve the garrison. This force sought to attack Grant's rear on the line of the Big Black River. Grant, who by this time was receiving reenforcements from the North, was fully on the alert, and confronted Johnston with ample force to keep the latter at a safe distance from the operations against Vicksburg.

Meanwhile, all sorts of stories were in circulation—nearly all favorable, however, to the Federals. At one time it was rumored Port Hudson, some three hundred miles down the river, had capitulated to General Banks; at another, that the Confederates could not hold out longer; again, that Richmond was taken, and then that Washington had been captured by Lee.

Of nights the mortar boats from the river shelled Vicksburg, and sometimes, with one or more comrades, I would go out upon a high hill in front of the hospital from whence the bombardment could be seen. The mortar boats were, perhaps, eight miles distant, and first a flash would be seen, then the discharge of the mortar, next a streak of fire, followed by a burning fuse; this would rise away up in the air and finally descend, and, just before reaching the ground another flash, the explosion of the shell, broke upon the vision. Some time elapsed after the flash was seen before the report could be heard. The shells thrown by these mortar boats were of one and two hundred pounds caliber, and all through the siege were thrown at regular intervals during the night-time.

One cannon, belonging to the Confederates, received the appellation of "Whistling Dick." The ball from it passed through the air with a peculiar whistling noise that could be heard by all on the southwestern aspect of the works. It was a fine breechloading rifled cannon of English mnaufacture.

Toward the latter part of June rumors of the impending fall of Vicksburg pervaded the command, and later, as the National anniversary drew near, it was said a most determined assault would be made on the 4th of July. Finally, preparations for this were in progress when, on the 3d of July, word came that the Confederates had already made propositions looking

Men lived like moles in the labyrinth of the extensive network of Federal fortifications at Vicksburg.

toward a surrender, and next day, the 4th of July, Vicksburg, after withstanding a siege of forty-six days, capitulated.

The command, though long expecting this event, was almost wild with joy. Some surprise was, however, felt that the Confederates should have yielded on the day they did; the belief prevailed that they had, in some way, gained an inkling of the intended assault and felt as though they could not withstand another determined effort on the part of the Federals. Up to date this was the most important success of the war. The number of men captured exceeded 30,000, with a vast quantity of small arms, cannon, heavy ordnance and munitions of all kinds. Indeed, more men capitulated at Vicksburg than were taken in one body at any other time during the war.

A day or two after I procured a pass and visited the city. It was alive with soldiers of both armies, All upon friendly relations, swapping yarns, telling experiences, trading curiosities, as if hostile words, much less shot and shell, had never passed between them. One tall young Confederate approached me and wanted to exchange a two-dollar Confederate note for the same amount in United States currency; he said, by way of explanation, that he would, in a few days, be going home over in Louisiana on his parole and wanted the "greenback" money to show his folks. This was, most probably, not true; Confederate money was wholly valueless in the Union lines, and the United States currency was doubtless wanted for immediate use.

The various places of interest about the city were visited. The several roads passing from the city, upon reaching the bluff, had roadways cut through this. In many places these cuts were twenty and thirty feet deep, and the walls of red clay perpendicular, or nearly so. But the clay composing these walls was of such tenacity that washingts never occurred, and the sides of the cuts remained as durable as if built of stone.

From the sides of these walls of clay caves were cut in which for security some of the citizens passed much of their time. I visited several of these caves, and found two or three of them carpeted and neatly furnished. Many places were seen where the immense shells from the mortar fleet struck the earth. When these failed to explode a great round hole was made in the ground, and in case of explosion after striking the ground, a large excavation was the result.

The great guns along the river front—the Columbiads of 9-, 11- and 13- inch caliber—were visited. It was these that blockaded the river and made the passing of even heavily-armored vessels hazardous. Some of the Confederate soldiers belonging to the infantry were about one of these huge guns, and one of them said within ear-shot:

"I'll bet this 'ere old cannon's killed many a blue-belly."

Passing out toward the outworks a Confederate regiment, containing not many more men than a full company, was seen draw up in line for inspection and roll-call, preparatory to completion of parole papers.

In conversation with the Confederates some said they had had enough of the war and hoped the South would make an end of it; others avowed their faith in ultimate success; the great majority, however, were non-committal regarding their notions of final success or failure.

The rifle-pits and works of the Confederates that crossed the railway and dirt road nearby were visited. The neighborhood of the dirt road seemed especially to have been the scene of most obstinate conflict; it ran along on a ridge and the approach was particularly well guarded. The space outside the Confederate works, between these and the Federal rifle-pits, was dotted all over with Union graves; if some dirt thrown over a soldier where he fell could be called a grave.

Grant meets with Pemberton on 4 July to accept the Confederate surrender of Vicksburg.

One of the most powerful guns in the Confederate arsenal at Vicksburg, an 18-pound rifle. The distinct sound of its screaming shells won it the name Whistling Dick.

A day or two after the assault the Union dead were buried under a flag of truce. The weather being very warm, before this was attended to, decomposition had already begun and the consequent stench would soon grow intolerable. Under thse circumstances both armies readily agreed to a short armistice for disposition of the dead. The time allowed was too short for regular interment, hence dirt was thrown over the dead bodies where they lay, and in cases where they could be identified, a piece of board put at the head, upon which, in rude letters, were the names and commands of the fallen ones.

Wherever an elevation intervened between the Union lines and Confederate works the tracks of bullets through the grass and weeds were surprisingly thick and crossed and cris-crossed each other in various directions, and at one point there was hardly an inch of space but what had thus been marked. This was near the Jackson dirt road, where the Confederates had an enfilading fire and used it to most deadly advantage.

Immediately upon the fall of Vicksburg, an expedition was started against General Joe Johnston who, during the siege, had been threatening Grant from the rear and on the line of the Big Black River. Under a broiling July sun the Union soldiers took up the line

of march and followed the Confederates under Johnston to Jackson, Miss., to which, for a time, they laid siege. Finally, however, realizing that he was outnumbered, General Johnston evacuated his works at Jackson and permitted the Federals to take possession for a second time within two months.

Meanwhile, with the regimental surgeon I was assigned to duty at the Thirteenth Corps Hospital, which was in the near vicinity of a farmhouse, though the sick and wounded were in tents and everything needed for their comfort and care was on a much more commodious scale than had been possible at the Division Hospital, where I was on duty during the whole forty-five days of the siege. One peculiar method of prescribing was in vogue here: A number of favorite prescriptions for sundry diseases were put up in quantity and each given a number; consequently, instead of having to write out a prescription and having it put up separately the surgeon had but to designate a given number, and in short order the patient would have the desired remedy.

During this period I, from time to time, secured a pass and visited Vicksburg, which was gradually settling down to the new order of things. The wharf at the river front, very soon after the Federal occupation, assumed a busy aspect. Steamboats with all needed supplies came down the river, I came near saying, in fleets. Many visitors came from the North, some to see friends in the army, some to see the newly-captured stronghold, some to look up new fields for trade and speculation, and some came on the sad

Grant after his tremendous success of the Vicksburg Campaign. His noticeable exultation over his recent victory is evident in the smile that curls around his lip. However, his earnest gaze reveals a determination to embark on the grueling and bloody campaigns necessary to bring a final termination to the bloody war gripping the nation.

mission of, if possible, finding the bit of earth that hid from view the remains of fallen loved ones.

General Logan, who commanded within the limits of Vicksburg after its furrender, had his headquarters in the Court House, which, from its location on a high hill, was a conspicuous object. Over the dome of the Court House floated the flag of the 45th Illinois Infantry Volunteers, an organization that was given the advance when General Logan's Division entered Vicksburg after its surrender and took possession. The 45th Illinois was thus honored because its members, many of whom were miners, had, during the siege, performed a great deal of duty of an exceptionally hazardous nature.

Toward the end of the siege, J. W. Spurr, Company B, 145th Illinois Infantry Volunteers, became the hero of a most remarkable adventure. He, somehow, managed to get possession of an old Confederate uniform and going to the Mississippi River at the extreme left of our lines went in the water during a heavy rainstorm after night and swam north, past the pickets of both friend and foe. Then, upon going ashore he at once went to some Confederates who were gathered about a campfire and engaged them in conversation. Later he left them and went to a house and asked for something to eat which was refused in consequence of the fact that, at that particular time, eatables in Vicksburg were at a very high premium. Finally, however, with the persuasive influence of a five-dollar bill both food and lodging for the time being were secured.

Young Spurr's hostess was an Irish woman, who was found to be a Union sympathizer, and who proved her fidelity by warning her guest that he was being watched. Consequently, after spending three days in the beleaguered city the daring adventurer, after night, found his way to the river's bank south of the city, went in the water and swam and floated down past the pickets of foe and friend alike, and upon reaching the Union lines was promptly arrested, but upon establishing his identity was as promptly released.

It is, perhaps, not too much to say that this feat had few, if indeed any, parallels in either army during the whole period of the Civil War's four years' history. That an eighteen-year-old boy, on his own intiative and impelled by nothing save curiosity and innate dare-deviltry, should plan, undertake and successfully execute such a hazardous feat as that of young Spurr, is hard to believe. As to credibility, however, the reader can rest assured that the above is absolutely true, and can be verified by the best of evidence. J. W. Spurr, the hero of the adventure, is a well-preserved veteran, and has his home in Rock Island, Ill.